Aristocracy of the Dead

Aristocracy of the Dead

New Findings in Postmortem Survival

by

Arthur S. Berger

FOREWORD BY
ANTONY FLEW

McFarland & Company, Inc., Publishers
Jefferson, North Carolina, and London

Library of Congress Cataloguing-in-Publication Data

Berger, Arthur S., 1920–
  Aristocracy of the dead.

  Bibliography: p. 195.
  Includes index.
  1. Spiritualism. 2. Future life. 3. Mediums.
  4. Psychical research. I. Title. [DNLM: 1. Parapsychology. 2. Spiritualism. BF 1281 B496a]
  BF1272.B47 1987   133.9′01′3   87-42501

ISBN 0-89950-259-8 (acid-free natural paper)

Printed in the United States of America.

McFarland & Company, Inc., Publishers
  Box 611, Jefferson, North Carolina 28640

ACKNOWLEDGMENTS

To Professor Antony Flew, the leading and most resolute sceptical philosopher considering the problem of postmortem survival, I wish to express my appreciation for his kindness in writing the Foreword to this book. My thanks go, too, to the Psychical Research Foundation, Carrollton, Georgia, whose grant in support of my research helped make the book possible.

I remember with gratitude also Dr. Gertrude R. Schmeidler, professor emeritus, Department of Psychology at the City College of the City University of New York and past president of the American Society for Psychical Research, who took the time to consult with me and to supply many helpful suggestions for the research reported here. I am grateful as well to Dr. C.B. "Scott" Jones for his suggestions. Any errors or shortcomings in the work, however, must of course be laid entirely at my door.

This acknowledgment would not be complete without thanking Joyce Berger, my wife, for her support and the hours she spent in editing the manuscript and typescript and in the preparation of the statistical data.

Arthur S. Berger

CONTENTS

FOREWORD

When Arthur Berger asked me to write this Foreword to *Aristocracy of the Dead* my first reaction was to regret that nothing I could write would be appropriate. For I have long been persuaded there is no coherently formulated survival hypothesis that is not already known to be false. This is a thesis I develop at length in my Gifford Lectures on *The Logic of Mortality* (Oxford: Blackwell, 1987).

But now that I have had a chance to study Berger's book it seems that there is after all something very constructive I can say. For, if some of the tests he proposes did turn out to have certain (by me and possibly by Berger) extremely unexpected results, then we should all be confronted with a formidable explanatory challenge. To meet this challenge we should be bound, at the very least, most strenuously to attempt to formulate some hypothesis of a kind which, I contend, is not at present available to us.

My own argument starts from the contention that we people simply are specimens of a very special kind of creatures of flesh and blood. This is, however, not a would-be factual claim, falsifiable by possible future scientific discoveries, but instead a contention about the very meaning of the word "people," and of all other person words. If, for instance, it were to be discovered that people contain some controlling component which is, in some explicable understanding, incorporeal, then this would be, like the actual discovery of the functions of the brain, not a discovery that we really are those components — souls or, as the case actually was, brains — but a discovery about the constitution and workings of the particular kind of essentially corporeal creatures that in truth we are.

Given that we people are just the flesh and blood organisms which indeed we are, then any suggestion either that some of us survive death or that we are all of us immortal must be either self-contradictory or factually false. For since when have the categories of "dead" and "survivors" ceased to be both mutually exclusive and together exhaustive? And who is not apprised of the fact that — with the possible exceptions of Elijah the Prophet and Mary the mother of Jesus bar Joseph — all humans are mortal?

There are of course three sorts of ways in which people have attempted to get around or over this enormous initial obstacle to any doctrine of survival—and, *a fortiori*, of survival forever, immortality. I have elsewhere named these: the Reconstitutionist Way, the Way of the Astral Body, and the Platonic-Cartesian Way. Only the third is immediately relevant. For what those who speak of "the survival hypothesis" in a parapsychological context usually have in mind is some complex Platonic-Cartesian contention: that we are composite of both corporeal and incorporeal elements; that the incorporeal element is the real me or the real you; and that this element will survive the dissolution of the other and corporeal element, the body.*

The almost always unrecognized trouble about this way of thinking is that no one has ever been able to explain how such a separable and incorporeal soul might be identified, or how it might be reidentified as the same after some lapse of time. Until this is done we simply do not have a coherent and scientifically testable survival hypothesis. It is not a bit of good here to insist that souls are by definition incorporeal. For that does not even begin to tell us what souls are or might be. Incorporeality is not a rather elusive but positive and particular characteristic. On the contrary: "incorporeal" is a word for the absence of most if not all the characteristics that we can think of.

This, as I see it now, is where *Aristocracy of the Dead* comes in. For Arthur Berger has here excogitated and explained various possible tests which, if they were to be made and if the results turned out to be unexpectedly positive, would constitute the formidable challenge to which I referred at the beginning. This challenge would be to think up some way in which such positive test results might be explained by reference, and related to some deceased person. We must presume that that is something which might conceivably be done: either by solving the problem of giving meaning to the notion of a detachable and incorporeal soul—showing how such putative entities might be identified, and reidentified through time—or else in some quite different and presently altogether unthinkable alternative way.

In *Aristocracy of the Dead*, therefore, Arthur Berger has achieved something which no one else has for a very long time achieved. He has taken a significant step forward in what used to be called, and what he himself would presumably still wish to call, "survival research."

Antony Flew

*See, for instance, Part V of Antony Flew (ed.), Readings in the Philosophical Problems of Parapsychology (Buffalo, NY: Prometheus, 1987).

Antony Flew is distinguished research fellow, Social Philosophy and Policy Center, Bowling Green State University, Bowling Green, Ohio.

PREFACE

Every year a torrent of books about a future life spews out from printing presses everywhere and descends upon the world. Why, then, do editors and authors go on flooding the world with more books on the subject and what has the reader to gain from reading another and yet another one?

The answer is that, whether we are sceptics or believers, we ought to read whatever and whenever we can about the subject of a possible postmortem existence in order to open up ever wider and deeper our understanding of it. The resolution of this question would have a shattering effect on science, philosophy and religion. It is this principle that justifies the writing and publishing of the present book. Although the subject is so old that it occupied the Neanderthals, this book has something new to say about it. It does what artists, writers and inventors do when they convert the simple and commonplace into the unusual: It looks at its subject from fresh and different angles.

Aristocracy of the Dead presents for the first time the results of independent research into fascinating questions oddly ignored by researchers and writers in the past. Scientific investigations by the societies for psychical research into mediumship and the important question of survival after death have been going on for a century. The results of these investigations are packed into thousands of pages in their journals and proceedings. Yet perhaps 100 cases can be found in which communications purportedly from dead people seem *prima facie* evidence of survival. What made these communicators special? Was it their sex? Their religious beliefs? Was it—well, what? And why is it important to know?

My purpose from the beginning was to use careful methodology to see if such questions could be answered. This book reports my procedures and my findings, sets up guideposts to answer these questions, and documents a rigorously controlled, never-before-published experiment that confirms my findings. This book, therefore, is not just a repetition of prior writings. It adds something new to our knowledge.

This book is special in a third way. If we should die tomorrow, or fifty years from tomorrow, and wanted to let our loved ones know that we had survived death, would we know what to do? Can we plan the evidence to be given of our continued existence? This book tells us.

I have tried to make the book unusual in still another way. Based on my findings and answers to the above questions, I have hit upon an entirely new strategy in the campaign to resolve the issue of the possible survivability of death. It involves making the attempt at resolution more democratic than it has been and mobilizing special teams from among readers. But why should readers wish to volunteer? Who will qualify and what will be their purpose? This book has a message and offers some answers.

Scholars know that in Semitic languages the words are written from right to left and books are read "backwards." Reading this book in reverse would allow its most interesting and original parts to be read first. But since the book must be read from front to back, these portions of the book necessarily follow chapters 1, 2 and 3. Although chapters 2 and 3 contain material with which few readers are familiar, it is not original and may discourage some readers at the start. Nevertheless, it seemed to me that chapters 2 and 3 were necessary to explain and lay the groundwork for the later chapters. Students of the subject already familiar with the contents of chapters 2 and 3 may elect to browse through them quickly and proceed to Chapter 4.

Although this book has been written for general readers not familiar with research on the subject of a future life, it ought to interest professional parapsychologists as well because it offers them statistics and references to sources of information. To the general reader the book offers an eye-opening text.

Arthur S. Berger

1
THE MAN OF UZ

From earth, as we look into an expanding universe, the light we see comes to us from galaxies as they existed billions of years before our births. What illumines the subject-matter of this book reaches us also from a place and time of long ago.

Between 2000 and 4000 years ago in that "land flowing with milk and honey" located in the Valley of the Nile where the Euphrates and Tigris Rivers emptied into the Persian Gulf, patriarchs and prophets, pharaohs, preachers and teachers, flourished. Their dreams and dramas, their laws and teachings, all destined to have a profound impact on the history and spiritual insights of the world, are recorded in the Old Testament.

Of all who lived, loved, killed, healed, prophesied, preached and died in the Promised Land and whose dramas, thought and faith are collected in the codes, psalms, songs, proverbs and accounts of the Bible, one alone deserves our attention: The man of Uz.

"There was a man in the land of Uz, whose name was Job." So begins the Book of Job, one of the wisdom books of the Bible. Uz, a small village in Judea, was real, but it is probable that Job never existed. Maimonides, the great Jewish thinker of the 12th century, doubted it. Nevertheless, the figure of Job provided the poet who wrote the Book of Job with a basis for his drama.

It is familiar enough. In the poet's imagination Job is virtuous and pious. Yet God tries him terribly. His sons are killed when a great wind destroys the eldest brother's house. His oxen, asses and camels are stolen and his servants are slain by the thieves. Job does not understand the ways of God but submits to them. He rends his robe, shaves his head and falls down to bless the name of the Lord. Again God tests him. Job's entire body is covered with painful boils. But Job refuses to curse God or to sin against him.

So far the poet has expressed the overwhelming power of God and the powerlessness of the human beings He created. But now the poet sets the stage for what will occupy us. When three of Job's friends come to comfort and commune with him, they sit with him in silence for a week until Job can stand his anger, grief and loss no longer. He becomes bitter, complaining and

1

rebellious against God. He accepts God's power but he no longer believes that God is just. Then Job asks the most stirring, the most human question in the entire dramatic story: "If a man die, shall he live again?" (Job 14:14).

This famous question, a jewel of Biblical literature, like a cut diamond, is multi-faceted. As we turn it in our minds, it presents some of the issues and subject-matter at which this book is aimed.

Some questions, such as the classic "Have you stopped beating your wife?", cannot be answered with a simple "yes" or "no." Job's question is another. How can the question be answered when the question itself must be questioned?

What does "live again" mean? These words have many and different meanings which depend on the philosophy and perspective of the place and time the question is asked, on the person asking and on the person answering. It is essential to clarify the varied and often inconsistent conceptions of living on after death and to specify which is intended when a question like Job's is asked or answered.

No effort is made here to describe all these conceptions. The author has done this fully elsewhere.[1]* It will do to point out that "live again" is susceptible of six different conceptions. Some of them are based on an indirect continuance after physical death through one's descendants, through one's work, through the influence of one's thought or spirit or through being remembered by loving relatives or friends. Interaction with physical objects may permit another form of indirect continuance. A "psi-field" theory in parapsychology, supported by such psychic phenomena as haunting apparitions and token object tests (in which psychics holding objects appear to get information about people associated with them), suggests that we may leave traces of ourselves in objects and that, long after we have died, these traces will survive in these objects and be transferred to the living with the help of extrasensory perception. A concept of postmortem continuance arises from the idea of a super-mundane storehouse that contains information about our lives and memories which may be retrieved later by persons with paranormal abilities. There is also the Neitzschean concept of "eternal recurrence" which asserts that the "I" who live and die in this instant, "I" who have lived and died repeatedly before, will be reproduced through eternity. It is possible as well to conceive of continuing after death by being absorbed into Nature with its flowers, earth, waters and stars, or by being merged into the One, the Absolute, the soul of the world. Finally, Job's question might be answered with a belief for which the burial customs of ancient races give us mute but unmistakable evidence. Tools and meat deposited next to corpses in their graves many tens of thousands of years ago attest to a conception of the survival after

*See Chapter Notes, beginning on page 187.

physical death of the same individuals who once lived and who would need weapons and food.

With qualifications it is this last conception of personal postmortem survival with which this book deals. If death were not involved, it would be unnecessary to use the word "survival." But death is involved and it produces the destruction of what we understand as life. We want to find out if something besides the physical body may exist and survive the death of the body. And survive for how long? For eternity or for some finite period of time?

When Job asked his question, he may have been thinking of life eternal. But the essential inquiry to which this book is directed is not whether we are immortal but whether something in us lives again for any period of time after bodily death. This first condition must be established before one can think seriously about the doctrine of immortality.

"Shall he live again?" Was Job asking whether the same individual who was alive would resume life with the same body he had had? And if not the body, what might be the something in us that might live again? Traditional replies would be the "soul" or "spirit." These terms, however, are vague and do not necessarily connote that the same old person we knew had survived death. Many writers, including L.E. Rhine,[2] Myers,[3] Lamont,[4] and others, have preferred to say that it is the human personality that lives again. But the personality is that which is perceived by others. "Arthur Berger" is recognized by his family and friends by his face, body, speech, walk, dress, mannerisms. Clearly, these physical aspects of his personality will not continue after his death. If anything of Arthur Berger's personality is to survive, it must be its mental aspects: thoughts, memories, attitudes, emotions. These aspects constitute the stream of consciousness that can be summarized in the single pronoun by which we describe ourselves, "I." But these mental aspects are purely private. Even those closest to Arthur Berger cannot be party to them. How, therefore, could anyone know directly that his consciousness had survived death? It would seem that only Berger would have direct knowledge that his "I" had continued after the death of his body.

Are living people, then, barred from ever knowing if a deceased human being has survived death? Not if the continuance of that person's "I" could be indicated in some indirect way. If, for instance, Arthur Berger's memory, as one aspect of his "I," could be authenticated following his death, it would suggest the survival of his stream of consciousness. Such authentication might be possible if, along with its memory and other mental aspects, the "I" of a deceased human being also possessed the ability to communicate with the living and, in addition, to communicate to them specific information that person had prearranged while alive.

Suppose the answer to Job's question were "yes." What then? Should there be a future life for the "I," and communications between that life and this were feasible, would the afterlife be a democratic state based on the principles of Locke and Jefferson in which all citizens would be able equally to communicate with people yet alive? Or would it be a feudal aristocracy in which only a privileged class would have this power of communication? This question is not so strange when we consider the startling fact that, out of the thousands of millions of human beings who have lived and died on this planet, only a tiny number have purported to interact with people still incarnate. This fact suggests a form of government practicing discrimination and inequality against which the Americans would have rebelled had it been an earthly one, a possible case of "many called, few chosen" (Matt. 20:16, 22:14) with the ability to interact with the living being granted only to deceased people with special qualifications.

If they exist, what might these qualifications be? The man of Uz was a pious and good man. If a special class is found in the postmortem state, would it be characterized by Job's piety and goodness or would the impious and evil be included, also? Might an answer to Job's question, with its reference to "man" and "he," suggest that only the male sex will be able to communicate after death, or will the female of the species be able to do so, also? If religious belief and sex play any role with respect to the postmortem ability to communicate, are there any other factors at work, and, if there are, what can they be? Interesting and important questions such as these generally have been neglected not only by the millions who have repeated it before and since Job but by religionists, philosophers and poets who have prayed, speculated and composed writings to express human hopes and fears concerning death. But now a central portion of this book will be devoted to them.

If Job was thinking of personal postmortem survival, his question becomes of interest from another viewpoint. Until his angry outburst, a this-life theme dominated the Old Testament. The concern of the Jew was for the immortality of Israel. The resurrection belief did not appear until the time of the Maccabees. Except for some reference to Sheol, a dark and gloomy spirit abode like the Hades of the Greeks, the Old Testament omits mention of a postmortem state for the individual. Some passages even deny personal survival: "The dead praise not the Lord" (Psalms 115:17); "They are dead, they shall not live . . . shall not rise" (Isaiah 26:14); "In death there is no remembrance of thee" (Psalms 6:5); "Before I go hence, and be no more" (Psalms 39:13). Job's question, therefore, represents the beginning of a new Hebrew hope and vision.

But it is contingent on God. Pious Job, despite his bitterness and inability to understand God's treatment of him, nonetheless could endure his losses and trials because he was able to grasp at the hope that ultimately God would remember his piety and patience and would permit the night of death to be followed by a dawn. For the man of Uz, God and living on after death were intimately and indissolubly related.

An obsolescent supposition? It is seen also in the lines of Alfred Lord Tennyson's *In Memoriam*:

That nothing walks on aimless feet;
That not one life shall be destroyed,
Or cast as rubbish to the void,
When God hath made the pile complete.

In the minds of two poets writing their poems thousands of years apart, one in Asia, one in England, the postmortem state is secondary to and dependent upon the existence of God.

Sometimes we find the order reversed. Survival after death comes first to give life and reason to God. When Unamuno, the Spanish literary genius, suggested to a peasant one day that there might be a God governing the heaven and earth and yet there might not be personal survival, the peasant replied, "Then wherefore God?"[5] But the relationship between God and a future life remains unbroken.

As a result of Job's question, still one more question is directed to us. Must we think of the subject of postmortem existence only in religious terms, as exclusively a matter of faith or as always hinged to the existence of God? Or can it be considered simply a question of fact: Does some component of the human being survive death or does it not?

Religion and science are said to travel along separate roads which, no matter how far extended, can never meet. Faith in God and in a future life are claimed to be beyond the realm of scientific inquiry. Even Francis Bacon, the father of modern science, embraced theological doctrines so strongly that he maintained that things divine must be left to faith and must not be invaded by scientific methods. Religion is "certainty without proof" while science is "proof without certainty."

It is interesting, then, to see the scientific spirit in Christianity invade the area of a future life. Stories of people rising from the dead existed before Christianity. Such accounts are recounted in Homer's *Iliad* and in the dramas of Sophocles and Aeschylus. Not very much was made of them. Christianity is unique in the high place accorded Christ's resurrection and the conclusion drawn from it that it gave people the right to hope for a future life. Its importance is indicated by Paul's admission: "And if Christ be not risen, then is our preaching vain, and your faith is also vain" (1 Corinthians 15:14). Christianity is also unique because of its demonstration in the New Testament that continuance after death was a matter of fact which required investigation as such.

To reinforce faith in Christ's resurrection, evidence was offered in the account of John (20:19–28) in which Jesus is said to have appeared in the absence of Thomas to his other disciples. He showed them his hands and side. But Doubting Thomas said he would not believe unless he could see the nail wounds in Jesus's hands, put his fingers in them and place his hands in Jesus's side. Eight days later when Thomas and the other disciples were together, Jesus reappeared. Thomas stopped doubting when Jesus told him: "[P]ut your fingers in my hands, your hand in my side." In the Gospel of Luke (24:36–43) Jesus is said to have appeared to other disciples, showed them his wounds, asked them to touch him, and to have eaten a piece of fish and some honeycomb.

In these New Testament narratives early Christians used the skills of lawyers and researchers to unfold, retell and substantiate the story of Christ's rising. Witnesses were sought and questioned and their evidence collected and recorded as would be done in any court of law. Implicit in these accounts is the admission that the resurrection — as a haunting, an apparition or a conversation with the dead — is no less a fact than is the sun.

This book takes the position, then, that the question of survival after death is a legitimate subject of investigation. The question of whether we live again after death is on a par with the question of whether there is life in outer space. They are both questions of fact. The question of life after death can be determined by more and better survival research, by which is meant a cautious, systematic effort to investigate, experiment and seek evidence bearing on the question of survival. If an "I" which once lived has persisted after bodily death and exists in an unseen domain, it may be possible to discover and focus on its existence and identity there with tools invented in our own sphere. In this investigation the existence of God does not enter and faith or the lack of it is irrelevant.

Accepting the legitimacy of survival research, Job's question prompts other inquiries related to it: Why, when and where did survival research begin? Has the evidence collected by it yielded an answer to whether we live again? We now turn to these queries.

2
HUMAN MORTALITY

The philosopher Unamuno began his classic work, *The Tragic Sense of Life* by defining himself as a man of flesh and blood, a "man who is born, suffers, and dies—above all, who dies."[1] It is this awareness of our mortality that forces upon us a consideration of whether there is a possibility of life beyond the grave. And if this consideration is not forced upon us by the awareness of our own mortality, then the awareness that others are mortal, especially those close to us, does so.

So it is that in almost every age and culture human emotions have given rise to the idea of an afterlife. In modern times the hope that had appeared in ancient cultures swelled into a powerful movement that maintained that the dead live on and hold converse with the living. It began with Swedenborg, the 18th century mystic and scientist. He is credited with obtaining by telepathy information about a fire fifty miles away in Stockholm. But that feat is nothing compared to the case of the silver service. After a goldsmith demanded payment from a widow for a silver service her husband had purchased, she asked Swedenborg to find out from her dead husband if he had paid for it and, if so, where the receipt could be located. Swedenborg agreed. Three days later he called at her home, and in the presence of her friends, told her that he had communicated with her husband. The receipt for payment would be found in a secret compartment in an upstairs bureau. The astonished lady and her guests went upstairs at once and, following Swedenborg's directions that a lefthand drawer in the bureau be pulled out and that a board which would appear be withdrawn, the secret compartment and unknown receipt were discovered.

The interest created by Swedenborg in receiving communications from another world was perpetuated by the work of Franz Anton Mesmer in the mid-1700s. Animal magnetism and somnambulism led to "mesmerized" subjects, such as Frederica Hauffe in Germany, who went into trance to talk with persons who had died.

A century later in the United States, the "Poughkeepsie Seer," Andrew Jackson Davis, accelerated the trend. He was 16 years of age and a shoemaker's apprentice when he became "magnetized." In trance strange phenomena began to appear. Soon he became what today some call a psychic healer who while in a state of trance, diagnosed illnesses and prescribed cures. Again, while in trance, he delivered public lectures. He also published philosophical books, including *Nature's Divine Revelation* and *Principles of Nature* in which profound observations were made and spirit communications were said to be a truth which soon would be demonstrated to the world. Davis was a prominent figure on the American scene and set the stage for what happened in a farmhouse in Hydesville, Wayne County, New York, owned by Mr. and Mrs. J.D. Fox. The family, which included two daughters, Catherine, 12, and Margaretta, 15, heard rapping sounds in the house in March 1848. At first they thought rats might be causing the sounds or that a neighbor might be pounding away with a hammer. Finally, on March 31, Catherine thought the sounds might have an intelligent source. She challenged "it" to repeat the snaps of her fingers and the challenge was accepted. Mrs. Fox was astounded. She asked questions of the invisible intelligence and received rappings which spelled out that the intelligence was the spirit of a man murdered for money and buried in the cellar of the house.

If a great spiritual force could arise from a Judean carpenter speaking to crowds from boats and in Galilean streets, it should not be a shock to find out that it might come also from two small girls and an unseen intelligence speaking from a wooden farmhouse in upstate New York to crowds of neighbors attracted to the Fox house by the news. Nothing could stop Spiritualism, especially when people like Horace Greeley, owner of *The New York Times*, and Harriet Beecher Stowe, who wrote *Uncle Tom's Cabin*, supported it. Spiritualism even entered the White House where Mary Todd Lincoln held seances attended by the President. Everywhere else there were seances, also, with apports of objects penetrating solid walls, musical instruments floating and playing, and spirits of the dead conversing, writing or even materializing or appearing as "extras" on photographs.

These phenomena were too provocative to remain within the confines of the United States. By the third quarter of the 19th century, Spiritualism had invaded Great Britain, Europe and Brazil. With its churches and mediumistic seances, Spiritualism was an attempt to harmonize religion, philosophy and quasiscience into one movement based on a belief in a spirit world and in efforts to establish spirit communications. It generated so much interest among the masses that, at last, the intellectuals and scientists could resist it no longer.

The idea of founding the Society for Psychical Research came from Sir William Barrett, a professor of physics who came to Cambridge, England, in 1881 to stimulate the interest of some scholars in Trinity College in the phenomena of Spiritualism. In 1881 the Society was constituted with Barrett as vice president and Henry Sidgwick, professor of moral philosophy at Trinity College, president.

The Society was formed, said Sidgwick in his inaugural address, because we all agreed that the present state of things is a scandal to the enlightened age in which we live. That the dispute as to the reality of these marvellous phenomena, — of which it is quite impossible to exaggerate the scientific importance, if only a tenth part of what has been alleged by generally credible witnesses could be shewn to be true, — I say it is a scandal that the dispute as to the reality of these phenomena should still be going on.[2]

The first number of the *Proceedings* of the Society stated what it proposed to do about this scandal:

It has been widely felt that the present is an opportune time for making an organised and systematic attempt to investigate that large group of debateable phenomena designated by such terms as mesmeric, psychical, and Spiritualistic.[3]

That the topic of survival after death was not expressly stated as a subject of examination has led some students of the subject to conclude that the survival question "was *not* one of the subjects the Society was set up to investigate *per se.*"[4] Indeed, Frederic W.H. Myers, one of the members of the first S.P.R. Council, in his elegy to Edmund Gurney, another member of the Council, gave as the primary aim of the S.P.R. the study of telepathy with hypnosis running a close second.[5]

Nevertheless, there can be little doubt that the question of whether an "I" was independent of the doomed body and could persist beyond it occupied a central place in the scandal the S.P.R. was established to investigate and was indeed the principal target of the Society's attention. The subject is implied in the word "Spiritualistic," the phenomena the S.P.R. was to explore. Moreover, that the subject was an explicit concern of the S.P.R. was made clear by the declarations of its early leaders. We are told, for example, by Eleanor Sidgwick, wife of the S.P.R.'s first president and herself a distinguished and brilliant worker in the Society and its president in 1908 and its president of honor in 1932, that the survival question was "one which from the foundation of the Society in 1882 has interested the majority of the members more than any other branch of our enquiries, because of the far-reaching consequences its solution would carry with it."[6] And six years after the founding of the S.P.R. Sidgwick said in his Presidential address:

[W]hen we took up seriously the obscure and perplexing investigation which we call *Psychical Research*, we were mainly moved to do so by the profound and painful division and conflict, as regards the nature and destiny of the human soul, which we found in the thought of our age. On the one hand, under the influence of Christian teaching, still dominant over the minds of the majority of educated persons, and powerfully influencing many even of those who have discarded its dogmatic system, the soul is conceived as independent of the bodily organism and destined to survive it. On the other hand, the preponderant tendency of modern physiology has been more and more to exclude this conception. . . . Now our own position was this . . . [I]t appeared to us that there was an important

body of evidence — tending *prima facie* to establish the independence of the soul
of spirit — which modern science had simply left to one side with ignorant con-
tempt. . . . We meant to collect as systematically, carefully and completely as
possible evidence tending to throw light on the question of the action of the
mind either apart from the body or otherwise than through known bodily
organs.[7]

In his third Presidential address, he said:

In truth, there is not one of us who would not feel ten times more interest in proving the action of intelligences other than those of living men, than in proving
communication of human minds in an abnormal way.[8]

One by one the early members of the S.P.R. systematically and with great
care labored to investigate whether the continuity of individual existence
could be proved. Across the Atlantic, others were conscious of the same scandal to which Sigwick had referred.

Under the leadership of William James, the philosopher and psychologist from Harvard, a committee consisting of James, G. Stanley Hall of Johns
Hopkins University, C.S. Minot of Harvard Medical School and other eminent
people, met in 1884 to consider the formation of an American society. As a
result of that meeting, the American Society for Psychical Research was
formed in 1885. The first number of its *Proceedings*, after describing the aims
of the English Society, states the aims of the American organization:

The Council of the American society feel that the evidence published by the
English society is of a nature not to be ignored by scientific men . . . [and] that
the duty can be no longer postponed of systematically repeating observations
similar to those made in England, with a view toward confirming them if true,
to definitely pointing out the sources of error in them if false.[9]

Once again, the survival question was not made an explicit topic of examination by the A.S.P.R. But the question occupied its leaders. James
discovered the medium from Boston, Leonore E. Piper, whose trance
mediumship was to dominate the next decades, and he had sittings with her
all his life. Two years after the establishment of the A.S.P.R., Richard
Hodgson, who had served on the Council of the S.P.R. and had distinguished
himself in an investigation of Madame Blavatsky whose phenomena he found
fraudulent, became secretary of the American branch. He, too conducted an
extensive examination of Mrs. Piper. Following Hodgson's sudden death in
1905, the A.S.P.R. became an independent society under the leadership of
Professor James H. Hyslop. Hyslop was known and respected for his rigid experiments with mediums and for his careful scrutiny of the evidence of
postmortem existence.

So it was that, with the formation of the two societies for psychical
research and the work of their early (and some later) members, for the first
time the subject of human mortality, which had been wrapped in human fears
and hopes, in religious doctrines and superstitions, in philosophical

arguments and in moral and ethical considerations, was approached coolly, critically and without reference to religion, philosophy or morals. The sole question concerning the debated reality of survival-related phenomena was whether good evidence would be found to confirm their truth or show them to be false. What was done to gather this evidence and how far has this evidence brought us?

3

THE CONTINUING SCANDAL

The Society for Psychical Research established several committees to examine various subjects and they set to work with zeal and vigor. A Committee on Mesmerism reported its work in the first issue of the *Proceedings* of the English society.[1] The study of thought-reading (later called telepathy) led to experimental reports by the American society[2] while Gurney, Myers and Frank Podmore, as active workers in the English society, carefully collected and appraised the evidence of telepathy and published their results in 1886 in *Phantasms of the Living*.

But there was "ten times more interest" in the two classes of phenomena relevant to the dominating issue of personal postmortem survival. In the first class were unexpected events and experiences reported by witnesses which included haunted houses, covered in the first issue of the English *Proceedings*[3] and apparitions which resulted in an extensive "Theory of Apparitions" published in the *Proceedings* of 1884.[4]

The primary emphasis of both the English and American societies, however, was upon the experimental investigation of mediumistic phenomena. Some mediums, for example Eusapio Palladino and Mina Crandon (also known as "Margery"), who purported to produce physical phenomena such as materializations of hands, faces and forms and the levitation of objects, were examined. But so many were publicly exposed as frauds or were under a cloud of suspicion that the American society was discouraged from actively pursuing the study of physical mediumship.[5] Attention therefore was concentrated principally on trance mediumship in which people claimed to possess the paranormal ability to be the instruments through whom dead people communicated.

Many issues of the *Proceedings* and *Journals* of the English society are filled with the results of long investigations into famous British mediums of the era: Mrs. Holland (pseudonym for Rudyard Kipling's sister, Alice Fleming), Mrs. Willett (pseudonym for Winifred Coombe-Tennant), Mrs. A.W. Verrall and Mrs. Helen Verrall (Salter) and Gladys Osborne Leonard.

The publications of the American society reported in full on the trance phenomena of American mediums. Hodgson conducted detailed investigations of Mrs. Piper,[6] James's "white crow," and one of the greatest mediums of her time. After Hodgson's death, James produced a lengthy study of messages seeming to come through her from Hodgson as the deceased communicator.[7] Mrs. Smead (pseudonym of Mrs. Willis M. Cleaveland) and Mrs. Chenoweth (pseudonym of Mrs. Minnie R. Soule) were the subjects of experiments conducted by Hyslop, who published numerous papers on his research.[8] The importance Hyslop attached to sittings with these mediums can be gleaned from the fact that many of the *Proceedings* of the American Society for Psychical Research from 1909–1913 were devoted to their work.

For a period of about fifty years following the founding of the English and American societies the question of survival engrossed men and women of letters and scientists on both sides of the Atlantic. The evidence was collected, sifted and judged by them in such books as Barrett's *On the Threshold of the Unseen*,[9] Hyslop's *Contact with the Other World*[10] and Sir Oliver Lodge's *The Survival of Man*.[11] Perhaps the most famous of the works was a collection of facts relating to hauntings, apparitions, mediumship, telepathy and other psychic phenomena in support of the author's theory of a Subliminal Self and his belief in survival. This work was Myers' posthumous *Human Personality and Its Survival of Bodily Death*, published in 1903. When James reviewed it, he confessed that "I find myself filled with an admiration which almost surprises me. The work . . . strikes me as at least a masterpiece of co-ordination and unification. . . ."[13] In praise of Myers, Lodge said, "We too have had a Bacon. . . . It is possible that in his two posthumous volumes we have a book which posterity will regard as a *Novum Organum*."[14]

In addition to these works, thousands of pages printed in the proceedings and journals of the two psychical research societies stand as careful records of all investigations made and the evidence of survival which had been amassed and evaluated.

In the decades following *Human Personality* trance mediums continued to be studied and to supply the richest evidence. Researchers tried to strengthen the value of this evidence by improving methodology to determine whether information provided by a medium was beyond what could be expected by chance. J.G. Pratt, for example, applied this methodology in his investigations of Eileen Garrett, considered the greatest medium of her era.[15] To combat the possibility that a trance medium might be getting information by telepathy from living persons instead of from a dead one, investigations with mediums continued along two lines. In one the living person who knew the facts was blocked off from the medium by several persons who acted as intermediaries and through whose minds, it was thought, a medium would have to penetrate to reach the living source.[16] In the second kind of investigation cases were studied in which neither mediums nor sitters had any knowledge whatever of the deceased persons purporting to communicate — the so-called "drop-in" communicator — so that mediums would be compelled to tap a variety of distant sources, if any indeed existed, for the facts reported.[17]

Recent years also have witnessed studies made of cases of the reincarnation-type,[18] death-bed visions and near-death experiences,[19] out-of-body experiences[20] and electronic voices recorded on tape recorders.[21] To review all the evidence collected on behalf of personal postmortem survival would merely repeat what has been done already by W.H. Salter and Alan Gauld,[22] Gardner Murphy,[23] Curt J. Ducasse[24] and others. The sole aim now is to try to describe how far the evidence collected over a century of survival research has carried us toward establishing the reality of a human "I" across the gulf of death.

What have clear-sighted and serious investigators, authorities in the field of psychical research, found upon appraising the value of the evidence? Various of these authorities concluded that the evidence did not warrant any inference of survival. Charles Richet, a professor of physiology, a Nobel Prize winner and president of the Society for Psychical Research in 1905, said: "I am forced to regard the spiritistic hypothesis, not only as undemonstrated, but, still more, as being in formal opposition to a great number of facts. . . . [T]he theory of survival has some extremely feeble evidence in its favour."[25] Eric Dodds, a classical scholar and president of the S.P.R. from 1961 to 1963, said, "I must regard survival as unproved."[26] If there is any name familiar to anyone interested in ESP or any opinion respected, it is that of Joseph Banks Rhine who founded the Parapsychology Laboratory at Duke University and was president of the S.P.R. in 1980. He wrote:

> A detailed scientific appraisal of [the evidence] brings out the fact that it was not adequate to meet the general critical requirements for proof. . . . [A]s we review the evidence on record to date, there is none that is completely unambiguous, that rules out all the counterhypotheses that have to be considered.[27]

In addition to the views of these three distinguished individuals, the opinion of the members of the Parapsychological Association should be considered. The P.A., which became affiliated with the American Association for the Advancement of Science in 1969, is an international organization of mathematicians, philosophers, lawyers, psychiatrists, psychologists, engineers, and others studying psychical phenomena. In a poll taken in 1980, 87 percent of the members said that survival after death was not the only explanation for the evidence.[28]

The attitude of other authorities is entirely contradictory. A physicist who was knighted in 1902, Sir Oliver Lodge was also president of the English society from 1901 to 1903. Some mediumistic communications persuaded him to say:

> The evidence needs careful and critical study; it is not in itself sensational, but it affords strong evidence of the intervention of a mind behind and independent of the automatist [or medium]. . . . [A] good case has been made out, and that as the best working hypothesis at the present time it is legitimate to grant that lucid moments of intercourse with deceased persons may in the best cases supervene.[29]

Ducasse, a professional philosopher, was occupied as few philosophers are with the survival question. His critical examination of the evidence of mediumistic communications and other types of evidence led him to say

> that the balance of the evidence so far obtained is on the side of the reality of survival and, in the best cases, of survival not merely of memories of the life on earth, but of survival also of the most significant capacities of the human mind, and of continuing exercise of them after death.[30]

Ian Stevenson, professor of psychiatry and director of the Division of Parapsychology at the University of Virginia Medical Center, has distinguished himself as one of the foremost survival researchers. He said, "I prefer only to record my conviction that the evidence of human survival after death is strong enough to permit a belief in survival on the basis of the evidence."[31]

Few people dominated the field of psychical research in the last three decades more than the late Gardner Murphy. He made many and monumental contributions to it in the form of lectures, articles and books. As president of the American Society for Psychical Research from 1965 to 1971 he administered its programs with the same strength and dedication demonstrated by its former great leaders, Hyslop and Walter F. Prince. But Murphy differed from them in that he himself conducted no investigations in the search for survival evidence. Yet he had a great interest in survival. His reviews and analyses of the evidence contained in three famous papers published by the American society[32] and his book *The Challenge of Psychical Research*[33] still remain among the best ever made. They left him unable to say whether the evidence was weak or strong. He found that it could not be bypassed or ignored. It was neither totally convincing nor totally unconvincing. It did not permit him to take a position one way or another. He described his stand in these words: "[W]hat happens when an irresistible force strikes an immovable object?"[34]

After 100 years of survival research the situation prevailing in the field is best described by recalling to mind a series carried a few years ago on American and English television called *The Long Search*. It was an exploration of the world's religions during which many parts of the world were visited. One of the programs originated from Jerusalem where a rabbi was interviewed. When he was asked whether Jews were argumentative people, he replied: "Where you find two Jews, you'll find three opinions." Similarly, among those who appraise seriously and critically the evidence on behalf of survival, there are three opinions. One, represented by Richet, Dodds, Rhine and the Parapsychological Association, speaking for the sceptics, is that the evidence can be explained by alternative theories and therefore does not support a belief in survival. A second opinion, represented by Lodge, Ducasse and Stevenson, speaking for the convinced, finds the evidence of sufficient strength to allow a valid belief in survival. A third opinion, represented by Murphy, speaking for the undecided, is that one cannot believe or disbelieve and that the entire case still rests upon dead center.

People who reflect on these different and conflicting points of view must find themselves in the predicament of one investigator who was asked to prepare a review of the survival evidence and to evaluate it. When he sat down to do so, his first words were: "Any attempt to survey the evidence for human survival of bodily death faces a dilemma."[35] If we follow one opinion, there is no evidence in favor of a postmortem existence. If we follow another, there is a great deal. And if we follow a third, we don't know what to believe and are unable to commit ourselves.

It is clear that, although investigators have been attempting to grapple with the problem of survival across the gulf for more than a century, as was said by Henry H. Price, the Oxford philosopher and twice president of the English society, "we are still nowhere near a solution of it."[36]

Since the resolution of the survival question would have a profound impact on science, philosophy and religion, and would make life bearable and meaningful for many, this situation causes us the greatest dismay. To repeat what Sidgwick said in his first Presidential address in 1881: It is a scandal that the reality of human survival of death should still be a matter of sharp dispute.

4
NEW PERSPECTIVES

New perspectives have always played a vital role in the history of science. Take falling objects, for example. When *Homo sapiens* first discovered fire and began to make tools, flying sparks and flint flaked from cutting edges fell to the floors of his caves. And, of course, a variety of other objects had always fallen to the ground and remained there. Yet millions of pairs of human eyes and intelligences had taken no particular note of them until one leisurely day in 1666, in Woolsthurde, England, when a falling round red object was observed by one special pair of eyes and one special intelligence. As Byron said:

> When Newton saw an apple fall, he found,
> In that slight startle from his contemplation, . . .
> A mode of proving that the earth turned round,
> In a most natural whirl called gravitation.[1]

The common sight of a falling apple, which had never before excited attention or speculation and which by Newton's own account sparked the basic idea of gravitation, led him on the path of one of the great discoveries in science. We can call the new-sight-of-the-apple an act of genius or a new angle of vision.

Job's question, repeated for centuries, suddenly became for us the "new-sight-of-the-apple" and stimulus for new angles of vision. So might the scandal that continues over the actuality of survival if it were approached without prejudice. It is interesting that although a plethora of books have been written for the general reader on the subject of a future life, none has acknowledged the opportunity presented by the scandal for more imaginative insights. We can explain this myopia by dividing popular books into two classes, which I call the "will to believe" class and the "will to disbelieve" class.

In the first class, writers seem so anxious to allay the fear of death or to paint a rosy picture of the postmortem world that they treat the evidence simplistically and without regard for alternative explanations and as if it led inescapably to the conclusion that we survive death.[2] In the "will to disbelieve" class, writers are so eager to demonstrate that survival is an illusion and that this life is all that there is, again oversimplifying the matter, they treat the evidence in a superficial and supercilious manner and brand it negatively.[3] Books in a third class, the "will to be realistic" class, as this one aspires to be, are rare if they exist at all. In this class, the approach to the subject is made with the honest admission that it is not simple but is complicated and perplexing. Such books, besides being campgrounds for people who cannot express an opinion, are arenas in which our best thinkers express conflicting opinions with respect to the evidence.

It is exactly the realistic and honest approach that is needed if innovative ways to stronger and clearer evidence on behalf of survival are to be discovered. Gardner Murphy took this approach. He wanted more convincing evidence which might push the case off dead center this way or that. His hope was for better research efforts to get it. "We need new perspectives," he said.[4]

If we sit back with Newtonian calm and contemplation and take the time and trouble to examine the subject through fresh and realistic lenses, four new and constructive perspectives might be developed. They are (1) the view of the fallen torch, (2) the view of the angle that has been neglected, (3) the view of death, the unequalizer and (4) the view of the future. These perspectives may afford us all a theoretical model for a more effective assault on the problem and the production of survival evidence of a more decisive nature. It is toward this ultimate destination that we are journeying.

The view of the fallen torch is our immediate concern. The rest of the perspectives will follow in due course. Virtually every review of the evidence on behalf of survival, whether in popular books dealing with life after death or in scholarly or scientific literature, are mirror images of one another, each reflecting with monotonous repetition the same experiments and cases which date back to the beginnings of psychical research. The "cross-correspondences," for example, first noted over 75 years ago by Alice Johnson, then research officer of the (English) Society for Psychical Research, are cited over and over again. Nothing new is presented. The age of the evidence does not render it valueless, and I do not propose to dump it out with the garbage. With rare exception, however, it is the absence of anything fresh that is significant. Why are there no reports of fresh investigations and why is there so little production of any new data? What happened to the quest for evidence?

As the years passed, the pioneers who started this quest died off. Even when dead, however, their concern with obtaining this evidence seems not to have waned as they looked to the living to take their places. After Edmund Gurney died in 1888, a message purportedly from him appeared in a medium's script:

It has been a long work—but the
work is not nearly over yet—It has

barely begun — Go on with it — go on —
We were the torch bearers — follow after us.[5]

How well have their successors followed? If we try to estimate the progress that has been made in picking up and carrying the torch dropped by Gurney and his contemporaries, we should be forced to measure it in terms of millimeters instead of kilometers. Should interest in the survival question be represented on a chart we would see that scientific interest reached its highest level between the 1880s and 1930s. From the 1930s to the 1960s, when Rhine and others generated enthusiasm for laboratory research into extrasensory perception and psychokinesis, interest in survival dipped sharply to its lowest point as attention was diverted from mediumship and reports of hauntings and apparitions. From the 1960s to the present, although a few notable exceptions, such as investigations of cases of the reincarnation type and deathbed visions, allowed interest to pick up slightly, survival interest has fluctuated uncertainly along a low level.

Several reasons for why Gurney's successors have dropped the torch left to them are discussed and criticized in the literature.[6] In consequence of them, as Rhine notes:

...the psychical research societies today are practically inactive on the survival problem.... [T]he issue has become almost a dead one.[7]

How dead is "almost dead?" Some facts indicate how few vital signs remain. Of the approximately 300 parapsychologists who attended the joint Society for Psychical Research and Parapsychological Association Centenary–Jubilee Conference held at Trinity College in Cambridge, England, in 1982, only three, including the author, continued to investigate survival. The loss of interest and the darkly pessimistic attitude toward the subject on the part of the remaining 99 percent of the attendees at the Conference were demonstrated clearly by the title of a paper on survival presented there. It was called "The Forlorn Quest" whose concluding words were: "Whether the quest for human survival will be resumed, we cannot tell."[8] Another good measure of the stage the survival quest has reached so far as the parapsychological community is concerned was an interview held in 1976 by a leader of that community whose responses apparently had the tacit approval of the American Society for Psychical Research because they were printed in its prestigious and refereed *Journal*. The interviewer asked: "Could you give me a definition of the parapsychology field? I am not sure what it includes..." The reply was: "Parapsychology is the study of the two phenomena, extrasensory perception and psychokinesis (PK)."[9] In the opinion of this speaker, a former president of the Parapsychological Association, survival had disappeared from the parapsychological map.

Yet it has not vanished completely. Four small centers continue to investigate the problem actively: The Survival Research Foundation of Pembroke Pines, Florida; the Department of Behavioral Medicine and Psychiatry (formerly the Division of Parapsychology) at the University of Virginia in Charlottesville; the Psychical Research Foundation at the Department of Psychology, West Georgia College, Carrollton; and the Metascience Foundation in Franklin, North Carolina. An International Foundation for Survival Research in Los Angeles seeks to raise funds for survival research. But we are discussing a handful of researchers and support organizations and a mere trickle of resources. There has thus been a near abandonment by Gurney's modern counterparts of the quest for evidence. What a contrast to the time when the subject of survival was of tenfold greater interest to the members of the English society than other psychic phenomena!

The present indifference to the subject is not only a departure from the passionate attitude of earlier researchers; it verges on the inexplicable when we consider that, among medical scientists, behavioral scientists, scholars, clergy, health care professionals, jurists, thanatologists, clergy and lay persons, the issues raised by death have become topics of intense interest and study: Can the dying be allowed to ask to die? When should artificial life support systems be turned off? When are patients dead so that their vital organs can be transplanted? Everybody has got into the act today. Many are wrestling with one of death's issues with all the intellectual and emotional strength they have. In the societies for psychical research only bored yawns are induced by this most important issue, death. What is it? Must it be feared as the final extinction of the individual? Or is it a "change of life?"

To these societies and their present members, and to all others, we say, along with French philosopher Blaise Pascal, that this "is a matter which is of so great consequence to us, and which touches us so profoundly, that we must have lost all feeling to be indifferent as to knowing what it is."[10]

The controversy which surrounds survival research is twofold. It consists on the one hand of the continuing dispute over the reality of survival and on the other of a virtual neglect of the question. It is an intellectual scandal that should arouse the feelings of every member of the intelligent and educated segments of society. It should bring them sharply out of the comfortable but false supposition that the subject is receiving serious attention from professional researchers. If a new model for investigation were offered to these researchers, as it will be here, would they turn their attention to it? We may need to realize that we can no longer rely on the psychical research societies and parapsychological associations to resolve this issue of survival which is of such momentous importance to us. We must act ourselves.

5
THE NEGLECTED ANGLE

For the founders of psychical research the late 19th century was "an opportune time for making an organized and systematic attempt to investigate" various of the phenomena that claimed public attention, especially those related to the actuality of survival after death. Although almost the entire parapsychological community has withdrawn from the survival problem, the late 20th century presents us with an even more opportune and critical time for such an attempt.

If, however, we make our own systematic inquiry into the survival question, why should our effort not tumble into the same pit of pessimism and apathy that has trapped professional researchers for the past 50 years? Why should our effort produce better evidence than has been collected over the past 100 years? The answer may lie in new perspectives.

We can begin to try to pick up the fallen torch of the early researchers by focussing on the contents of the pages of the mainstream publications issued by the primary centers of psychical research. A survey of the reported cases and experiments dealing with mediumship discloses that the mediumistic situation has been looked on as a straight line drawn from the medium at one end to the experimenter at the other. Intensive studies were made of the medium's end of the line. Mental mediums were wired to EEG machines, were given psychological tests both in trance and in normal states, had their verbal material assessed, were subjected to ESP tests and even followed by detectives to ensure that they did not come dishonestly by the information they gave. Recently, the role the experimenter plays has been recognized so that the methods and attitudes of investigators in the achievement of psi results have been examined to determine their significance. But there has been little realization that mediumistic communication requires a partner (albeit a dead one), and the deceased partner has been all but ignored in favor of the medium and the experimenter.

But suppose we shift our point of view. In ESP tests the situation is not thought of as a straight line but as a triangle with the target, the experimenter and the subject at the three angles. Here, "the subject is obviously the most important angle."[1] If we think of the mediumistic situation as triangular, the investigator is at one angle, at the second is the trance medium and at the third angle the deceased communicator. The role of the communicator is probably the "most important angle," but even if we give equal importance to the medium, we cannot fail to see that the communicator is highly significant.

"The search for gifted subjects has always been an important concern of the inquiring parapsychologist."[2] Some of the most convincing data for ESP, for example, came from the Parapsychology Laboratory at Duke University because J.B. Rhine and J.G. Pratt conducted such a search and chose for their card-calling experiments Hubert Pearce who had demonstrated telepathic ability. In the quest for survival evidence, one would have thought that, consistent with this selective policy, researchers would have been as concerned and discriminating in the choice of communicators as in the choice of ESP subjects. But attention was riveted on the medium and only the most limited studies were made of communicators.[3,4] Thus the discovery that the communicator has been neglected redirects our thinking. Why were researchers not more concerned over whether the personal histories, qualities and circumstances of communicators might hinder or set free their power to produce mediumistic phenomena? What did they assume that might have diverted them from this angle of approach?

Pratt, a distinguished researcher, said: "Research is never free of assumptions, whether they are explicitly stated or only implied. Either way, they strongly influence the investigator at every stage...."[5] Research on the question of survival is also heavily charged with express and implied assumptions. Two of these are working assumptions.

In order to investigate we must suppose that it is possible that the human personality is independent of the physical body and survives it after bodily death. This assumption is the *sine qua non* of research in this area. Unless there is some provisional acceptance of the possibility of survival, there can be no investigation of it. It was this assumption, in fact, that permitted survival research to begin in the first place. The Society for Psychical Research did not go out blindly to collect facts relating to hauntings, apparitions and mediumship. The presidential addresses of Sidgwick quoted in Chapter 2 make it clear that the investigation of such evidence was motivated and preceded by a dualistic theory and started as an effort to get facts that might confirm or refute the theory.[6] The dualistic assumption is adopted not only as a rudder for the research but as a way of expanding our knowledge:

> *Research effort should be increased when we are confronted with an "either-or" situation, and we should actually favor the more novel explanation, in this case the possibility of survival, during the evidence-gathering stage of the research.*
> If as a consequence, the novel explanation should eventually prove to be the correct one, science would have benefited through our venturesomeness.[7]

Another assumption which is an indispensable condition of investigation is that communication with the dead is possible. It is obvious that every effort to make contact with deceased persons must be hinged to this assumption. Telepathy has been shown by experiences in daily life and repeated laboratory experiments to be a real phenomenon. We can therefore assume further that, if the minds of living people can communicate unrestricted by space, a human mind surviving death may have the power to communicate telepathically across the great gulf with a living mind, as in mediumship. As an alternative to telepathy, if a human mind survives death perhaps it can communicate with the living via electronic instrumentation, such as the tape recorder, and affect the electromagnetic tape in some unknown way, perhaps by psychokinesis (mind over matter), so as to cause it to register a voice. We can hypothesize other forms of communication as well: A decedent might temporarily take over the organs of a living person in order to speak or write as in cases of apparent possession; or might project a surviving consciousness so that it can be seen or heard as in apparition cases or hauntings.

A pair of widely held assumptions, however, like blinders, seem to have narrowed the view of survival researchers and prevented them from studying the attributes of communicators. One of these assumptions is that, if there is survival after the grave, all people will survive equally. There will be no exceptions. In the words of one respected student of the subject "survival is automatic and universal."[8] There is a corollary to this "all survive" assumption: If a human mind has the ability to communicate with living minds, this ability is automatic and universal as well and is possessed in the same degree by all survivors of death. The afterlife can be thought of as governed by the same democratic philosophy and self-evident truths that are, for example, expressed in the Declaration of Independence: It is a place where all are created and die equal, where all are endowed with the same rights and where all privilege is extinguished.

The importance of the ability to communicate posthumously cannot be overemphasized. Even if a human being survives death and does so with the stream of consciousness uninterrupted by death, if the ability to manifest the fact of survival to the living does not exist, that fact cannot be authenticated and badly needed evidence cannot be obtained. The "equal ability" assumption, however, declares that the ability to give evidence is universal and that every deceased person can be the source of such evidence.

Both these assumptions are not only unnecessary for the investigation of the survival problem, but, if false, either or both may have severely retarded the search for better evidence. It is certain that any approach through mediumistic experiments based on these assumptions to try to obtain messages from a specific deceased person cannot be successful, no matter how ingenious the experimental design or how powerful the medium, if that person has not survived death or does not have the capacity to communicate

posthumously. The prospect for evidence on behalf of survival may improve
if these assumptions are discarded. It is therefore of crucial importance to take
a good hard look at them. Why are they generally accepted? Do they stand
up to logic? Is there any systematic way to test them?

6
THE DEMOCRACY
OF THE DEAD

Cemeteries reflect many of our basic beliefs about the society of the living. One of the great poems of 18th century English poetry, Gray's *Elegy Written in a Country Churchyard*, perceived in the cemetery the leveling of all persons, a kind of democracy:

Let not ambition mock their useful toil,
   Their homely joys, and destiny obscure;
Nor grandeur hear with a disdainful smile,
   The short and simple annals of the poor.
The boast of heraldry, the pomp of power,
   And all that beauty, all that wealth e'er gave
Awaits alike the inevitable hour:
   The paths of glory lead but to the grave.

Cemeteries present to us an image of the society of the dead that has given rise to the "all survive" and "equal abilities" assumptions. This image is reflected in the poem *Death the Leveler* by James Shirley, a 17th century poet:

The glories of our blood and state
Are shadows, not substantial things;
There is no armour against fate;
   Death lays his icy hands on kings:
      Sceptre and crown
      Must tumble down,
   And in the dust be equal made
With the poor crooked scythe and spade.

This notion appealed to political minds, too. John James Ingalls, a senator from Kansas whose statue was placed by that state in Statuary Hall as a tribute to his oratory and writings, articulated it:

In the democracy of the dead, all men at last are equal. There is neither rank nor station nor prerogative in the republic of the grave.

But this egalitarian conception of the society of the dead has not been alone responsible for producing the "all survive" and "equal ability" assumptions; they have arisen also from a failure to take into account the several contingencies of the postmortem state.

Let us suppose that eight people (Mrs. V, Mr. V, Mr. W, Mr. X, Mr. Y, Mr. Z, Ms. A and Master B) have died.

Possibility 1 is that all eight individuals are identical with their bodies and will be no more after their brains and bodies perish.

Possibility 2 is that some core factor existing in Mrs. V, unlike her physical body, will persist after death, be reincarnated in a new human body with the aptitude to give evidence of her former life by the recognition of people or places connected with it or by statements about it that can be verified.

Possibility 3 is that some core factor existing in Mr. V, unlike his physical body but possessing his antemortem memories, traits, habits of speech or writing, his skills or knowledge, will persist after death in a disembodied or quasiphysical state, such as an astral or spiritual body, and will be able to manifest clearly all his characteristics to the living.

Possibility 4 is that a core factor residing in Mr. W and possessing all the marks of his antemortem personality will persist after death disembodied or in some quasiphysical form but will be able to give only some slight evidence of personal identity and nothing more.

Possibility 5 is that a core factor in Mr. X, unlike his everyday body but possessing the components of his antemortem personality, also will persist after death disembodied or in quasiphysical form but will be either partly unable or somewhat reluctant to manifest personal identity.

Possibility 6 is that some core factor existing in Mr. Y unlike his normal body and possessing all his antemortem memories, traits, etc., will persist after death disembodied or in a quasiphysical state but will be totally unable or unwilling to give evidence of personal identity.

Possibility 7 is that some core factor existing in Mr. Z unlike his normal body will persist after death disembodied or in a quasiphysical state but will be devoid of all that made up his antemortem personality.

Possibility 8 is that a core factor existing in Ms. A during her life unlike her normal body and capable of persisting after death as the vehicle of her antemortem traits, etc., nevertheless ceases to exist simultaneously with her body and brain so that the effect is the same as if she had perished when her body and brain did.

Possibility 9 is that, unlike the other seven people, no core factor ever existed in Master B which could have persisted after death. He was identical with his body.

These possibilities show that the "all survive" and "equal ability" assumptions are unreasonable. Even in the republic of the grave people are not clones. Any research effort we undertake must see them in this new light so that they represent different shades of interest for us depending on the contingencies which may befall them. For example, Mrs. V reincarnated and Mr. V as a clear and full-blown communicator would be of great interest to us and our search for evidence should be built around them. Mr. W also would be of some interest. On the other hand, Mr. X as a feeble or uncertain communicator would be of limited interest while Mr. Y and Mr. Z would be of no interest since they would be incapable of giving evidence. Ms. A and Master B would be a sheer waste of time.

In the light of world population figures, the "all survive" assumption seems purely gratuitous. From time to time there have been attempts to count people. Moses numbered the males of the family of Levi and found 7500 (Numbers 3:15–22) and Caesar ordered a census of the Roman Empire for the purposes of taxation and administration. But for thousands of years and prior to the 17th century, no serious studies were made of the world population. We can merely speculate that a great number of men, women and children once occupied this planet.

Firmer estimates can be made for the population of the world since 1600 as a result of improved population censuses and studies. According to the *Encyclopaedia Britannica* over six billion people have lived on earth during the last 300 years. If we add to this figure an indeterminate large figure for the earlier periods, we unmask the "all survive" assumption as absurd. For out of this enormous ocean of people who have lived, died and disappeared without a trace, we have but a cupful of paranormal phenomena related to human survival of death.

When W.G. Roll surveyed poltergeist disturbances over four centuries in the United States, the British Isles, Europe, Indonesia, India and Mauritius, he found 116 cases.[1] If we accept that all these strange breakages and movements of objects were suggestive of the agency of dead people and were not caused by the energy emanating from a living adolescent or emotionally disturbed person, where is the deluge of poltergeist phenomena which would indicate the agencies of billions of dead persons?

Ian Stevenson reports that in his files at the Division of Parapsychology at the University of Virginia, there are 1300 cases of the reincarnation type, most of which he and his colleagues have investigated in India, Sri Lanka, Thailand, Lebanon, Turkey, Alaska and elsewhere.[2] Shouldn't Stevenson's files be bulging with tens of millions of cases to be investigated in these countries and cultures?

There is a similar feebleness in the numbers of authentic mediumistic communications, hauntings, apparitions of the dead and cases of possession. Were survival universal, why would the numbers be so small? Why aren't dead people communicating, haunting, being seen as apparitions and possessing the living in numbers approaching the number of 20th century deaths, estimated at about 100 million, from bombs, guns, gas chambers and prisoner of war camps?

The answer to all these questions may be that survival after death is not universal and that it has been wrong to assume that it is. Survival seems to be infrequent and restricted.

Yet, although we seem to have good and logical grounds for thinking that the "all survive" assumption is ridiculous and has done and is doing great mischief to survival research, we cannot devise any means to dislodge the assumption. That billions of people may have disappeared, left no traces and were never heard from again—whether as poltergeists, apparitions, persons with memories of past lives or as communicators through mediums—does not necessarily mean that these people have ceased to exist. Their remaining in utter silence after death could signify possibilities 1, 8 or 9 but might also mean possibilities 5, 6 or 7. In our ignorance and inability to produce one iota of evidence that these people have not survived death, we can asseverate nothing. We have no way of solving the problem of nonsurvival. We cannot prove a negative and can go no further with it.

Like the "all survive" assumption, the assumption of "equal ability" may be just as simplistic. It ignores our everyday, workaday common knowledge: that human society is a mosaic of diversities and inequalities. Some of us are strong, others weak. Some are rich and others poor. Some are leaders, some followers, some masters, some servants. Some have greater talent, some lesser. Is it any different in the world of the paranormal? Parapsychologists are very much aware that some people have out-of-body experiences and some do not, and some have near-death experiences and some do not. In ESP tests, some people, like Hubert Pearce in the United States and Basil Shackleton in England, have been stars, some have displayed only a modest range of psychic gifts and others have shown a lack of psychic talents.

On these grounds, it is logically possible to attack the "equal ability" assumption and argue that only some people may be stars able to give clear evidence of their survival and that some may have only a fair ability to do so and some may have no ability at all. It is entirely reasonable to say, as did Hodgson, "it may well be that the aptitude for communicating clearly may be as rare as the gifts that make a great artist, or a great mathematician, or a great philosopher."[3]

In addition, even if the aptitude for communicating were shared equally by all prior to death, the blow of death or the strange environment of an afterlife—if one exists—may make some people less able than others to give evidence of their survival and identity, and this lessened ability, or the complete loss of it, may last a very long time. But the "equal ability" assumption is old and influential and not easily dislodged by theoretical considerations. And it is not a question of logic; it is a scientific question. The only certain way to settle the issue of whether the "equal ability" assumption is true or false is by determining whether the evidence sustains or contradicts it.

Unlike "all survive," "equal ability" may not be impervious to systematic investigation. Our aim now will be to place it on the operating table for the first time and to examine ostensible communicators from the "other side" to find out what makes them tick, to see if they possess things in common and, if not, what makes them different. A doctor, asked by a patient, "Doctor, will this operation be successful?" replied: "That's what we're about to find out."

7

SAINTS AND SCOUNDRELS

How can we test the belief of poets, politicians and pessimistic psychical researchers that death is the great equalizer? There is a method, important in both law and psychical research, that may show the way.

The common law of Great Britain and the United States derives from cases which have been decided by the courts and published in thousands of reports. Lawyers and judges study the reported cases and use them as precedents in deciding later cases with similar facts. This case method is equally valuable in psychical research. It is from the study of spontaneous case reports of thousands of people describing their natural, everyday experiences that much has been learned about the nature and functions of ESP, and the cases have given direction to the avenues of research and experiment.

The case method was used here in the hope that it would provide some needed guidance for us as we try to determine whether the dead are equal in their ability to communicate. Twelve cases were examined and their subjects classified according to the strength of the evidence their communications provided toward establishing postmortem identity.

If the egalitarian assumption were correct, as seems to have been taken for granted, all persons in all cases, whether during life they were high or low in the social scale, saints or scoundrels, or had similar or dissimilar attributes, should have had the same abilities to give evidence of personal identity in their postmortem communications. But if the assumption were incorrect, as it seemed to be on the surface, we should expect that some of these persons would be good, some bad and some very bad communicators.* Unequal abilities to manifest postmortem identity would decisively contradict the assumption.

Before we could place communicators in categories, however, certain

*Readers are reminded that the investigation of the survival question involves the tentative acceptance of the possibility of survival and postmortem communication. These are working hypotheses. Words like "communicator" or "medium" are used for the purpose of clarity and not to imply any belief that survival and communication have been proved.

criteria needed to be established in order to classify a case. Necessarily, some degree of subjective judgment and some arbitrariness were involved in deciding how to apply these criteria. Since the cases studied will be made accessible to readers, we will all have the right to disagree with any determination made here and to substitute our own judgment in any case.

The following four categories were set up along with their criteria:

CATEGORY 1

Cases where decedent (a) has clearly established evidence of personal identity; and (b) has recognized people or places involved in a former life or made statements about it that are corroborated; or (c) has conveyed verifiable information unknown to a living person; or (d) has shown antemortem traits, abilities, knowledge or other indicia of personality.

CATEGORY 2

Cases where evidence of personal identity has clearly been supplied by a decedent but neither element (c) nor element (d) mentioned above is present.

CATEGORY 3

Cases where a decedent has not given satisfactory evidence of personal identity, i.e., the evidence is doubtful or insufficient.

CATEGORY 4

Cases where a decedent has not been able to give satisfactory evidence of personal identity or any other evidence.

The categories described cover the possibilities discussed earlier. Mrs. V and Mr. V (possibilities 2 and 3) are examples of Category 1 decedents. Mr. W (Possibility 4) is a Category 2 decedent while Mr. X (Possibility 5) is placed in Category 3. Mr. Y and Mr. Z (possibilities 6 and 7) belong in Category 4 as do Ms. A and Master B. In Category 4 we cannot and need not differentiate among possibilities 7, 8 and 9.

It was decided to study the case histories of two population samples. But the immediate problem was to select the source from which the samples were taken. In the last decade there has been a massive surge of interest in the subject of life after death. A flood of magazine articles and religious, psychological and popular books have come pouring off the presses. Caution was obviously necessary. Sensational accounts, such as are reported in the *National Enquirer*, and reports in Spiritualist-oriented books and newspapers that would have us believe not only that everyone is a Category 1 communicator but that all discarnate communicators are paragons of wisdom and great spiritual teachers, had to be avoided. The decision was made to study samples selected from cases published in the serious parapsychological literature in the belief that the good faith, integrity and competence of the impartial investigators who witnessed or conducted experiments or investigations and of the editors who published case reports were not open to question.

The publications of the English and American societies for psychical research were searched for mediumistic experiments and, as a beginning, 12 cases reported in them analyzed. In making these analyses the reports were accepted as written, an independent judgment being made thereafter on the evidence presented to determine if the persons involved in the cases demonstrated equal or unequal abilities to give evidence of postmortem identity. (Readers wishing to review these cases will find that Appendix C refers to each case by number and gives a reference in the literature.)

These initial 12 cases were divided in half. One-half consisted of a population sample of six people considered representative of the general population. These six people came from different backgrounds, had dissimilar aims, interests and values and disparate social stations, educational levels and intellectual abilities. They were a moneyed businessman and sportsman, a roustabout writer, a middle-class spinster, a politician who became a college president, a clergyman-publisher and a poor housewife. The immediate concern is not the lives of the six, which will be summarized only very briefly in what follows, but an examination of how they performed (if they did perform) after their deaths. If the afterlife is governed by democratic principles, regardless of their prior differences each member of this heterogeneous group should have performed equally after death. One of these cases, in which both William James and Richard Hodgson were involved, came from the mediumship of Mrs. Piper, one of America's great mediums. The remaining five cases were taken from the mediumship experiments conducted by Hyslop with Mrs. Chenoweth.

Case 1. John Jacob Astor IV

Millionaire John Jacob Astor IV not only raced cars and built hotels; he was an inventor and writer. He went down with the *Titanic* in 1912. During 1913 and 1914 Professor Hyslop held a series of sittings with Mrs. Chenoweth at her house in Boston (34b, 35c, 36c)* (Hyslop, 1925, p. 433fn).† There is

---

*Figures in parentheses inserted in the description of all cases refer to the List of Special Factors which will be explained later in Chapter 8, "The Making of a Communicator."
†All references are to Appendix C.

no indication in the record that either Hyslop, who was to the sitter, or the medium had any prior dealings with Astor (39s, 40d).

In the spring of 1913 Mrs. Astor had some sittings during which no evidential material was given. Unknown to the medium, Mrs. Astor was to have returned for a sitting with Mrs. Chenoweth on October 20, 1913. A few days before the sitting, however, Mrs. Astor cancelled her appointment (Ibid., p. 50 fn). Nevertheless, Hyslop proceeded with the sitting. While the medium was doing automatic writing (38b), a communicator* supposed to be William T. Stead, who had died when the *Titanic* sank on April 15, 1912, came through her. Various references were made to his sister, son and secretary. Toward the end of the sitting the communicator complained that he was dizzy as if he were whirling around like a whirlpool in the ocean. Then he said, "Where did Astor go?" (Ibid., p. 50).

Astor, of course, had been drowned with Stead and others as Mrs. Chenoweth was bound to know. *The New York Times* and other leading papers carried stories on the front pages with titles such as "Colonel Astor Went Down Waving Farewell to His Bride" and "The Titanic's Rescued Tell of Colonel Astor's Heroism as Ship Went Down." Yet the explicit reference to Astor is of interest because it was made during a sitting to which his wife was to have come. Although interesting, it is not evidence of Astor's identity.

On November 25, 1913, sitting again with Mrs. Chenoweth who was doing automatic writing (38b, 41a), a communicator appeared who seemed to want to give information. Hyslop tried with difficulty to find out who was communicating. The communicator complained,

"If I could only write my own name it would help so much" (p. 144). The communicator wanted to tell a number of people of his return. Then the automatist wrote the letter "J." Then the pencil fell from her hand. Thereafter the letters "a–s–t" appeared after which the pencil fell again.

On January 20, 1914, still doing automatic writing, Mrs. Chenoweth's script recorded a reference by a communicator to his wife and his wish to help her because of "sweet burdens" that were to fall on her. He was upset about fatherless offspring coming to a widowed mother. Again, Hyslop asked who the communicator was. "J . . .Jack" was the reply. The communicator described himself as having been killed very suddenly and as having tried to come through to Hyslop the previous year. When Hyslop asked the widow's name, the initial "M" was given. The reference to "sweet burdens," fatherless offspring to come and to "M" could have related to Mrs. Astor who was pregnant at the time of Astor's death and whose name was "Madeline." The reference to "Jack" might have been correct since people called Astor "Jack."

Whenever "communicator" or the names of "communicators" are used, terms such as "purported" or "alleged" are intended as qualifying terms.

At the start of the sitting of January 21, 1914, an article not described in the report was placed on the table after which Mrs. Chenoweth went into a trance. After a pause she whispered, "What did we hit?" She repeated the phrase. The communicator then asked Hyslop: "Do you know anyone named Nan?...I don't mean Nancy, but I hear Nan or Nanny." He added, "It is funny what a mixed up condition is here. Ugh!"

With Mrs. Chenoweth writing automatically the communicator said he was glad of the safe deliverance of the child (p. 197)—a statement that related directly to the sitting of the day before, which dealt with a coming offspring. Now in a trance, Mrs. Chenoweth exclaimed: "Oh, who shot me? Who shot me?" The relevance of this exclamation was not clear. Then the medium's chief control, Madame, apparently took over Mrs. Chenoweth and demanded to know the name of the man who was holding up in his hand a letter "M" as if for someone he knew. When he was asked for the name, it was given as Madge, then Maud, then Madeline and finally Marion was spelled out. Madeline was Astor's wife, but Marion was the correct name of the wife of another communicator Hyslop wanted to reach (p. 199 so that the evidence here is doubtful).

Some months later, at the sitting of May 19, 1914, once more a package wrapped in oiled silk and whose contents were not known to Hyslop was placed on the table. With the medium doing automatic writing, a communicator appeared and said that there was much to be said and that friends were anxious. Then Mrs. Chenoweth wrote and spoke: "I belong to that article. She sent it to me." Hyslop wanted proof of who was communicating. There came a pause, the pencil fell and there was heavy breathing by the medium. The communicator tried to give his name. The initials "I" or "J" and "G" were given and then the alphabet up to "W," the communicator groaning and saying that he thought he could stop when he reached a letter but he could not. Ultimately, a questionable "J" appeared, then "Jh." After a pause the letter "R" was repeated while the medium's hand struggled to control the pencil. Then the communicator said, "My name does not begin with R...I am J—yes that is right." He gave the name "John," then "John J." He then said he was "John R." He was evidently distressed at not being able to get his name right and the sitting soon ended (pp. 394–398).

The following day, May 20, a communicator wrote through Mrs. Chenoweth, "I am John J." An "a" was written after "J" but erased. Then "Jacob" was written and soon "Astor." Astor was, in fact, the owner of the wrapped article which the medium never touched. Thereafter the medium went into trance. The communicator seemed disturbed and complained that it was very cold. He said he felt so cold and so wet. He thought he was drowning. Then he said he was not drowning; he was freezing and paralyzed. The communicator then asked for Mr. Stead who had been on the *Titanic* (pp. 400–402).

At the sitting of May 25, 1914, with Mrs. Chenoweth doing automatic writing, an article belonging to a Mr. T— was placed on the table by Hyslop. A communicator identified himself as "J.J.A." and said that he wished to send a message to help humanity whereupon T—'s article was removed and Astor's article replaced on the table. The letter "W" was written, then erased, and the letter "M" was written three times followed by "Ma," "Man" interspersed with pauses. The communicator said he would name the one to whom he wanted to send his message. After several efforts: "Ma," "Made," "Madeleen" (with "een" erased), "Madeline" was written. The communicator then expressed his love for his wife and said that he was glad that she did not go when he did (pp. 402–405). Since she had accompanied Astor on the *Titanic*, by "did not go" the communicator must have meant that she did not die when he did.

On June 1, 1914, a communicator appearing in Mrs. Chenoweth's automatic writing was identified as "J ast" and then as "John Jacob." In answer to Hyslop's query whether he knew a clergyman who was interested in the subject of life after death, the communicator gave the name of "Heber...E. Horber New...Newton" (Ibid., p. 417). This person was described as an Episcopalian rector.

At the start of the sitting of June 8, 1914, the automatist wrote "vin" and then "J.J.A." The "Vin" might have related to Astor's son, William Vincent Astor. The communicator was asked if he remembered speaking of a clergyman, and he replied, "Yes R.H.N." When asked if he could recall any incident involving the minister Newton, the communicator said that they had talked of various things of mutual interest. But Newton, when asked to verify the communication, could not remember any such conversations. It was also said that the clergyman would recall a portrait of the communicator's father, but this statement could not be verified, either. Similarly, the communicator's reference to a lectern having to do with a church seemed meaningless. The sitting ended with the communicator saying, "so cold, so cold . . . an awful sea to swim in. Sinking, sinking. She is gone. The ship" (pp. 425–429).

On June 9, 1914, "J.J.A." related the experience he had had when the *Titanic* went down — He had no chance — no one could live in such a sea — cold and suction — life belts would have been useless in the cold water. (In fact, he had not donned a life belt, possibly for that reason.) Mrs. Chenoweth then went into trance and the communicator referred to a watch and a tomb but they could not be verified (pp. 429–431).

On June 10, 1914, "J.J.A." put in another appearance and complained that he had to be very cautious of many messages from him reported by spurious mediums. What proved to be an interesting feature of this sitting was the communicator's giving the name of "John F. Pater" as someone who was helping or with him. He said that "Pater" was more significant than "Father" because the person referred to was French. The communicator also said that, because his name was so well known, he would use his title: "Colonel." In fact, he had been a lieutenant-colonel during the Spanish-American War.

So far as is known there is no further reliable record of Astor's appearance through a medium. We are therefore left to judge his classification on the basis of the evidence in the record just reported.

There was nothing evidential in the sittings of November 25, January 20 or May 25 because all the facts related, i.e., the initial of Mrs. Astor's first name, her pregnancy and that John Jacob Astor was called "Jack" and the name "Madeline" were all well known to Hyslop and can be explained as easily by the theory that the medium had obtained them from him by telepathy as by the explanation that they came from the dead Astor.

Much of the material in the sitting of January 21, 1913, is of no value as evidence, either. Half the world knew the *Titanic* had struck an iceberg, so the question, "What did we hit?" is not impressive. Similarly, the description in the sitting of June 9, 1914, of the communicator's plight in a sea in which life belts were no use is valueless. It was well known how those on the ship perished.

The same observation can be made about the statements in the sitting of January 21, 1913, which expressed the communicator's happiness that the Astors' child had been delivered. It was common knowledge that Astor's widow had given birth.

Similarly, in the sitting of May 20, 1914, the communicator's complaint that he was freezing is of no value nor was his inquiring after Stead. Everyone at the time knew that the *Titanic* had gone down in an icy sea and that William T. Stead was among the famous passengers.

The sitting of June 8 produced little of worth, either. Since the newspapers had publicized marriage of Astor's son, Mrs. Chenoweth could have known and Hyslop undoubtedly would have known Vincent Astor's name, which could have explained the reference to "Vin." And the references to a watch and a tomb given in the sitting of June 9 could not be verified.

On the other hand, the communicator's reference to "Nan" is interesting and might support a spiritistic theory. The question "Do you know anyone named Nan? I don't mean Nancy...." (probably Viscountess Nancy Astor, his cousin's wife) suggests that the source of information was probably not Hyslop, who might have been thinking of Nancy Astor, but rather some external source. January 21, 1914, 21 months after Astor's death, can therefore be considered his first communication (32g).

Again, in the sitting of May 1, 1914, the communicator's difficulty in getting his own name right does not seem to have stemmed from Hyslop who knew Astor's name perfectly and would neither have had nor conveyed any difficulty with it to the medium.

The sitting of June 1, 1914 (32g), however, is extremely interesting as survival evidence because the communicator named Heber Newton as a clergyman interested in the survival question. Minot J. Savage was the clergyman at the time known to be greatly interested in the subject and was the person Hyslop undoubtedly knew. It was therefore Savage's name that Mrs. Chenoweth would be expected to have written. Although no incident reported by the communicator which involved Newton could be verified, R. Heber Newton was the pastor of Astor's church. The record does not show that Hyslop knew of this clergyman's connection with Astor. If he did not and Mrs. Chenoweth did not—and the record implies that they did not—the communication of Newton's name is a good piece of evidence.

Perhaps the most valuable piece of evidence came at the last sitting of June 10, 1914 (32g). Hyslop reported that five days earlier a woman in New York who knew nothing of the work Hyslop was doing gave this message: "Why should a Monk John come to you? John Jacob Astor came along with him. The Monk was tied up as if with ropes and Astor was mixed up too, tied up, needed straightening out" (p. 433 fn). The connection between Father [Pater] John or Monk John and Astor thus seems corroborated by an outside record. (A later experiment Hyslop conducted with the woman in New York, however, provided no more evidence.)

All in all, there seems enough in this case to support a conclusion that John Jacob Astor IV, while not a "star" communicator, seems to have given some evidence of his identity. He is classified in Category 2.

Case 2. *Samuel Langhorne Clemens*

Samuel Langhorne Clemens was a vagabond, showman, poet, writer and lecturer under the nom de plume of Mark Twain. He was born when Halley's Comet appeared and died in 1910 when it appeared again.

Using a ouija board, Pearl Louise Curran and Emily Grant Hutchings had purportedly received communications from Patience Worth in 1913 which some consider impressive evidence of survival. Thereafter, Mrs. Hutchings, who was a psychic, discovered Lola V. Hays. Using the ouija board once more, the two women claimed that Mark Twain communicated stories through them for the book *Jap Herron*. It was duly published by Mitchell Hennerly and offered for sale as the posthumous work of Mark Twain.

We would have a stronger case for spirit authorship had Mark Twain and his writing been unknown to the two women. But Mark Twain was an eminently successful writer and both were familiar with his writings, Mrs. Hutchings more than Mrs. Hays. Besides, Mrs. Hutchings had spent her girlhood in the town where Mark Twain had lived as a boy. She probably had a great interest in him, and since she was a writer herself, she might have tried to follow his style. And there were other facts suggesting unconscious imitation of Twain and his books. Not only was Mrs. Hays an admirer of Twain's who had hoped he would come through her, but she was a humorist as he had been.

Another explanation for the receipt of the material for the book is the theory of the unlimited extrasensory abilities of the women. Some living mind could have been tapped by their ESP for the material which came through them as *Jap Herron*. Or they might have gotten it, either normally or clairvoyantly, from Mark Twain's works.

But the case does not end with *Jap Herron*. Rather it begins there. It led Hyslop to a cross-reference experiment with Mrs. Chenoweth in Boston in which both Mrs. Hutchings and Mrs. Hays as sitters each had five different sittings. The medium did not know their identities or that there was any connection between them. Between the sittings given by Mrs. Chenoweth, Hyslop sat with Mrs. Hays and Mrs. Hutchings who used their ouija board (Hyslop, 1920). But we will deal only with the main sittings with Mrs. Chenoweth, the purpose of which was to see whether Mark Twain would appear as author.

In the first sitting with Mrs. Hays on May 28, 1917, Mrs. Chenoweth automatically and correctly wrote that the sitter was a "light" — a term used for a psychic (Ibid., p. 53). This striking hit at the very start of the sittings suggests that the medium's mind was sharply attuned at once to the minds of the sitter and Professor Hyslop and presages much of what follows in the sittings. There was not at that time, however, the slightest suggestion of Mark Twain's presence.

In the second sitting with Mrs. Hays on May 29, 1917, there appeared in Mrs. Chenoweth's automatic writing someone referred to as a "guide" for Mrs. Hays. The communicator claimed to have used Mrs. Hays' hands to make sounds for her at home "on the paper" (Ibid., p. 58). Since Mrs. Hays denied making raps, "on the paper" might have meant that the communicator was writing a book through her. But there was nothing to identify the communicator with Mark Twain.

On May 30, 1917, a third sitting was held with Mrs. Hays. A communicator referred to "sittings at home," a possible reference to her use of the ouija board. There was also a reference to the "man who comes often and . . . is a person of some activities and who had been over here awhile" (p. 68). Toward the end of the sitting there seemed to be a change of control and the words "Jests are made" were written (p. 69). These two phrases could have referred to Mark Twain, but of course both Mrs. Hays and Hyslop knew that Mark Twain was a man who, she claimed, came often through her, that he was a prominent writer and lecturer ("of some activities"), that he had been dead for seven years ("over here awhile") and that he was a famous maker of jests. These statements are therefore of no value in establishing Mark Twain's survival, and there was no other clear indication of him in this sitting.

On May 31, 1917, still with Mrs. Hays as sitter, a communicator appeared in Mrs. Chenoweth's automatic writing who gave no identification. After a change of control, a reference was made to music that might have related to Mark Twain because his daughters, Clara and Susy, had been singers and Clara had married Ossip Gabrilowitsch, the famous pianist. Mark Twain also had played the piano a little. But the reference is too tenuous to establish his presence at this sitting.

At the last sitting of June 1, 1917, with Mrs. Hays, the letter "M" followed by a letter which might have been an "A" came through Mrs. Chenoweth's automatic writing (p. 85) and might have been the beginning of an attempt to write "Mark." But we must remember that the sitter and Hyslop were trying to have "Mark" identify himself. The communicator then referred to the work he was putting on paper at home and described it as "the type which is philosophical" (p. 86). Mark Twain, however, would not have described the book in this way, for it was not philosophical. If, therefore, Mrs. Chenoweth was not tapping living minds for her information, she might have been receiving it from a deceased communicator other than Mark Twain. Later in this sitting, while the medium was in trance, she said, "Who is Moses?" Hyslop said he wanted someone else. There was a pause and then: "You want another man, don't you. . . Is that MZ or two" (p. 89).

The "M" might have been an effort to convey "Mark" and "MZ or two" might have referred to the source of Clemens' pseudonym, "Mark Twain," which means two fathoms deep. On the other hand, although the medium might not have known who the communicator was supposed to be or whom Hyslop wanted, nevertheless Hyslop's mind could have been the target of Mrs. Chenoweth's telepathy and not the deceased Mark Twain's.

Shortly afterwards, the medium said "S" and "T," possible references to "Samuel," Clemens' first name, or to "Twain." Then she said "Mar. . . Mar. . . Is it Mark?" (p. 91). For the first time we have Mark Twain's first name mentioned as would be expected if he were the communicator. But the same result would have been obtained if the medium were "reading" Hyslop's mind (i.e., receiving information from him telepathically).

In the first sitting with Mrs. Hutchings on June 2, 1917, Mrs. Chenoweth, before the pencil fell from her hand, wrote automatically "S. . . S. . . Sam. . ." (p. 93), a possible reference to "Samuel," Mark Twain's real name. After the pencil was restored to her hand, the medium wrote, "C. . . Cl. . . Funny man cannot write his own name" (p. 93). Here is another possible reference to "Clemens" and to Mark Twain's humor. Then the words "one must inevitably make a mark in the world of literature" (p. 94) were written and might have been a double entendre: "mark" for Mark Twain's first name and also for his having become famous as an author. A statement about "a Connecticut Yankee" (p. 95) could have been a reference to Mark Twain's *A Connecticut Yankee at the Court of King Arthur*. And there was also the statement, "the

2 Marks my name" (Ibid.). Then the communicator said, "You know who I am now" (p. 96). After that, "Lighten the burden with a laugh" (p. 97) could have been an attempt to reveal Mark Twain's real character, for behind the whimsical Mark Twain was the pessimistic Sam Clemens.

Such references now rather clearly identify Mark Twain: of that little doubt can be entertained. But what is their value as evidence? Everything received could have been gained by Mrs. Chenoweth's extrasensory powers from sources other than the mind of the deceased Mark Twain. (There is also the possibility of an impersonating communicator.) At the end of the sitting Hyslop asked the communicator to relate some incidents in Mark Twain's life involving psychical research. The communicator described "a vision like a mist rising and forming a picture before me and that was clairvoyance" (p. 98). This vague and ambiguous description of a psychic phenomenon was most uncharacteristic of Mark Twain who had had many startling and interesting psychic experiences and should have been able to tell much more about "mental telepathy" than was told here.

In the second sitting with Mrs. Hutchings on June 4, 1917, the communicator called himself "Mark" (p. 103). After a change of control, the initials "S.C.C." were given and then "M.T." (p. 106). If the first set of initials were supposed to relate to Mark Twain, they should have been "S.L.C." for Samuel Langhorne Clemens. "M.T." is self-evident. The communicator then made the most evidential statement to this point. He asked Hyslop, "Do you know P.T. Barnum?... This spirit knew him" (p. 107). Here was a piece of information known neither to the medium nor to Hyslop nor, apparently, to the sitter. Mark Twain's daughter confirmed that her father and Barnum had been acquainted.

In the sitting of June 5, 1917, with Mrs. Hutchings, a communicator stated that a book had been completed in an effort to contribute a posthumous work to literature (p. 112). This first reference to a book composed after death can be explained by the theory that the medium was tapping the minds of the sitter and Hyslop.

Mrs. Hutchings was still the sitter on June 6, 1917 when the communicator said, "I never did like to ride backward and this is sort of a backward ride" (p. 115). But Twain's surviving daughter remembered no such dislike and so this statement has no evidential value (p. 115 fn). During this sitting the communicator identified himself as "Same old Mark" (p. 115). He corrected the initials "S.C.C." to "S.L.C." for Samuel Langhorne Clemens, and he gave the name of his surviving daughter, Clara, correctly (p. 117). The sitting closed with Mrs. Chenoweth making two vertical and parallel lines while the communicator said "my mark" and repeated the two vertical and parallel lines (p. 119). All this could have referred to the communicator's identity: Mark Two, 2 Marks or Mark Twain. Once again, the possibility of psi abilities among the living makes their value as evidence questionable.

The final sitting with Mrs. Hutchings was held on June 7, 1917. Almost at once the communicator stated that he had seen his wife's face as he died. But his daughter, Clara, who had been with him when he died, knew of no death bed vision and could not corroborate the statement (p. 126 n). The communicator then acknowledged authorship of the book by referring to Mrs. Hutchings, the sitter, as "my friend who is here my amanuensis. . . I shall continue writing through these girls if I am allowed the privilege. . ." (p. 126). A little later he referred to the work being done on a small table and to a "oujiha" or "planchette" and to "two girls. . . each working for the same thing" (p. 127).

All these references were highly pertinent to the writing being done by Mrs. Hutchings and Mrs. Hays on the ouija board. Their importance as evidence, however, is another matter, for everything was well known by Hyslop and the two operators of the ouija board. Toward the conclusion of the sitting there was a change of control thought to be Mrs. Hays' mother. This control referred to a man in white clothes (pp. 129–130) which seems to refer to Mark Twain's habit of dressing in white. But it was not merely his habit: It was Mark Twain's trademark and well known to everyone so that the reference is valueless.

After the sittings with Mrs. Hays and Mrs. Hutchings were concluded, Hyslop held a series of sittings alone with Mrs. Chenoweth. In these Mark appeared again and sometimes gave his name as Samuel Clemens, as in the sitting of June 26, 1917. Nothing reported by Mrs. Chenoweth as having been said by Mark Twain, however, was outside Hyslop's knowledge. And any statement supposedly made by Mark Twain that was outside Hyslop's knowledge could not be verified. For example, the communicator said, "I could never seem to remember the things I have written until I had gone over them several times" (p. 170). His daughter knew nothing about her father's having such a problem.

In what category shall we place Mark Twain? If the extended sittings with Mrs. Chenoweth provided "abundant" evidence of Mark Twain's identity and of his authorship of the book *Jap Herron*, as Hyslop believed (1917, p. 364), the case of course belongs in Category 1. To resolve the question to our own satisfaction we must look at the book and then at the sittings.

Was there anything intrinsic in the book to show that Mark Twain was its author? When it was reviewed by *The Nation*, the reviewer said, "[A] good deal of the detail does 'sound like Mark' — as an echo sounds like a voice." But "its Twainish flavor, are external and occasional. . . . At the worst, it could be called a decent parody of Mark Twain." The relationship between the book and Sam Clemens is therefore remote. It becomes more so with the examination of *Jap Herron* by Albert Bigelow Paine, Twain's close friend, the editor of two of his books and his literary executor. In the book's introduction, he said that he found some things characteristic of Mark Twain, some not. But as to the story itself, "Mark Twain in life would never have written a line of it" (Hyslop, 1920, p. 43 fn).

On the whole, we cannot conclude that Mark Twain was the author of *Jap Herron*.

In making an independent evaluation of the sittings, we have to consider these points:

(A) In support of his view of the sittings with Mrs. Chenoweth, Hyslop said, "The most important point is the appearance of Mark Twain where there was no reason in the situation to suggest it and where it was usual to have family relatives appear" (1920, p. 363). We must answer that on the contrary there was every reason for Mark Twain to appear because both sitters, although not related to him, wanted him to do so and to support their claim that he was the author of *Jap Herron*. Hyslop himself, as objective and careful as any researcher of his time could be, was anxious to see if Mark Twain would appear. Mrs. Chenoweth, excellent psychic that she was, was sensitive to their wishes.

(B) Every piece of evidence of Mark Twain's personal identity lay within the knowledge of Hyslop and the two sitters or could have been obtained from material he wrote or that was written about him. It does not seem possible in this case to defend the spiritistic explanation from the "Super ESP" hypothesis, which would grant Mrs. Chenoweth great psi abilities by which she tapped living minds or documentary sources.

(C) There is only one bit of information which might provide evidence of personal identity and which neither Hyslop nor the two women knew. This one exception was Twain's acquaintance with P.T. Barnum which his daughter confirmed. Hyslop obviously did not know this fact or he would not have had to ask Clara. Mark Twain's biographers do not mention Barnum either as friend or enemy. So we have here a fragment of recondite information about Mark Twain which has evidential value for that reason.

(D) There were enough significant mistakes in the record to suggest that, even if there were a spirit communicator, it was an impersonator of Mark Twain and not the dead man himself. The reference to *Jap Herron* as a philosophical work, the inability to relate any of Mark Twain's psychical experiences and the mention of a dislike of riding backwards, all of these were incorrect.

Were it not for the confirmed evidence of his having known Barnum, Mark Twain would have to be consigned to Category 4 because no other evidence of his personal identity had been furnished. But given the confirmed Barnum account, it is possible that at least some of the remaining evidence of personal identity might have come from the dead Twain. The Mark Twain case, therefore, is classified in Category 3, one in which no satisfactory evidence of personal identity has been supplied.

Case 3. Hannah Wild

A milliner by occupation, Hannah Wild was an outspoken champion of women's rights. She died in 1886.

Hannah's sister, Bessie, was extremely interested in the question of survival and had asked Hannah if she would write a letter to her with the idea of communicating its contents posthumously. If the contents could not be communicated, then there would be no proof of Hannah's survival. The two sisters discussed the experiment for a period of several weeks.

Hannah suffered from cancer of the stomach. She had many "bad spells." On the occasion of each, Bessie reminded her that the letter they had discussed had not been written. One week before her death, Hannah decided to delay no longer; she knew she would not live long. She said to Bessie, "Bring pen and paper. If spirit return is true, the world should know. I will write the letter. It will prove that the dead do not lie asleep in the graves waiting for a resurrection like the Second Adventists teach" (Hodgson, 1892, p. 69). Hannah Wild wrote and sealed the letter and put it in a tin box with a bank book. When Bessie was given the box to hold, Hannah said, "If I can come back, it will be like ringing the City Hall bell."

Bessie never touched the letter. After her marriage to Dr. Blodgett in 1886 in the winter after Hannah died, it was put in his safe. Having seen William James' name in a paper, Bessie wrote to him about Hannah's letter. James, who described the experiment as "what would have been a good test of actual spirit-return" (1890, p. 657), received the letter from Bessie Blodgett and initiated a sitting with Leonore Piper early in 1887. The sitter was J.M. Piper, the medium's father-in-law. Some articles of clothing that had been worn by Hannah Wild were used. The exact date of any of the sittings is not given, but, if they began in the spring of the year, the first attempts to reach Hannah Wild were made about seven or eight months after her death.

At the time of the sitting Mrs. Piper knew nothing of either Bessie Blodgett or Hannah Wild. During the sitting, Phinuit, the medium's control who claimed to be a French physician, correctly gave the name of the writer of the letter as "Hannah Wild," had some awareness that Hannah had something to do with the *Woman's Journal* and also gave Bessie Blodgett's name. Several more sittings were held over a period of weeks to get the contents of the sealed letter. At length, Phinuit came up with a rather long letter that he said he was certain had come from Hannah Wild. On the receipt of this letter, and with Bessie's consent, James broke the seal on the envelope and compared the contents of the original letter with those of the letter Phinuit had dictated. "The two letters," wrote James, "had nothing in common" (Ibid.). In addition, many of the statements and details contained in the letter, such as living in a house with an attic, leaving a trunk, having jewels, having a sister-in-law named Ellena, a friend named Margaret Dow, were all wrong. Besides this, Phinuit's description of Hannah Wild as having dark brown hair with gray in it which she combed straight back and as having peculiar looking teeth, did not correspond to the real Hannah Wild.

In May 1888, still anxious to see if Hannah could establish her identity, Bessie came to Richard Hodgson's office in Boston where a sitting was arranged with Mrs. Piper. Mrs. Blodgett was not identified to the medium. Bessie brought a small bag containing articles that had belonged to Hannah. Without Mrs. Piper's knowledge she placed the bag behind her chair. She also brought along Hannah's original letter wrapped in a rubber cloth. Phinuit began by correctly naming Hannah Wild and Bessie Blodgett. The medium then groped for the bag, found it and placed it in her lap. The bag was opened and Phinuit found spectacles, hair and a picture in the bag that Bessie had not known was there and identified them all as Hannah's. Phinuit said, "Do you remember I told you it would be ringing a church bell?" His references to Bessie's rubbing Hannah to make her feel better and to a big silk handkerchief of Hannah's were correct. About Hannah's letter, Phinuit said, "Sacred and religious. I remember something about elevation of myself." This was clearly wrong, as were other statements.

Another sitting was held in August 1888 in which Hodgson was the sitter and Bessie was absent. By this time, however, Mrs. Piper knew the identity of Bessie Blodgett. At the August sitting, with the aid of a lock of Hannah's hair, Phinuit once more dictated a letter claimed to be from Hannah in which she told why she had not married someone she had loved. Bessie acknowledged that this indeed "was the one sorrow of sister's life." But, when James again compared the contents of the dictated letter with the original letter, he said it was not what Hannah had written.

At a further sitting in October 1888 Phinuit produced a lengthy letter that dealt with subjects either entirely wrong or which had no relation to the letter Hannah had written. Bessie was not present.

Two more sittings were held in May 1889 when Bessie was a sitter along with Hodgson. In the first of these, on May 28, Bessie tested Phinuit with more articles of Hannah's, 11 in all, such as a waist and bird's eyes. Phinuit was correct about four of them, but about some, especially the bird's eyes which Hannah would have known, was wrong. The most interesting product of this sitting was the answer to Bessie's question about who was present when Hannah wrote her letter. Phinuit said that Bessie and another lady were present, and then Phinuit appeared confused and changed the subject. A little later Phinuit said correctly that Bessie and her mother, Alice, had been there, that Hannah wrote the letter on a stand and sat in a chair with big arms on it and leaned back in it because she was tired. Phinuit then proceeded to discuss the contents of Hannah's letter and, again, James said Phinuit's statements were incorrect.

In the sitting of May 29, 1889, after learning that James had rejected his description of Hannah's letter, Phinuit grew angry and said that James ought to "sharpen up his memory." Phinuit once more described what was supposed to be in the letter and James once more said that the letter contained none of these statements. Two final sittings with Mrs. Piper were held by Mrs. Blodgett in May 1891. In neither sitting did Phinuit try to describe Hannah's letter or refer to it.

The principal test of Hannah Wild's survival and identity failed. It was finished effectively after the first sittings in 1887 when James was authorized to open Hannah's letter and to read its contents. From that time on the test was compromised and any letter that Phinuit might have dictated that matched the original letter would have been subject to the objection that its contents had been gleaned telepathically from James's mind. As it was, no letter corresponding to the actual letter was produced by Phinuit during the next seven sittings in 1888, 1889 and 1891. If Hannah survived death and was able to communicate, her pledge to her sister had been that she would try to prove survival, if it were true, through the specific means of communicating the contents of her letter. She did not or could not fulfill her pledge. The conclusion is therefore that she did not give evidence of her personal identity and does not fit in either Category 1 or 2.

But is this too harsh, too strict, a requirement? Perhaps Hannah tried to give evidence of her survival in other ways through Phinuit. Phinuit made three kinds of statements; none require a spiritistic interpretation. The first kind of statement consists of assumptions or guesses Phinuit might reasonably have made, such as when, during the sitting of May 7, 1888, he identified a picture in the bag which Bessie had not known was there. The second kind are statements every one of which might have been received paranormally from Bessie Blodgett's mind when she was the sitter. Mrs. Piper was known to have possessed extraordinary extrasensory powers so that it is perfectly legitimate to think that Bessie could have been the source of Phinuit's identification of Hannah's hair and spectacles and of the reference to Hannah's big silk handkerchief, to Bessie's rubbing Hannah, to the ringing of the church bell so similar to Hannah's remark about ringing the bell at City Hall (sitting of August 1888), to Hannah's failing to marry which caused her sorrow (sitting of August 1888) and to the circumstances under which Hannah wrote her letter (sitting of May 28, 1889).

These references or statements, although correct, are not even doubtful evidence of Hannah's identity. We have to agree with Bessie's and Hodgson's evaluation of the case. She said of Mrs. Piper's mediumship, "It was all true, yet not one word I did not know. . . . Really he [Phinuit] is doing wonderfully well as far as thought-transference goes, but positive proof that it is not Hannah" (Hodgson, 1892, pp. 74, 83).

Hodgson wrote, "The evidence, then, in this series of sittings seems to be very far from proving the presence of Hannah Wild. Most of the statements made by Phinuit are explicable by the hypothesis of thought-transference from Mrs. Blodgett's mind" (Ibid., p. 15).

Then there is the third kind of correct statement made by Phinuit in the first sitting of 1887 when Bessie was not present and was not yet known to Mrs. Piper and Phinuit. These statements included Phinuit's naming of Hannah Wild as the letter writer and of mentioning Bessie Blodgett's and Hannah's connection with *Woman's Journal*. Of all Phinuit produced, these statements come closest to being evidence of Hannah's identity. But they can still all be explained by "Super ESP." Bessie's mind could have been the target of Mrs. Piper's telepathy and could have supplied some of the information. The articles that had belonged to Hannah, such as her glove, which had been provided to the medium might have worked as psychometric objects and been the source of impressions about their former owner.

"Hannah Wild" appeared as a control for Mrs. Piper on other occasions (see, for example, *Proceedings of the S.P.R.*, Vol. 28, Pt. lxxi, p. 291), but the real Hannah Wild must be consigned to Category 4 because she failed to give evidence of personal identity or any other evidence worthy of consideration in connection with this study.

Case 4. Carroll Davidson Wright

Educator and recipient of appointments from presidents Theodore Roosevelt, Grover Cleveland and Chester A. Arthur, Carroll Davidson Wright died in 1909.

A reading of the record of Hyslop's sittings with Mrs. Chenoweth at her home (34b) in Boston (33) thirty miles from where Wright had lived and died (35a, 36a) shows several in which communicators made direct or indirect references to him. On October 27, 1910, an allusion was made to "Clark University" (Hyslop, 1912a, p. 186), of which Wright had been president. On November 3, 1910, the communicator kept repeating the name "Carroll," said that he and William James had been close friends and described "figures, figures, figures, mathematics whatever it is" in relation to "Carroll" (Ibid., pp. 240–241). In the sitting of November 11, 1910, the William James personality also alluded to Wright and their friendship (p. 268).

On December 2, 1910, the Hodgson personality alluded to "Wright" and "C–" (p. 360), and in yet another sitting on April 8, 1911, the personality of "G.P." made a number of references to Wright (many of which were wrong) (p. 518).

A little over two years after he died (32h), on April 8, 1911, Wright seemed to be trying spontaneously to give evidence of this identity through the communicator "G.P." (p. 517). Writing automatically (38b, 41a), Mrs. Chenoweth recorded in her script: "C.W. places both hands on the table and says he thought all the physical phenomena was easily explained by magnetic vibratory influence or simple fraud..." (p. 518). During his lifetime Wright had observed table tipping so that this statement had a good ring to it. The medium also wrote, "I see also a great pile of papers, some printed, some compiled for printing and all in a stack on the table, a matter in which he was engaged at the time of his last illness" (p. 519). This statement also has the ring of truth because Wright had been working on a book which he finished only a month before he died.

In the same sitting of April 8, the question was asked, "Who or what is Adams?" (p. 521). It was determined later that Adams was a friend of Wright's. In this sitting also it was said, "I see a glass of water there [referring to Wright's library] as if he frequently kept one near him as he worked" (p. 523). Subsequent inquiry showed that this statement was true because Wright needed to relieve his stomach trouble with lithia tablets.

But did Wright ever appear directly to Hyslop through the medium? We are told that Mrs. Chenoweth "knew nothing about Mr. Carroll D. Wright" (p. 7). She was a stranger to him (40d). As for Hyslop, he never had any personal relation with Wright (39e), but he knew of Wright as United States Labor Commissioner. Nevertheless, during Hyslop's sittings with Mrs. Chenoweth in Boston on November 26, 1910, and April 7, 1911, the control changed suddenly in the middle of both sessions so that the medium wrote automatically (39b) "Carroll Wright" in the one (p. 328) and "Carroll D. Wright" in the other (p. 59).

The 1910 sitting contained allusions to Professor James and Mrs. James and other items but nothing relevant to Wright. The 1911 sitting contained these statements, "Fractions and decimals prepare the way for algebraic and higher arithmetical work.... Some facts like figures stand strong and uncontradicted..." (p. 510). The sitting contained no clear effort to reveal evidence of Wright's identity, but these references to Wright's special skill with figures and statistics possibly pointed to him. In the same sitting, after a change of control, the names "Mary" and "Gertrude" were brought up as having to do with Wright (p. 512). A dead sister of Wright's wife had been named Mary, but it is also as common a name as can be. The name Gertrude was not recognized by Wright's family. These data, as well as allusions made to a place Wright was supposed to have worked, are worthless as evidence.

In another sitting on December 19, 1911, when Wright seemed to be the communicator, he described his casket as having a wreath with red leaves on it and that baskets of flowers were near, while over the casket were banners on spearheads (pp. 363–371) — a reasonably accurate description of Wright's funeral.

Hyslop thereafter arranged for a cross-reference series of sittings to be held in Boston with Mrs. Chenoweth in which Wright's daughter, not identified to the medium, was to be the sitter (39j). An arrangement was made for a friend of Hyslop's to take notes and for Mrs. Chenoweth to go into trance

(38a) and use her "Starlight" control. The medium was not told that there was any relation between these sittings and those in which Hyslop had been the sitter and in which she had done automatic writing. The detailed record of the sittings with Wright's daughter was not published because it contained a mass of garrulous talk. Hyslop discussed their content, however (Hyslop, 1919). The main points of these sittings were:

1. Some of the incidents to which references had been made in the sessions in which Hyslop had been the sitter were repeated.

2. An aunt was described as was a grandfather whom the daughter recognized.

3. Correct hits concerning the initial "J" and the name "Arthur" were made, "J" having been Wright's son-in-law and "Arthur" a dear friend.

4. The medium described a big sheet of music and made reference to the communicator's singing, possibly with a choir or quartette associated with a church, which was true.

5. The medium correctly described Wright's habit of sitting and resting in a big brown chair after he came home.

6. She also correctly described a gold watch fob on a ribbon that was to be given to someone when he got big enough for it — a grandson as it turned out.

7. Wright's impatience with white lace bedspreads was indicated correctly.

8. The medium described a place in which people wore caps and gowns — recognized by his daughter as Clark College.

9. The medium referred to a small bottle with pellets or globules in it that the sitter's father had taken "for some trouble, more like a medicine" — an entirely correct reference to Wright's lithia tablets.

10. The medium referred to a charm, a small key that symbolized his belonging to something, a "watch key" — a correct reference because Wright wore a Masonic emblem with a key on his watch chain.

11. The medium referred to someone "with a short name beginning with 'H,'" a big man, a politician, who helped Wright — again a correct reference to Senator George F. Hoar, who persuaded Wright to become president of Clark College.

In assessing the value of the evidence and deciding in what category to place Wright, the numerous allusions to Wright in the sittings of October 27, November 11 and December 2 are not important enough to consider. Where conspicuous persons are concerned, a more rigid evidential standard should be required than in the cases of ordinary people. Much more is known about the lives, habits, thoughts and backgrounds of the great or near great (or notorious) or could easily be learned from reading publications or statements or newspaper accounts about them than ever could be known about an average man or woman. Wright was such a public figure.

Besides being president of Clark College Wright had been a Massachusetts state senator and chief of its Bureau of Statistics of Labor. In addition, President Theodore Roosevelt had appointed him to the United States Anthracite Strike Commission, President Grover Cleveland had appointed him to complete the 11th Census and President Chester A. Arthur had appointed him United States Labor Commissioner. Mrs. Chenoweth's disclaimer of any knowledge about Wright, especially when the College of which he was president was only about 35 miles from her Boston home, cannot be accepted. It is likely that all information she gave about him could have come from her normal knowledge about him. Moreover, Hyslop can be presumed to have been familiar with enough of Wright's life to have been the target of the medium's ESP. For example, Wright's mathematical ability (April 7, 1911, sitting) was public knowledge.

But then there were more striking references, those in the sitting of April 8, 1911, to items of information about which Hyslop knew nothing until the family verified them and which were highly suggestive of Wright: his placing his hands on a table which was suggestive of his early experience with table tipping; the papers on which he was working just before his death which suggested the *Century Book of Facts* completed one month before his death; the reference to Adams, his friend; and to a glass of water he kept near in order to take medicine as he worked.

These facts alone, however, are not evidence of Wright's identity because of the theoretical possibility that they all were known to living persons and might have been obtained from the family by Mrs. Chenoweth's roving extrasensory powers. If these references and others received when Hyslop was the sitter were all we had in this case, Carroll Wright might be placed in Category 4. But they are not all. They must be taken in connection with the sittings with Wright's daughter in which almost a dozen rather specific and correct references were made to people, events and objects in Wright's life. All the things to which references were made, however, were known to Wright's daughter so that she could have been the target of the medium's ESP. Yet that is not the position taken here.

It seems to me that the "faggot theory" can apply to the Wright case. Unlike cases such as Hannah Wild's (Case 2) that rest on one type of evidence — sittings with one sitter who might have been the target of ESP — we have in the Wright case two types of evidence emerging from two independent series of sittings. Each type, weak in itself because subject to counterexplanation, becomes strong when combined with the other. Hyslop expresses this idea:

> The evidence for Mr. Wright's personal identity is extraordinarily good tho this was not apparent in the automatic writing [Hyslop's sittings]. . . . [T]he Starlight sittings [with Wright's daughter] were unusually good ones and justify the inference which the more meagre incidents suggested. . . . Collectively the mass of

evidence makes [Wright's] personal identity perfectly manifest" [1912b, pp. 383–384].

When taken together the two independent series of sittings make the spiritistic hypothesis more probable than any other and place Wright in Category 1 as an example of a posthumous communicator able to establish clear evidence of his identity.

Case 5. Isaac Kauffman Funk

Isaac Kauffman Funk was a clergyman who made outstanding contributions to the literary world and who was known also as a psychic investigator. He died in 1912.

Isaac Kauffman Funk was a friend of Hyslop's. On March 28 and again on March 30, 1917, Hyslop sat with Mrs. Chenoweth. Through her control references were made to a Bible in which records of births and deaths in the Funk family were kept. Seven names, one of which began with "R," were said to be recorded. But neither Hyslop nor Funk's son knew anything about such a Bible. After some investigation the son found an old family Bible with two groups of names in it. Although no name began with "R," one group did contain six or seven names. Between the groups was a space for more names (Hyslop, 1919, pp. 308–309). This communication would be of interest if a family Bible were not used very commonly as such a record. And it does not identify Funk himself.

Another indirect communication came from Henry Ward Beecher who had been pastor of Funk's church in Brooklyn. Beecher communicated on at least two occasions through Mrs. Chenoweth to identify Funk as a surviving personality. On June 12, 1917, he said he had appeared on a prior occasion "with F.I.K.F." (Hyslop, 1920, p. 137) and before that, on June 27, 1916, after referring to "your friend, I.F., Isaac Funk, who is my friend . . . and he was to write today. . . ." Beecher told the story Funk had related in his book *The Widow's Mite* of how Beecher had given Funk a message about money (an apparent reference to a coin Beecher had lent Funk that was lost and then found as a result of Beecher's message) (Hyslop, 1919, pp. 296–298).

But evidence of his identity coming directly from Funk would be far more persuasive. Walter F. Prince reported a mediumistic message from Funk but with very little elaboration (Prince, 1925, p. 97).

It was through Mrs. Chenoweth in her Boston home (33, 34b, 35c, 36c) with Hyslop as the sitter that Funk appeared as a serious communicator while the medium both did automatic writing (38b, 41a) and was in trance (38a). He appeared first on October 2, 1912, a little less than six months after he died (32e) (Hyslop, 1919, p. 283). Mrs. Chenoweth claimed not to have known Funk or to have read any of his books or any published by Funk and Wagnalls

(40d). Hyslop, on the other hand, was familiar with Funk's books, knew him and had conversed with him very often (39p). At the time of this first sitting Funk's initials were given. The Funk personality then alluded to the opinion people had of him, that he had been credulous in his investigations of psychic matters. Years later, on June 16, 1916, we find him alluding to others thinking him an idiot in these matters (p. 293).

On October 7, 1912, the Funk personality spoke of the cemetery in Brooklyn in which he had been buried and of letters he had left whose contents he was to reveal posthumously (p. 284). During this same sitting the Funk personality denied being the credulous dupe people supposed him to be. He said he had adopted a pose so that he could get evidence to consider later.

On October 8, a secret sign known to Hyslop was given to identify Funk (p. 286) and on October 9, referring again to this sign, Funk mentioned "riddle" and asked Hyslop if this word signified anything. In the same sitting Funk, beginning with the letter "C," gave the name "Carnegie" as someone who was interested in simplified or phonetic spelling.

On January 14, 1913, Funk appeared again and spoke of civilization and God's law. Apart from this general discourse he said that he had once fathered a dictionary. He also referred to the Orange Mountains and described a church there which, on subsequent investigation, could not be identified (p. 288).

On January 15, 1913, the Funk personality made reference to sisters who made spirit paintings, gave their names as "L...L...M...Bangs" and told of a picture or painting made by them which he thought was a good likeness of his mother (pp. 289–290). In fact, Lizzie and May Bangs were mediums in Chicago who did this kind of work.

Some years passed. Then the Funk personality reappeared in June 1916. On the 15th of June he discussed a theory of language and communications (pp. 291–292) and on the 16th, besides mentioning that people thought him easily fooled as a psychic investigator, he discussed the relation between incidents in the Bible and psychical research and referred to the dead as "plain people returning in plain fashion" to distinguish them from the exalted beings they are generally supposed to be (pp. 293–294). Funk thereafter made several more appearances. On June 29, 1916, Funk referred to his living son and his dead brother, Benjamin (p. 300). On February 9, 1917, Funk referred to a "bronze piece" or "medallion" (p. 303). A few days later, on February 12, the Funk personality again related psychical research to holy books and biblical themes (p. 304) and on February 13, 1917, he spoke of his brother again and of Funk's "N.J. home, Mountain View" (p. 306).

In deciding in which Category to place the Funk case, we must remember what we have said about conspicuous figures. Funk was a public figure as a publisher. He had a reputation as a psychic investigator. His books *The Widow's Mite* and *The Psychic Riddle*, which dealt with psychic phenomena, were widely read. Although Mrs. Chenoweth said she had not read them, we must assume that she could have heard them discussed or had read about them. Thus, many of the references made by the Funk personality can be explained on the ground of the medium's normal knowledge of him, viz, the references to people's opinions of his credulity given at the sittings of October 2, 1912, and of June 16, 1916; the allusion to "riddle" (part of the title of his well-known book) during the October 8, 1912, sitting; in that same sitting the reference to Carnegie since it was public knowledge that Andrew Carnegie had helped finance Funk's drive to simplify spelling; the reference to the Orange Mountains on January 14, 1913, and to his "N.J. home" on February 13, 1917, because it was known that Funk had lived in Montclair, New Jersey; the reference to the Bangs sisters on January 15, 1913, is not surprising since they were a controversial pair investigated by Funk and who had been called frauds by some, including Hereward Carrington, and genuine by others; nor is the reference, in the sitting of June 29, 1916, to Funk's son surprising. In spite of Hyslop's saying that "the fact that he [Funk] had a living son [was] not . . . known to the psychic" (p. 300), she could have known because the name of "Wilfred J. Funk," identified as Funk's son, was published in the April 5, 1912, issue of the *New York Times* in an article dealing with Funk's death. Finally, the reference to the "bronze piece" in the sitting of February 9, 1917, ought not to have surprised anyone, either, since a bronze coin figured prominently in Funk's *The Widow's Mite*.

Apart from her own normal knowledge, we must consider the possibility that the medium could have obtained knowledge paranormally from Hyslop's mind concerning: (1) the initials given at the sitting of October 2, 1912; (2) the letters left by Funk, a fact known not only to Funk but to Funk's son, Wilfred; or (3) the statement made during the October 7 sitting that Funk was not the fool he was thought to be (known to Hyslop from conversations with Funk) (Hyslop, 1915).

But less susceptible of easy explanation is the reference to the Brooklyn cemetery in the October 7, 1912, sitting. At that time neither Hyslop nor the medium knew of Funk's burial there. Of special interest, also, is the sign given by Funk to Hyslop at the October 8, 1912, sitting. While the medium might have gained this knowledge paranormally from Hyslop's mind, Hyslop reported that the same sign was given to him later on two separate occasions through persons who knew nothing of Hyslop's sittings with Mrs. Chenoweth or of Funk or his sign (p. 286). Although one manifestation of the sign might be explained by ESP between the living, it seems to be stretching the explanation too far to cover three. In this case it is simpler to think that all three manifestations came from one source: the dead Funk.

There are also other things to be taken into account. For example, Funk's theory of language in the sitting of June 15, 1916, his interest in biblical themes and psychical research and the conception of the unexalted dead expressed at the sitting of June 16.

Hyslop said that the expressions and thoughts in relation to these subjects were entirely characteristic of Funk and that "Mrs. Chenoweth did not know the man well enough to reproduce him in this manner" (p. 299). We must take Hyslop at his word.

All in all we have in the Funk case a bag of mixed evidence, some explainable, some not. Has Funk given evidence of his identity? What is "evidence" in his case? Hyslop answers for us:

> The collective import of these facts ought to be clear. We may find fault with any one or each incident by itself as measured against all knowledge of such phenomena in other cases. But it will not be easy to offer normal explanations for the complex and articulated whole. . . . [T]heir collective significance is not to be despised, and it is synthetic or collective import that constitutes scientific evidence [p. 309].

We have here in this "complex and articulated" mass of evidence a pointer in the direction of a surviving personality that has supplied clear evidence of personal identity along with a demonstration of former characteristics. Funk is a Category 1 case.

Case 6. Emma Fischer

Emma Fischer, wife of a drunkard, living in squalor and mother of 13 children, died in 1906.

The case of Doris Fischer, Emma's daughter, is a celebrated case of multiple personality. Following Emma's death, Doris developed two and then four secondary personalities, making five in all, each with its own thoughts, memories, expressions, voice, each appearing to control for a longer or shorter time.

In 1910 Walter Franklin Prince, a clergyman and once president of the American Society for Psychical Research, was drawn to Doris. He adopted her in 1911 and finally cured her. Thereafter Doris seemed normal and happy. Prince's classic report of the "Doris Case of Multiple Personality" was published in the *Proceedings of the American Society for Psychical Research* (1915, 1916).

One of the personalities, Sick Doris, had never seen or known Emma Fischer because she developed after Emma died. But sometimes she thought she felt Emma walking next to her. On two occasions in 1911, while Prince was trying his cure, the original personality, Doris, claimed to have seen Emma's apparition (Prince, 1923, p. 7).

After Doris was cured, Prince decided to use her as a sitter in experiments with Professor Hyslop and Mrs. Chenoweth in Boston about 600 miles from

Pittsburgh in or near which Emma had died (35d, 36d). Doris travelled alone from California in 1914 for this purpose. Mrs. Chenoweth knew nothing about Emma Fischer (40d) and nothing about Doris. (Her case did not appear in print until after the sittings.) During the sittings Doris, who sat behind the medium, was neither seen by Mrs. Chenoweth nor identified to her (39j). As usual, Mrs. Chenoweth did both automatic writing (38b, 41a) and went into trance (38a) in the course of the sittings. During the sitting of November 19, 1914, the dead Richard Hodgson came through as a communicator to compare Doris's case with the Beauchamp case, another famous instance of multiple personalities (Prince, 1923, pp. 113–114). This communication is interesting because the medium did not know Doris's condition and yet she identified it correctly. This communication, however, has nothing to do with the question of the identity of Doris's mother. It is to this we now turn.

The first sitting with Doris and with Hyslop as scribe was held in Mrs. Chenoweth's Boston home (34b) on November 9, 1914 (32j). A communicator came through who said that she had not wanted to die and that she had been needed. She gave the letter "M" followed by "Mother—Mother." This "Mother" personality said it had come for the comfort it might bring and to prove itself. It said also that it wanted to make clearer statements than it had made before. Then it tried to identify itself: "...I am...her your h... My...WWW I love her...She is my W...She is my dear W...M...Child" (pp. 28–30). This quotation was interspersed with gibberish and confusion and struggle and initials or parts of them written and then erased. Then the communicator complained of being very cold and later remembered violets with white roses at the funeral (pp. 31–32).

At the very start of the sitting of November 10, 1914, "Mama loves you" came through (p. 34) with the statement, "I did not want to die.... It was a surprise to me to die and I did not want to go" (pp. 35–36). The communicator also said, "I have been able to show myself on two or three occasions.... You know who E is do you not? ... I have S with me over here" (p. 38). When Hyslop said that "S" was not recognized, the medium wrote, "No wonder for it (is) someone she [Doris] never knew" (Ibid.). If "S" were Emma's Aunt Susan, Doris had obviously not known her.

The sitting of November 11, 1914, produced these statements: "nor will I bring restraint upon her mental power but hope to add to it.... She was not so able to care for herself as some girls." When asked what was the matter with Doris, the communicator replied: "I do not know what you refer to if you mean the physical condition I should say not that so much as a child-like dependence mentally ... which needed all my care and foresight to keep her as she ought to be." The communicator went on: "I know that my last thought and my first one when I was free was for her to do something to help her in her especial dependence on me and my work and planning ... everything that was connected with her was my constant care.... The play with other children was never as children usually play but was left as a part of my care for her. We were companions my little one and I in a strange way" (pp. 47–49).

Two interesting statements were made at the sitting of November 16, 1914. References were made to "a little curl that was cut from baby's head and kept by me ... very like flax" (p. 64), to "Methodists" (Ibid.) and to "the hill — down the hill to the stream" (p. 66). When asked for the name of the stream, the communicator replied, "Yes and C...A...A not O but A" (p. 67). These references were all correct. Emma had cut a curl from Doris's flaxen hair when she was a baby; Emma's parents were Methodists, the Fischers' house was near a hill sloping toward a river and the "C" and "A" might have referred to the Allegheny River and an old canal connected to it which were not far from the Fischer house.

In the sitting of November 17, 1914, "Mamma" described her purpose to protect and develop her daughter and described other things of no evidential value. But then a correct statement was made about "a swing out of doors and a step where I used to sit. I mean a door step where I sat and worked ... and in the swing my little girl had played and had some pleasure" (p. 70). The communicator continued: "[T]here was also a game we played together out of doors I mean and I wonder if she recalls a game with balls we played out of doors." Asked what the game was, the communicator replied, "croquet" (pp. 70–71). "Mamma" then said, "I wonder if she recalls how a game won by her always meant shouts and jumps and a great crowing on her part regardless of how Mamma might feel and I can hear that laugh..." (p. 71). Commenting on this last statement, Prince observed: "This is a most realistic and life-like description of *Margaret's* [one of the personalities'] manner, when exultant, as I so often saw her in later days. 'Shouts,' 'jumps,' 'a great crowing,' 'regardless of how Mamma might feel,' 'I can hear that laugh,' these graphic bits of delineation can hardly be improved upon" (Ibid.).

Doris had been present as a sitter at all the sittings until November 30, 1914. (She began to dislike having to get up early in the morning to come to Boston in the crowded train.) Immediately, the medium's pencil wrote, "My baby did not come" (p. 79). A more striking assertion was that Doris had been possessed by a kindly Indian spirit (p. 84). Actually, "Minnehaha" was the part the Margaret personality used to dance every year at the annual dancing exhibition of the dancing academy (p. 85).

Minnehaha also appeared as a communicator in the sitting of December 1, 1914, from which Doris was again absent. The communicator was asked by Hyslop if she knew what caused Doris's trouble, i.e., spells, before Emma died. Turning to Doris's mother who was supposed to be near, the communicator answered: "Accident — accident is what she says. All right before the accident and all wrong after it ... and some shock which seemed to make her afraid afterwards" (p. 90). Asked to describe the accident, the

communicator said, "Fall." These statements are correct. When she was about
three years old, Doris had been thrown violently to the floor by her drunken
father.

In the sitting of December 7, when Doris was again absent, there was a
direct communication from Emma: "I had an undeveloped brain to manage"
(p. 98), a correct statement of the special care "Mamma" had to give her
strange and retarded Doris.

On December 14, 1914, with Doris present, the communicator made a
great effort to identify herself: "E m...Ma" was written by the medium (p.
98) followed by "M is for me.... Mother name" (pp. 98–99). But the writing
was done with struggles and pauses and the name "Mary" (not recognized) was
given three times. Again, on December 29, 1914, with Doris there, the communicator struggled at identification: "M M Ma...Mar...My name is M M
M Marg...Mother Marg..." (p. 108).

During the sitting of December 21, 1914, a communicator expressed
satisfaction that Hyslop was taking an interest "in this child of mine" and "my
baby girl" (pp. 100–101). Then the communicator said: "I want to say
something about Skippy Skippy" described as a "little pet of long ago ...
Skippy dog" (p. 101). It turned out that Doris remembered no dog by that
name; however, the family had had a lame cat called "Skippy." After some
talk about candy and a metal cup, the communicator said: "I wonder about
B...Bun...bun...bunn...Bunny...B...I cannot get it as I want it...
Animal...B o...milk...Bossy-milk Bosy's milk," describing the animal as
a little cow (pp. 103–104). During this communication there were pauses,
struggles, doubts and groans. Doris, however, did not remember any such
animal.

In deciding to which Category the Fischer case should be assigned, we
must consider the sittings and their evidential weight. On the minus side of
the ledger is much of the material produced at the sitting of November 9,
1914. The statement about not wanting to die and of being needed fits Emma.
"Mother" also tended to identify Emma. References to the sitter as "her" and
"child" were also right, as was the mention of being cold as Emma had been
before her death. The allusion to prior messages may also have been right.
But, of course, all these bits of information were well within the knowledge
of the sitter, Doris.

The reference to violets at the funeral could have been correct because
they were Emma's favorite flowers, but no verification was possible because
Margaret, a secondary personality, attended the funeral, and her memory was
not Doris's.

The statements made during the November 10 sitting were all entirely
consistent with Emma's story. Doris called her "Mamma"; her death probably
had been a surprise to her because she was well and working in the customary
way on the day she died. Doris claimed to have seen two apparitions of Emma

and "E" probably stood for "Emma." Yet we must repeat that Doris knew all these things. Her mind could have been the source of the medium's information and not the deceased Emma's. The reference to "S" was not clear, although it might have been Emma's late aunt whom Doris had not known. Doris did know of her, however, so again the information could have been gleaned paranormally by Mrs. Chenoweth from Doris.

Although all the statements made in the sitting of November 16 were correct, the same objections can be made to the references to a baby's curl, Methodists, the hill and stream and the initials that could have been an allusion to the Allegheny and its canal: Every fact was in Doris's memory and supposedly accessible to Mrs. Chenoweth's paranormal powers. The reference to "Minnehaha" in the sitting of November 30 as the Indian spirit who possessed Doris fits in with the character portrayed by Margaret in her yearly dances at the academy, but the name could have been a coincidence since "Minnehaha" had been popularized in Longfellow's *Hiawatha* and was a likely name for an Indian girl.

In the sitting of December 1, 1914, when the communicator Minnehaha was asked the cause of Doris's condition, she turned to Doris's mother for the answer since the communicator had come into the picture a year after the incident and would not be expected to know what had happened. The answer is correct if "accident" and "fall" are interpreted to mean Doris's being thrown to the floor by her father. This incident brought on her dual personality, and she was, in fact, "afraid afterwards" of him. But an advocate of "Super ESP" would argue that, although Doris was not at the sitting, these facts were very well known to her and therefore known as well to the medium's unlimited ESP.

In the sitting of December 21 Skippy was said to be a dog. It was, in fact, the name of a stray lame cat. But it turns out that a stray dog, also lame, had been taken in by the family and might have been called Skippy, too. Nevertheless, the name, whether of a dog or a cat could have been learned paranormally from Doris who knew it and cannot be given much evidential weight.

On the plus side of the ledger, much interesting and suggestive material was produced at many sittings. There was, for example, the November 9 sitting in which reference was made to roses at the funeral. Doris said there were none. But when the record of this sitting was read by Mrs. Prince, she recalled that Margaret had said she had put roses into Emma's dead hands. Indeed, Prince had a small box containing the flowers that Margaret had taken from the coffin. The box contained two white roses, two pinks, a fern and a sprig from another plant.

Also interesting are the confusion and struggle that took place in the sitting when the communicator was trying to show who it was. The struggle is suggestive of a foreign intelligence trying to get through the medium's mind.

In the December 14 and 29 sittings the communicator tried to give her name and identify herself. She did so on December 14 but did not quite succeed on December 21 unless we accept "M" for "Em" so that "M Ma" becomes "Emma." Since Doris surely knew her mother's name, this difficulty may suggest that the medium was getting the name from a source other than Doris. The struggle to say "Bossy" and her milk suggests once more that the medium was struggling with another intelligence she could not quite grasp.

The mother did not know of Doris's split personality, but she did know of their little games and Doris's strange ways when Margaret was in control. All the statements during the November 11, 1914, sitting referred to that knowledge and to Doris's dependence on her. It was a knowledge and a memory of Doris's mental state that was peculiar to Emma based on what she had observed. Doris did not have this knowledge because, when the childish personality, Margaret, emerged, the Real Doris did not know what she had done. As Prince said: "Real Doris had no memory of the intervals when Margaret was out" (Prince, 1923, p. 3), that is, in control. So it does not seem that Mrs. Chenoweth could have received this knowledge from Doris's mind or from any history of Doris which she might have seen. The evidence suggests an outside source, i.e., Emma.

Similarly, in the sitting of November 17, 1914, the references to the swing outdoors and the game of croquet were known to Doris and could have been obtained telepathically by the medium. But Emma's references to "shouts," "jumps," "a great crowing," "that laugh" after winning a game of croquet could not have been known by Doris if, as Prince writes, these were actual and "graphic" references to the Margaret personality. Again, there is the suggestion that what the medium recorded came from elsewhere than Doris's mind.

We conclude that Emma Fischer was a Category 1 communicator who gave clear evidence of personal identity and recognized past situations. Wrote Prince:

> There has probably never been printed a more evidential group of communications than the one here presented. The conditions under which it was produced could hardly have been more nearly perfect. Let those who lightly dismiss all claims of the "supernormal" come forward with a theory consistent with the facts, to explain how the "Mother of Doris" came to be almost inerrant in her statements regarding an unknown sitter.... The purported messages from the Mother of Doris constitute a comparatively short though monumentally strong case.... I am willing to state that, taking the intrinsic factors and qualities of the messages purporting to come from the Mother of Doris and placing them on the background of other great evidential cases, it appears to me that the spiritistic solution has the logical advantage over the telepathic" [1923, pp. 1, 18].

And Hyslop wrote:

> The record shows that the mother of the sitter, Miss Fischer, gave good evidence of her personal identity" (1917); and again:

She did excellent work to prove her identity, by trivial incidents which were unusually good for the purpose" (1919, p. 394).

Taking the six persons just studied as part of the general population and the survey of them as indicative of the posthumous abilities of the general population, we see that there is no universal equality in terms of ability to communicate after death. If people have diverse values and are socially and intellectually unequal during life, why should we expect equality in the postmortem state?

But the question now arises, would the "all communicators are equal" principle be borne out and would the result be different, if, instead of dealing with a sample of the general population, we studied a carefully chosen sample consisting of people who were not only similar in many respects but who were under a compulsion to perform posthumously and well for the sake of the group to which they belonged?

Although human beings at times can be unpredictable and violent, they are basically completely subordinate and intensely loyal to their special groups with their aims, creeds and duties. These groups range from families to small tribes to colossal conglomerates called nations.[1] Similarly, Arthur Koestler[2] conceived of "Janus-faced holons." His holons are hierarchies of autonomous entities made up of similarly autonomous parts which are always subordinate to the interests of the next higher level—as individuals are subordinate to society, platoons of soldiers are to the battalion and battalions are to the army. The individual parts correspond to the need of the whole. This need, if strong enough, controls their actions; in the case of warring creeds or nations, this need can force individuals to lay down their lives.

These arguments place human beings on a par with ants and bees who are also social animals working for the good of the group to which they belong. But, as far as we know, ants and bees are not interested in telepathy or in survival after death. What happens when the need of the next higher level is for evidence of this sort? Very little that is different from what happens when the need is for food or a victory over enemies: The human beings associated with the group attempt to provide it. They may not always succeed but when they do the success can be marked.

Among the most successful of family examples were the telepathic experiments carried out by Professor Gilbert Murray with his eldest daughter, Mrs. Arnold Toynbee, and those carried out by husband and wife Upton and Mary Sinclair. The remarkable Pearce-Pratt experiments can also be seen as responses to the need of the Parapsychology Laboratory at Duke University for evidence suggestive of ESP.

If the need of the group to which persons are loyal is for more striking evidence that communications from the dead are genuine and establish personal identity, the individuals subordinate to the group will endeavor to supply it. They will do so in their roles during life as investigators, automatists, philosophers, scientists or people of letters. Their loyalty is so great that they will even try to do so after death. Witness the suggestion made by Frederic W.H. Myers that dead persons form groups to furnish such evidence.[3] Witness, also, one incident in which, apparently pursuant to this suggestion, the dead Myers teamed up with the dead Gurney to operate together and to help one another give evidence through the medium Mrs. Holland. And witness the famous cross-correspondences in which Myers and Gurney played prominent roles. These cross-correspondences can be interpreted as responses by the dead members of the holon known as the Society for Psychical Research to its need for striking survival evidence.

It is from this kind of holon, one composed of the English and American societies for psychical research, that six subjects have been selected to make up the special sample. All were presumably devoted to it, and all presumably would subordinate themselves to its need for survival evidence. Their histories not only make clear that they all were functioning parts of the exclusive holon which had its branches in England and America; they make clear that these people were linked by other factors.

Renée Haynes describes some of them:

> They shared the same cultural background, they took the same values for granted, and they were closely linked not only by their academic studies and by their intellectual and aesthetic values, but also by their family connexions . . . clearheaded philosophers, mathematicians and scientists who were not too deeply conditioned by their studies to recognize that things did happen which could not be explained in any terms known to them.[4]

In addition, the members of this holon had personal ties of family or friendship. They had the same purposes and interests. All were prominent and esteemed people who belonged to a brilliant and unique circle of academics and scientists deeply interested in the phenomena of Spiritualism and their implications. All produced or helped produce the British and American societies for psychical research. They were Eleanor Sidgwick, Henry Sidgwick, Frederic W.H. Myers, Edmund Gurney, Frank Podmore and William James.

Given the devotion of these six to their holon and its needs, were they all able to respond to that need in the same way? Under the prevailing assumption they should have been able to: If some of them were able clearly to communicate evidence of their personal survival and identity, they all should have been able to do so; and if some of the dead members of the holon were unsatisfactory or doubtful communicators, all should have been — all should have been equally good or bad in the democracy of the dead if the assumption is right.

Case 7. Eleanor Sidgwick

Born in 1845, dead in 1936, Eleanor Sidgwick was a remarkable woman who served as president of the Society for Psychical Research and supplied a lifetime of important contributions to psychical research. She was a zealous worker, keenly interested in survival, who studied with meticulous care every significant line of evidence—the mediumship of Mrs. Piper, the cross-correspondences, the book tests, the phenomena of Spiritualism—and was painfully aware of their strengths and weaknesses and of the necessity for good survival evidence.

Yet in Mrs. Sidgwick we have a conspicuous example of one who has uttered not a single word or given the slightest sign since death. In looking for evidence of her appearance, besides examining the literature in vain, I tried to determine what attempts had been made to reach her after her death and, to this end, corresponded with people who should have known, including Dr. Alan Gauld, Miss Renée Haynes, the Society for Psychical Research and Mrs. Sidgwick's nephew, the Hon. G.R. Strutt. No one knew of any such attempts. According to the literature, however, such attempts are not essential to the appearance of any communicator who wishes and is able to make an appearance, the case of Flight Lieutenant Irwin of the ill-fated R-101 being an example. So, even if attempts were not made to reach Eleanor Sidgwick, she should have been motivated strongly enough, if she were able, to have tried to fulfill the need of her holon for satisfying evidence of survival and to have made one final contribution to psychical research by "dropping in" on one of the many mediumistic experiments conducted by investigators since her death in England and America or by otherwise making an appearance in the dreams of colleagues or friends. But she has not done so.

For this reason we conclude that Eleanor Sidgwick's death, combined with her absolute silence these last 48 years, makes her a Category 4: One who has given no evidence of personal identity or otherwise.

Case 8. Henry Sidgwick

One of the founders of the Society for Psychical Research and its first president, Henry Sidgwick was also a professor of philosophy at Cambridge. He died in August 1900.

The first sittings to try to communicate with Henry Sidgwick began in December 1900 with the medium Mrs. Rosina Thompson who had worked with the Society for Psychical Research from 1848 and who knew both Frederic W.H. Myers and Sidgwick (40a). Although the record does not so state, it is presumed that the sittings with Mrs. Thompson took place in her home in Hampstead (34b), about 57 miles from where Sidgwick had lived

(35b) and 90 miles from Terling Place, Essex, where he died (36b). The sittings were conducted by J.G. Piddington, an original member of the SPR Council and one of Sidgwick's colleagues (39q) (Piddington, 1903–1904).

At the first sitting, at which Sidgwick's sister was the sitter, there were no results of value. Three further sittings produced no evidence relating to Sidgwick, either. During the fifth sitting on January 11, 1901, the sitters were a Mr. and Mrs. Percival who were unrelated to Sidgwick. Doing automatic writing (38b, 41a) with information coming from the Percival control, Mrs. Thompson wrote: "Trin y Henry Sidg." (Ibid., p. 236). The writing did not resemble Sidgwick's. Nevertheless, this seems to be the first reference to him and to Trinity College, Cambridge.

After the sitters left, with Mrs. Thompson in trance (38a), the Sidgwick personality seemed to take control and spoke in a voice and style so lifelike that Piddington said, "[H]ad I been ignorant of Professor Sidgwick's death and had happened to hear the voice without being able to tell whence it was issuing, I think I should have unhesitatingly ascribed it to him" (Ibid., 32e).

At the next sitting on January 21, 1901, the Sidgwick control appeared and again had a powerful effect on Piddington who called the impersonation "extraordinarily lifelike" (p. 237). He summed up the two sittings in the following language:

> The only two occasions on which I have been *émotionné*, or have experienced the slightest feeling of uncanniness during a spiritualistic séance, or have felt myself in danger of being carried away, was during these two manifestations of the Sidgwick control. I felt that I was indeed speaking with, and hearing the voice of, the man I had known; and the vividness of the original impression has not faded with time [Ibid.].

Mrs. A.W. Verrall had joined the SPR in 1889, had carried out experiments at Myers' request and was lecturer in classics at Newnham College, Cambridge. There can be no doubt that she knew Sidgwick (40a). In her scripts of May 11, 1904, which she wrote in the rooms of the SPR in London (34e), there is an indication of the Sidgwick personality writing: "Take it [a book] and open where the mark is..." (Verrall, 1906). Mrs. Verrall knew Sidgwick's writing and said that the hand resembled his (p. 26), but the value of this evidence is weakened exactly because the medium knew his writing and unconsciously could have imitated it. The content of the script turned out to be meaningless.

In an earlier sitting, however, the evidence was more impressive. On January 21, 1901, while Piddington was sitting with Mrs. Thompson, the Sidgwick control said that Myers was with him and declared it would write. While the medium held the pencil, which moved in an ordinary way, not deliberately as if the writing were being forged, these words appeared in the script: "I don't think Myers is here...." Alice Johnson, Sidgwick's long-time secretary, was familiar with his writing and confirmed the likeness of the script to his writing. Others also concurred (Piddington, 1903–1904, pp. 236–238).

There is no indication that Mrs. Holland (Mrs. Alice Kipling Fleming), who got in touch with Alice Johnson in 1903, ever knew Sidgwick or ever had any linkage with him (40d). She left India in 1904 and was travelling when Sidgwick is said to have appeared as one of her controls. In her automatic script of February 21, 1905 (38b), he is described: "One has a long white beard and he is nearly bald. His eyes are grey very shrewd yet very kindly—His nose is rather long—and it is a scholar's face." One of the names following the description was "Henry" (Johnson, 1907–1909, p. 246).

At a later time, on July 27, 1905, Mrs. Holland, while dozing in a place not disclosed, received the impression of an "old man with white beard and glasses," again a description of Sidgwick (Ibid., p. 264). Mrs. Holland, however, although she had not known Sidgwick, had seen his portrait.

In 1906, when, besides Lodge, another close friend of Sidgwick's was present (39q, 39p), Mrs. Holland wrote: "Patience and ever Patience. Wait for the slow blossoming of the aloe." After this the letter "H" was written (Ibid., p. 367). The sentence following was signed "F" (for Frederic Myers?) and read: "I'll tell you how he looks, he paces slowly with bent head—when he thinks one hand is generally in his beard" (Ibid.). This last script, however, as Alice Johnson remembers, was probably the result of the presence of Sidgwick's intimate friend and the medium's having read about Sidgwick's habit of pacing with his hand in his beard.

Early in 1901, a series of communications seemingly planned by dead communicators, one of whom was Sidgwick, was received. These communications, which came to be known as "cross-correspondences," consisted of messages in Greek or Latin which demonstrated classical scholarship and which were given at about the same time through different mediums. The messages were broken into fragments, one part appearing in the automatic script of one medium, another part in another script, another while a medium was in a state of trance. These bits of a message were not clear or understandable and, in themselves, were not evidence. Only when all were woven together and seemed to relate to a single subject or theme did they become evidence of a surviving mind or group of such minds behind them. For purposes of comparison, the passages of different mediums in different places but written about the same time are set out in tabular form:

Miss Rawson	*Mrs. Thompson*
(In France, place not disclosed)	(In England, 33, 35b, 36b)
(33, 35c, 36c)	
January 23, 1901:	January 21, 1901:
Sidgwick control:	Sidgwick control:

I have not seen my dear friend
Myers yet, but I am more thank-
ful than I can say that he has
come here (Piddington, 1903–
1904, p. 295).

Mrs. Verrall
(In Cambridge, England) (33, 35a,
36a):

September 22, 1903:

Myers control:

Henry Sidgwick has a message to
give before Christmas, through
you if possible.... But you must
give another message correctly
first and then ask her to open
my envelope (Verrall, 1906,
p. 419).

October 7, 1903:

Myers control:

Henry Sidgwick's message is next
to come ... (Ibid.).

October 8, 1903:

Myers control:

Sidgwick has not got the message
right yet ... (p. 420).

November 17, 1903:

Myers control:

Complete the message now.
(p. 422).

Mrs. Verrall
(Now in Algeria) (33, 35e):

January 17, 1904:

(Control not given):

S is the letter. S in the envel-
envelope ς and on a seal Σ.
(p. 422).

He's [Myers] not with me.
He's not within range at all.
(Sidgwick writing): I don't think
Myers is here...." (Ibid.)

Mrs. Holland
(In India) (33, 35e)

January 17, 1904:

Myers control:
How am I to make your hand
docile enough how can I convince them? The sealed envelope is not to be opened
yet—*not yet*—I am

unable to make your hand form
Greek characters and so I cannot
give the text as I wish—only
the reference—1 Cor. 16-13 (Johnson, 1907–1909, p. 234).

Note that the words in the biblical passage referred to in Mrs. Holland's
script are: "Watch ye, stand fast in the faith, quit you like men, be strong"

and, except for the words "be strong," were written in Greek over the gate of Selwyn College, Cambridge. This gate would have been passed by Sidgwick and his wife when going to Newnham College where they lived. In addition, Mrs. Verrall lived at 5 Selwyn Gardens (as in Selwyn College), Cambridge (Johnson, 107–109, p. 235).

Many other "messages" from Henry Sidgwick were unverified — for example, one attributed to him which described a talk between Mrs. Verrall's husband and someone (Verrall, 1906, pp. 277–278). But without these we have enough to proceed to an evaluation of Sidgwick's case.

Sidgwick was a distinguished scholar so that much of the information supposedly from him could have been obtained from his writings or from material printed about him. For this reason much evidential importance is attached to the handwriting in one of the scripts which convinced his secretary, Alice Johnson, and to the manifestations of Sidgwick which so impressed Piddington, a critical and careful investigator who had been Sidgwick's colleague and who had published many ingenious studies of mediums in the *Proceedings* of the Society for Psychical Research of which Piddington became president. In addition, however, the connections among the scripts of mediums in France, England and India which alluded in the one case to the absence of Myers and in the other to a sealed envelope and Greek characters also suggest that Henry Sidgwick was a full-blown genuine communicator who gave ample evidence of personal identity and characteristics. He is placed in Category 1.

Case 9. Frederic W.H. Myers

Poet and classical scholar, Frederic W.H. Myers became honorary secretary of the Society for Psychical Research and later its president. His major contribution to psychical research was the classic *Human Personality and Its Survival of Bodily Death*. Death came to him in 1901.

When Myers died, James was sitting outside his hotel room in Rome. James was too grief-stricken to go to the bedside of the dying Myers. Instead, he sat in a chair next to the open door with a pen poised over his notebook, for they had made an agreement that the one dying first, as he passed over into the spirit world, would convey a message to the other. As Myers died, James covered his face with his hands. The notebook remained blank.

Myers had made another pact. He left a sealed envelope with Sir Oliver Lodge and, as evidence of his survival, intended to communicate its contents posthumously. On July 13, 1904, Mrs. Verrall's script recorded a reference from the Myers personality to this letter with the statement that the letter contained a passage from Plato's *Symposium*. Again on July 18, the Myers control urged that the letter be opened and its statements tested (Verrall, 1906,

p. 301). Lodge and others yielded to this urging and the envelope was opened on December 13, 1904, in the rooms of the Society for Psychical Research in London. It was determined that there was not a literal match between the contents of the script and the contents of the letter so that many, but not all, took the view that Myers had failed to provide survival evidence. Those taking exception to this view included Lodge and Alice Johnson who felt that Myers' test had been partly successful. Since then, Salter has argued that, if Mrs. Verrall's script is interpreted correctly, it has a clear connection with the contents of the envelope (Salter, 1958).

In two books, *The Road to Immortality* and *Beyond Human Personality*, the medium Geraldine Cummins gave descriptions of the afterlife that she said came from Myers.

If we had only Myers' failure at the time of his death to communicate with James, his supposed communication of a test message that was open to argument and doubt, and the kind of unprovable allegations about communications from the dead that are made by mediums in general, we could not classify Myers as a good communicator. But we have much more.

1. The first real communication from Myers may have been received 13 days after his death (32e) through Mrs. Rosina Thompson, who had known Myers and with whom he had had several sittings (40a). On January 30, 1901, she was at her home in Hampstead (34b) about 57 miles from where Myers had lived at Leckhampton in Cambridge (35b) and over 1000 miles from Rome where he had died (36e). She was making no attempt to reach him; no sitter was with her (39t). She was at home writing a letter when suddenly she found herself writing spontaneously: "May I come?...Myers North must be here again on Thursday." Then the initials "H.S." and "F.W.H.M." followed. The signature "F.W.H. Myers" appeared at the lower right portion of the paper and was said to be "extraordinarily like" specimens of Myers' signature in the weeks before he died (Piddington, 1903–1904, p. 241). Myers' handwriting was also said to have been reproduced in the automatic script (38b) of January 22, 1903 (Verrall, 1906, p. 26), of Mrs. A.W. Verrall who knew Myers and, in fact, at his request had conducted experiments, including sittings with Mrs. Piper (40a). The place where this automatic writing was done was not given.

2. On March 22, 1905 (32h), while she was travelling about the Continent, Mrs. Holland recorded in her script: "My friends—my dear friends—if I could but convince you of my identity—My name—look for my name among the Fragments for this year—A calendar look up moonshine—F— without the final k" (Johnson, 1907–1909, p. 256). Mrs. Holland had a calendar called "Fragments for 1905." A list of authors, among them, F.W.H. Myers, was given in it. Concerning "f—without the final k," Myers omitted the k from Frederick from his title pages.

3. The cross-correspondences described in connection with Henry

Sidgwick (Case 8) when the Myers control made statements appear in the Verrall script (38b, 41a) and the Holland script (38b, 41a) are equally good evidence here. At the time, Mrs. Verrall was in Algeria (33, 35e, 36e) and Mrs. Holland in India (33, 35e, 36e). In Mrs. Verrall's script the letter "S" appeared while in Mrs. Holland's there was an allusion to a text inscribed over the gate of Selwyn College which Sidgwick had to pass on his way to and from his living quarters. There is also the indirect allusion in Mrs. Holland's script to Mrs. Verrall, for "Selwyn" was both the name of the college and of the road where Mrs. Verrall lived.

4. A good description of Myers appears in Mrs. Holland's script (38b) of February 21, 1905: "The third man has a short pointed beard — His dark hair is thin and turning grey it has receded from his forehead making the brow look very lofty — He has fine dark eyes . . . pathetic and appealing in their expression" (Ibid., p. 246). It was a rather accurate description of Myers, but Mrs. Holland had seen his portrait.

5. There were marked attitudinal similarities in the scripts of the two mediums, Mrs. Verrall and Mrs. Holland, when messages from the Myers personality were recorded. In the Verrall script of December 29, 1903 (32h, 38b), the control is a voice crying in the wilderness; in the Holland scripts of January 5 and 12, 1904, the reference is to shouting into the wind and waiting unheeded like the wind (p. 222).

The possible beginning of a cross-correspondence experiment to demonstrate survival through several mediums instead of just one is suggested by certain messages from the Myers control during the same approximate period. On October 19, 1903, Mrs. Verrall's script in England (38b) recorded: "Write this week but not for evidence. That later for you through others. . . ." On December 7, 1903: "Sit regularly alone or with others and that will bring results — you will see." Just prior to this message, on November 26, 1903 (32b), the Myers control had expressed frustration in Mrs. Holland's script written in India: "The nearest simile I can find to express the difficulties of sending a message — is that I appear to be standing behind a sheet of frosted glass — which blurs sight and deadens sound — dictating feebly — to a reluctant and somewhat obtuse secretary. A feeling of terrible impotence burdens me — I am powerless to tell what means so much — I cannot get into communication with those who would understand and believe me" (Johnson, 1907–1909, p. 208). Mrs. Holland seems never to have known Myers. She had read his book *Human Personality* (40c) and had gotten in touch with Alice Johnson to whom in 1903 she sent the scripts (39t).

On December 3 of that year (32h), Mrs. Holland's script recorded this message from the Myers control: "It will soon be three years now — and yet I seem no further from earth though perhaps no nearer than I was on that January day [he died on January 17, 1901]. . . . No no not rapping or Planchette . . . a pen in the hand of a sensitive. That is the way. One does so little alone." And on December 5, 1903, once more through Mrs. Holland: "I fear you will never be really responsive trying alone—at least not to influences unknown to you while they lived. You need the connecting bond." (Johnson, 1907–1909, pp. 230–231).

A good example of a cross-correspondence in which the Myers control seems to be the mind behind certain messages is the "Lethe" case. George B. Dorr was sitting in America (35e, 36e) with Mrs. Piper who had known Myers when she visited Cambridge (40a). On March 23, 1908 (32i), testing the control's knowledge of the classics, Dorr asked the Myers personality what the word "Lethe" suggested to him (Piddington, 1910). In reply to this question, Lethe was identified during Dorr's subsequent sittings with Mrs. Piper as a beautiful underground river in Hades and Ovidian details with which neither Mrs. Piper nor Dorr was familiar were given. Some scholar, such as Myers, who knew the recondite details might therefore have been the source of the information. Two years later, in England, Sir Oliver Lodge mailed this same question to the medium Mrs. Willett and asked that it be put to the Myers control. Mrs. Willett had not been a member of the Society for Psychical Research, had not known Myers and had had no prior linkage with him (40d). She could not reasonably have known of the experiment with Mrs. Piper (Lodge, 1911). On February 4, 1910, Mrs. Willett put the question to the Myers control. In her script of that date various classical allusions were made to the "River of Forgetfulness," "pain forgotten" and to "Valle Reducta" [sheltered vale], which is Virgil's phrase describing the river Lethe. Other classical references were made as well in this and later scripts. The Myers control also seemed to recognize the advantage of using two mediums to express a single theme and also recognized the purpose of doing so.

On February 10, 1910, the message "That I have to use different scribes means that I must show different aspects of thought, underlying which unity is to be found," appeared in Mrs. Willett's script. And again: "Myers yes I am ready I know what Lodge *wants* he wants me to prove that I have access to knowledge shown elsewhere" (Lodge, 1911, p. 148). On February 5, 1910 (32j), this message was recorded: "It is I who write Myers...," and almost immediately the name "DORR" was given (Ibid., p. 126).

Both Lodge and Ducasse thought that the "Lethe" case suggested most strongly that the scholar Myers had survived death. We conclude from it and the other evidence summarized above that Myers was a good communicator who supplied clear evidence both of his identity and of his characteristics and memory. Myers belongs in Category 1.

Cast 10. Edmund Gurney

Myers' friend Edmund Gurney became the first honorary secretary of the Society for Psychical Research and collaborated with Myers and Frank

Podmore in writing the well-known *Phantasms of the Living*. He died in Brighton in 1888.

The medium Mrs. Holland had not known Myers. Nor had she known Gurney (40d). Yet on December 19, 1905, seven and one-half years after his death, she seems to have seen his apparition. On entering a brightly lighted sitting room, she saw a tall man standing with his back to the fire. He had a long face with a moustache and was in early middle age. Again, on March 11, 1906, she saw him one evening lying on his left side on a bed facing away from her. At the sight of him, she was shocked for the moment and her foot seemed to kick a small empty bottle on the floor. (A bottle had been associated with Gurney's death.) The figure vanished. When she looked, no bottle was to be found (Johnson, 1907–1909, pp. 286–287). But these apparitional phenomena, however interesting, are not persuasive evidence of Gurney's identity and cannot be considered in evaluating this case.

The evidence for his postmortem identity comes principally from his appearances through the automatic writings of several mediums although these scripts were not always persuasive, either. For instance, he seemed to come through Mrs. Piper in the United States in 1889, William James being the sitter. James, however, found the appearances totally unconvincing and without "the slightest inner verisimilitude in the personation" (James, 1890, p. 656).

Thereafter Gurney seemed to develop as one of the main sources of the cross-correspondences and as one of the principal communicators through Mrs. Willett in England in sittings with the Earl of Balfour. She had not known Gurney and had had no prior contact with him (40d). Likewise, Gurney had had no previous linkage with Mrs. Piper through whom he also appeared (40d). Then, after his death in 1889, she came to England at the invitation of a special S.P.R. committee and stayed with Myers and Sidgwick at Cambridge and with Lodge at Liverpool (Lodge, 1909). Lodge, of course, had known Gurney and had come into psychical research because of him (3p, 39q). A sitting held on December 21, 1889, with Lodge taking notes, is of interest for two reasons.

Mrs. Piper, after being given a letter from Edmund Gurney, went into trance (38a). Her control, Phinuit, said that the letter had Edmund's influence on it and that it had to do with a person in trouble. Then, according to Lodge, the personality of Phinuit seemed to change into Gurney's. "He spoke so naturally that for a time I forgot to take notes," said Lodge (p. 144). Although nothing of an evidential nature was said, this sitting, held in an experimenter's home (34d) in Liverpool (33, 35b, 36b) one and a half years after Gurney's death (32g) may be the first evidence of his appearance and identity. Then, after a brief exchange with the Gurney control, Lodge wrote: "My extant notes here come to an abrupt end, the lower half of the page being cut off, presumably because something concerning Gurney's private affairs was said which I was asked not to remember" (Ibid.). Perhaps what was said might have cleared up the question of whether Gurney's death had been accidental or a suicide.

Two and a half years later, on February 24, 1901 (32h), the Gurney personality appeared as one of the controls of Mrs. Diana Forbes, who had never known him (40d) (Verrall, 1906, p. 220). Mrs. Verrall, however, to whom he appeared as a communicator, had known him (40a). On July 21, 1903, 15 years after his death, he seemed to want to instruct her on how to help her mediumship. On that date she recorded in her automatic script (38b, 41a): "a definite message to me from Mr. Gurney." It was: "Sit with some one else—so that you may be free for the impression. [Y]ou would help—and you would learn." On September 17, 1903 (32i), her script (38b) read: "I cant do much more through you alone but sit with others and learn to help" (Ibid., pp. 102–103).

Mrs. Verrall compared her automatic scripts with those of other sensitives to see if there were any connections. An interesting one appeared in 1904 (32j) between her script and a script of Mrs. Forbes'. In the latter's script of October 14 there was a message signed "E.G." to the effect that Mrs. Verrall should sit on October 16 and that "I will send the scene to Mrs. Verrall to be read by you" (p. 269). Mrs. Verrall received word of this message on the morning of October 16 and sat at 10:30 P.M. that evening. Her script recorded: "Tell this. in the fire-lighted room she & the dog alone, and the thought came to her as she held up the screen before the fire—and the dog stirred in his sleep—he felt that I was there" (Ibid.). While writing, Mrs. Verrall had the impression that Mrs. Forbes was sitting in her drawing-room with the door to the greenhouse open. On being questioned, Mrs. Forbes said she was sitting in the drawing-room. There was little light: only one small lamp was behind her. One dog only was with her (she usually had two with her constantly). She was holding in her hand a piece of paper as a screen. The door to the greenhouse was open. Except for "fire-lighted," Mrs. Verrall's script and impression were confirmed.

Mrs. Holland, as we know, had a special interest in Myers and his book but not in Gurney, whom she had not known (40d). Nevertheless, while she was still in India (34b, 35e, 41a) (which she left in April 1904 to visit her father's house in the south of England), her scripts record several utterances from Gurney. For example, "It has been a long work—but the work is not nearly over yet—It has barely begun—Go on with it—go on—We were the torch bearers—follow after us—The flame burns more steadily now—E.G. 1888" (Johnson, 1907–1909, p. 193). The initials are Gurney's and the date is the year of his death. But since Mrs. Holland had read Myers' *Human Personality*, she would have seen the date in Volume 1, page 8, of that work.

Like Myers, Gurney seemed to be thinking of cross-correspondences and of sending fragments of messages to several mediums in order to improve the evidence. In Mrs. Holland's script of November 7, 1903 (32j) a Gurney message read: "One person alone does so little," and another recorded in her script of January 5, 1904 (32j) ". . . one feels that words said—shouted sung to the wind—may perhaps some time—some time reach you as an echo—a whisper—distorted perhaps but yet with a purpose with a meaning—not for you—but for others" (Johnson, 1907–1909, p. 231).

The Gurney control sometimes seems to be standing next to the Myers control, as if the two were cooperating to supply evidence to their holon. On January 12, 1904 (32j), Mrs. Holland's script recites first, in pencil, a message from Gurney: "Now I want you to do something different this morning—Instead of the frequent interruptions of little broken messages . . . which trouble F. so and break the thread—your *hand* will be left alone—but *you* are to write down as much as you can gather of a message transmitted to your brain alone—I think it will be easier for F. Don't trouble to pick up phrases—jot down what is put into your mind—Throw it on the paper as it were. . . ." Then Mrs. Holland took up a pen and recorded in her own writing a message apparently from Myers in the midst of which the writing changes into that of the Myers control becoming more and more emotional as the writing grew larger: ". . . Does any of this reach you reach anyone or am I only wailing as the wind wails—wordless and unheeded—" Then abruptly the words of the Gurney control are recorded by Mrs. Holland in pencil: "Why did you let your hand yield to the writing—You have stopped and exhausted him now—and he might have gone on dictating" (Ibid., pp. 232–233).

A cross-correspondence involving the Gurney personality is set out in tabular form:

Mrs. Verrall (in England) March 15, 1905	Mrs. Holland (now in England) March 22, 1905 [32j]
The clock has passed the hour to strike—I hear no stroke—Send these five notes [and five notes of music are shown in the script] [Ibid., pp. 254–255]	The ivory gate through which all good dreams come. . . . E.G. [followed by five notes of music]

The occurrence of the same number of musical notes in the scripts of the two mediums along with an apparent reference to Gurney in Mrs. Holland's script is suggestive. But we note that Mrs. Verrall's script was received by Mrs. Holland on March 23. Her script, although dated March 22, was not sent to Alice Johnson until March 24, or after her receipt of Mrs. Verrall's script, so that the evidential value of Mrs. Holland's script is weakened.

A description of Gurney also appears in Mrs. Holland's script: One [of three men she was describing] looks young—Tall and very thin—long limbed and loose jointed—He has a long mustache [sic]—The strong rounded chin is clean shaven — The face is long and the eyes look tired." Besides "Henry" and "Fred," the other name in her script was "Edmund" (p. 246). As we know, however, Mrs. Holland had seen portraits of Gurney, Sidgwick and Myers.

A review of the evidence in the Gurney case shows that some of the incidents or messages are weak, others strongly suggestive. Taken as a whole, the evidence seems to indicate that Gurney identified himself and was a Category 1 communicator.

Case 11. Frank Podmore

Before his death in 1910, Frank Podmore served as joint honorary secretary of the Society for Psychical Research and, with Myers and Gurney, wrote *Phantasms of the Living*. He was known as the S.P.R.'s "prosecuting attorney" because of his sharp criticisms of psychic phenomena.

The accounts of two mediums in the United States contain questionable references to Frank Podmore. On September 26, 1910, in a sitting with Hyslop, Mrs. Chenoweth recorded: "Don't fret about Podmore. We know he came here . . . he wants to kep [keep] right on doing the same thing. He did that all his earthly life" (Hyslop, 1912, pp. 144–145). This communication is of no value, however, because not only did Podmore himself not communicate with the medium but because, at the time of the sitting, Mrs. Chenoweth knew of Podmore's death and in all likelihood had some familiarity with his work.

Prior to this sitting, about the last week in August 1910, Mrs. Chenoweth had been awakened in the middle of the night by the sensation of water coming through the window and over her. It seemed to be raining on her face and it frightened her badly (Ibid.). Although Hyslop ventured that this might have been the first attempt of Podmore to communicate (1914, p. 513), it is very hard to accept this explanation. There seems to have been no communicator, and, if there were one, there was no effort by the communicator to identify himself. That the medium sensed water and that Podmore had drowned on a rainy night do not require the conclusion that it was Podmore communicating.

In a sitting held on October 4, 1910, by Mrs. Smead (Mrs. William M. Cleveland), with her husband the sitter, the word "Poundr" was given and the "P" began with lines suggesting an anagram for "P" and "F" (Hyslop, 1912a, p. 131), which this medium also said that she saw again on February 1, 1911. These reports are somewhat suggestive but they are far too weak to be considered evidence.

On May 29, 1911, when Hyslop was sitting with Mrs. Smead, her script read: "So sure always he was just right did not like to open out to all the truth as coming from us" (Ibid., p. 824). Here, however, the communicator was supposed to be Hodgson, not Podmore, so that we still have an absence of any direct communication from Podmore. Moreover, by the time of this sitting Mrs. Smead knew that Podmore had died and probably was familiar with what his critics had said of his books: That Podmore was too ready to choose only events his theory could demolish while ignoring those he could not. The communication she received was of this tenor.

Beyond the vague lines suggesting an anagram, a reading of the long record of sittings left by Hyslop shows no material of evidential value pertaining to Podmore. As "prosecuting attorney" of the S.P.R. who pointed up the deficiencies of automatic writing and trance mediumship and the trickery of physical mediumship, he was painfully aware of the need for stronger survival evidence. Yet, although his colleagues, including Henry Sidgwick, Myers and Gurney seem to have met this need and were Category 1 communicators, "[i]n the case of Podmore," as Lambert writes, "there was silence" (1959–1960). The evidence is not merely faulty; it is nonexistent. Podmore is a Category 4 case.

Case 12. William James

Physician, psychologist and philosopher, William James had many interests, not the least of which was psychical research. He was a president of the Society for Psychical Research and a founder of the American Society for Psychical Research. He died in 1910.

With the exception of one English medium to whom Susy Smith refers in her *Book of James* and whose manuscript was never published, there are no indications that James ever made any appearance through the scripts of sensitives in the British Isles. Since James had had warm friendships with Gurney and Myers, and held high office in the S.P.R. from 1890 to his death—had, in sum, close personal and intellectual ties with most if not all researchers in England, it is significant that he did not appear to someone there.

In her book, Susy Smith describes communications she received from "James Anderson," whose history corresponded to William James's. Under questioning this entity said he had been using a pseudonym and actually was William James. But, although the book presented the reader with some inspiring words of a transcendental nature, Miss Smith does not claim that she had been in direct contact with the real James.

Others, however, have claimed to have received messages from William James. One such claim was made in October 1912 when a young woman wrote to Hyslop that she had been doing automatic writing when a message from "Prof. James" came to discuss God's plan and to give some moral precepts. Hyslop dismissed them abruptly: "The alleged messages from Professor James do not present evidence of identity in any form that is scientifically recognizable" (1913, p. 433).

In 1914, Dr. John E. Coover sat with the medium Mrs. Key in the offices of the American Society for Psychical Research, then in San Francisco. The medium was described as an "American gentlewoman of refinement and culture . . . known for her high moral character" (Coover, 1914, p. 201). At a seance held on April 18, the control "Katie" declared that "Professor Wm. James" was there but no proof was given. On May 2, during an experiment with scales to see if the James entity could exert psychic force on an apparatus consisting of a platform spring-balance and a scale pointer, "Professor James" was said to have exerted one and three-quarter pounds of pressure on the scale with his right hand. Investigation by the experimenter, however, indicated that the psychic's body had been used to produce this remarkable phenomenon. The experimenter, when the seance room was dark so that neither psychic nor sitter could have seen it, had covered the platform of the scale with lampblack. It was found that "Professor James" had wrapped a left hand in a fabric made of silk as if attempting to leave no traces or fingerprints (Ibid., pp. 230–233).

When the experimenter asked "Professor James" a question of psychological or technical nature, "James," reports the experimenter, "most unnaturally disappeared" (p. 242).

Several levels above the mediumship of the very refined and moral Mrs. Key was Mrs. Smead's. On August 27, 1910, the day following James's death, she reported seeing his apparition. She said she was wiping breakfast dishes when she saw a dark shadow in a long black gown coming across the floor toward her. At the time Mrs. Smead lived in the mountains of the South where news of the outside world did not come quickly — no radio or television then! When she said that she had not heard of James's death until after this event, she can be believed. Later, upon being shown James's picture, she identified him as the apparition (Hyslop, 1912a, pp. 94–96). Was this James's first manifestation? Possibly. But Mrs. Smead's statement really is of no evidential value. It was not recorded until after she had learned of James's death. If an event is not recorded at once, before memory fades and before facts are learned, it is not worth very much.

Mrs. Smead was used in experiments conducted by Hyslop in New York. His record of these experiments as well as those with Mrs. Chenoweth (in Boston) (Hyslop, 1912a) is as thick as a telephone directory and involves more details than can be gone into here. But some of the experiments are worth a little attention.

On August 31, 1910, a letter from James was placed near Mrs. Smead's hand, but the sitting was inconsequential. On September 1 the medium tried to make some semicircles, then tried to draw the Greek letter omega and heard some other Greek letters spoken. Some mention was made of a sign. James, however, did not know Greek, and nothing about the sitting implies his appearance at this time. At a subsequent sitting with Mrs. Chenoweth on September 26, 1910, however, the G.P. control took over and said that it would be desirable to give James a sign or name by which he could be known. The Hodgson control entered to speak with James, but James did not appear. On September 29, 1910, in another sitting with Mrs. Chenoweth someone referring to Mrs. James and Harry (James's son) came through the medium and, near the end of the sitting, said: "Here is my sign. Omega" (Ibid., p. 157).

In evaluating James's ability to manifest his identity, we must recall the comments made previously in connection with conspicuous* figures, of whom James was one. In such cases an extremely strict evidential standard is necessary. In order to establish personal identity, we must look for information that is not generally known. Was this information supplied? Much of the purported James material reported by the mediums was wrong; some of the incidents communicated were correct. Still, ESP among the living might explain those successes. Hyslop tabulated the incidents that were known to him and those which had not been at the time the messages were received (pp. 43–47). Twenty had been unknown to him; he knew 16 so that more things unknown than known had been communicated. Yet the ESP abilities of the sensitives might have drawn the information from the minds of absent living persons who knew about the incidents.

We cannot say that James established his identity unless we consider the Omega sign an effort to do so. Mrs. Smead's receipt of this sign on September 1, 1910, was not known to Mrs. Chenoweth on September 26 when it came through her. Arguably, this Greek letter then might be considered an effort by James to prove his identity. But Professor Hyslop was the sitter in both sittings and the sign was known to him. That Mrs. Smead had received it in the earlier sitting could have been picked up paranormally from Hyslop's mind by Mrs. Chenoweth.

If the Omega were really James's sign, did he perhaps communicate it to some medium with whom Hyslop did not sit and so make his attempt to identify himself clearer and stronger? In fact, Hyslop did receive letters from someone with whom he had not sat and who described herself as an automatist who was "telepathically clairvoyant." The letters were postmarked in June and July of 1912. The woman said that she had had communications from "William James" who drew circles and crosses (Hyslop, 1915). The circle, she said, was a symbol of endless continuance. Assuming that the circles were intended to be an omega — and, of course, an omega is not a circle — was this James communicating? Probably not. The sign can be explained just as well on the ground that the woman had read the reports of the Smead and

---

*See comments re: Wright (Case 4), Funk (Case 5), and Sidgwick (Case 8).

Chenoweth sittings in the May 1912 issue of the *Proceedings* prior to "receiving" the sign. Hyslop dismissed the messages as not evidential (Ibid., p. 520). He observed that the circle had an association with the woman's sick child and she might somehow have connected James's name with it.

Addressing himself to James's total performance as a communicator Hyslop also said, "On the whole the incidents purporting to come from Professor James are not as satisfactory as was desirable. . . . He was not a good communicator" (1912a, p. 40). What James said about the totally unconvincing nature of Gurney's appearance through Mrs. Piper in 1889 — not "the slightest inner verisimilitude — is equally applicable to the nature of James' appearance and leads to the conclusion that he belongs in Category 4.

Logically, if all people survive death with equal abilities to communicate with the living, and if one person in a group turns out to be a Category 1 communicator, then all should be Category 1 communicators. Or, if one in the group falls into Category 2, all should, and, similarly, if one were a Category 3 or 4 communicator, all should occupy the same categories.

What does the study made show us? That in the general population sample, three people were Category 1 communicators, but the other three fell into Categories 2, 3, and 4 respectively. In the special sample, half of the people were Category 1 communicators and half, Category 4. Those in the two samples showed altogether different aptitudes for communicating and fell into different categories. Although the group studied was small, results like these hint strongly that the doctrine of natural equality which overthrew regimes in the 18th century, helped generate the American and French revolutions and found its way into their constitutions, is otiose in the afterlife. The "all men are created equal" conception of the postmortem world is a misconception. There is no evidence for the "equal ability" assumption. The afterlife seems to be not a democratic state, but an aristocratic one.

8
THE MAKING
OF A COMMUNICATOR

The neglected angle of the mediumistic triangle permits still another view of the subject of survival, another aspect of it, possibly the most provocative of all: Death is the great unequalizer. Some people are privileged to be good communicators and others are not.

What confers this privilege? Are there correspondences between what people are, do or believe or what happens to them and their becoming good postmortem communicators? This question has never been asked before. To try to answer it, our probe that began as a test of the "equal ability" assumption enters its next phase.

The results of the research reported in this chapter and the two that follow are only a beginning, but perhaps a good enough beginning. Future research may make our findings obsolete or may establish their truth.

For the purpose of the exploration carried out here, "star" or "good" communicators are those in Categories 1 and 2 while "poor" ones are in Categories 3 and 4. To resolve the important question of what correlates may produce or influence the ability to be a good communicator, and since no previous study of this kind had been made, a new methodology had to be developed. A full grasp of all the details of the approach that was taken is not required to understand the results of the research. These details are presented, however, to help the few professional researchers and all general readers who may be interested in the procedures.

Four methods were used. Two, the subjects of this chapter, included the preparation of a list of *special factors* and the analysis of case histories.

List of Special Factors

A list of items, any or all of which might be special factors, was compiled and is tabulated below. They run along three basic lines of inquiry.

PERSONAL DATA

1. Decedent's birth
   Hour: 1a. 6 A.M.–6 P.M.
          1b. 6 P.M.–6 A.M.
   Month: 1c. January
          1d. February
          1e. March
          1f. April
          1g. May
          1h. June
          1i. July
          1j. August
          1k. September
          1l. October
          1m. November
          1n. December
   Day of Month:
   Year:
   Weather at Time of Birth:
          1o. Mild (sunny, calm)
          1p. Inclement (cold, stormy, rainy, windy)
2. Geographical Location of Birth
3. Place of Birth:
          3a. Family home
          3b. Home of another
          3c. Hospital
          3d. Vehicle (auto, boat, airplane, etc.)
          3e. Hotel
4. Sex: 4a. Male
          4b. Female
5. Race: 5a. White
          5b. Black
          5c. Brown
          5d. Yellow
          5e. Red
6. Marital Status:
          6a. Married
          6b. Unmarried
          6c. Divorced

6d. Separated
6e. Widowed

7. Children:
    7a. Childless
    7b. 1 to 3
    7c. 4 to 10
    7d. More than 10

8. Occupation:
    8a. Psychical research
    8b. Science
    8c. Education
    8d. Philosophy
    8e. Religion
    8f. Art, music, poetry
    8g. Business, government
    8h. Professional
    8i. Literature
    8j. Architecture
    8k. Family
    8l. Other

9. Educational Level:
    9a. Advanced
    9b. Moderate
    9c. Low

10. Intellectual level:
    10a. Advanced
    10b. Moderate
    10c. Low

11. Traditional religious beliefs (based on Christianity, Judaism, Hinduism, Buddhism, etc.):
    11a. Strong
    11b. Weak
    11c. None

12. Special Interests:
    12a. Psychical research
    12b. Science
    12c. Education
    12d. Philosophy (including Spiritualism)
    12e. Religion
    12f. Art, music, poetry
    12g. Legal and social issues

           12h. Political issues
           12i. Economic issues
           12j. Literature
           12k. Family
           12l. Sports
           12m.Other

13. Personality:
           13a. Important to achieve
           13b. Showman
           13c. Introvert
           13d. Extrovert
           13e. Optimist
           13f. Pessimist
           13g. Aggressive
           13h. Passive
           13i. Gentle
           13j. Persistent
           13k. Easily discouraged

Interest in Survival after Death:
           14a. Strong
           14b. Weak
           14c. None

Belief in Survival after Death:
           15a. Strong
           15b. Weak or uncertain
           15c. None

Wish to Survive Death:
           16a. Yes
           16b. No
           16c. No indication one way or the other

How Wished to Identify Self:
           17a. Mediumistic message (general—name, love, humor, memories)
           17b. Mediumistic message (specific—describing object unknown to living or unknown solution to puzzle)
           17c. Apparition or materialization
           7d. Haunting
           'e. Movement of physical object (stopping clock, turning picture, poltergeist disturbance, etc.)
            f. Possession
            g. Reincarnation
            h. Other

17i. No indication of how wished to do so

17j. No wish to identify self

CIRCUMSTANCES RELATING TO DEATH

18. Decedent's death

    Hour: 18a. 6 A.M.–6 P.M.

                18b. 6 P.M.–6 A.M.

    Month: 18c. January

                18d. February

                18e. March

                18f. April

                18g. May

                18h. June

                18i. July

                18j. August

                18k. September

                18l. October

                18m. November

                18n. December

    Day of Month:

    Year:

    Weather at time:

                18o. Mild (sunny, calm)

                18p. Inclement (cold, stormy, rainy, windy)

19. Geographical Location of Death

20. Place of Death:

                20a. Family home

                20b. Home of another

                20c. Hospital

                20d. Hotel

                20e. Other institution

                20f. Vehicle (auto, boat, airplane, etc.)

                20g. Other

21. Cause of Death:

                21a. Disease

                21b. Suicide

                21c. Accident

21d. Homicide
21e. Old age
21f. War
21g. Execution
21h. Undetermined
21i. Drowning
21j. Other

22. Unfinished Business at Death:
22a. Yes
22b. No

23. Death Expected:
23a. Yes
23b. No

24. Acceptance of Death by Decedent:
24a. Accepted
24b. Not accepted

25. Kind of Death:
25a. Peaceful
25b. Painful or unpleasant

26. At Time of Death Decedent's Age Was:
26a. Younger than 30
26b. Between 30–40
26c. Between 40–50
26d. Between 50–60
26e. Between 60–70
26f. Between 70–80
26g. Over 80

27. At Time of Death Decedent Was:
27a. Alone
27b. With friend
27c. With family
27d. With doctor
27e. With nurse
27f. With clergyman
27g. With strangers

28. Autopsy Performed:
28a. Yes
28b. No

29. Disposition of Body:
29a. Cremated
29b. Embalmed

29c. Not embalmed

29d. Entombed

29e. Buried in ground

29f. Metal coffin

29g. Wood coffin (or similar)

29h. Buried at sea

29i. Frozen (cryonics)

29j. Other (devoured by beasts, blown up, etc.)

30. Lapse of Time Between Death and Disposition of Body:

30a. 1–2 days

30b. 3–4 days

30c. 5–7 days

30d. 8–10 days

30e. 11 days or more

31. Geographical Location of Disposition of Body

CIRCUMSTANCES RELATING TO POSTHUMOUS
COMMUNICATION OR MANIFESTATION

32. Lapse of Time Between Death
and First Communication of Manifestation:

32a. 1–5 days

32b. 6–10 days

32c. 11–20 days

32d. 21–60 days

32e. 2 months–6 months

32f. 6 months–1 year

32g. 1 year–2 years

32h. 2 years–4 years

32i. 4 years–8 years

32j. Over 8 years

33. Geographical Location of Communication or Manifestation

34. Place Where Communication or Manifestation Occurred:

34a. Family home

34b. Home of medium

34c. Home of sitter

34d. Home of experimenter

34e. Psychical research offices or laboratory

34f. Outdoors

34g. Other

35. Distance Between Location of Communication
or Manifestation and Where Decedent Lived:

35a. 1–50 miles
35b. 50–200 miles
35c. 200–500 miles
35d. 500–1000 miles
35e. over 1000 miles

36. Distance Between Location of Communication
or Manifestation and Where Decedent Died:
36a. 1–50 miles
36b. 50–200 miles
36c. 200–500 miles
36d. 500–1000 miles
36e. over 1000 miles

37. Weather Conditions at Time of Communication:
37a. Mild (sunny, calm)
37b. Inclement (cold, stormy, rainy, windy)

38. Form of Manifestation or Channel of Communication:
38a. Mediumistic speaking in trance
38b. Automatic writing in or out of trance
38c. Apparition or materialization
38d. Haunting
38e. Movement of physical objects (stopping clock, turning picture, poltergeist disturbance, etc.)
38f. Possession
38g. Reincarnation
38h. Other

39. Relationship to Decedent of Sitter Receiving Communication
or Person Witnessing Manifestation:
39a. Grandfather
39b. Grandmother
39c. Father
39d. Mother
39e. Brother
39f. Sister
39g. Wife
39h. Husband
39i. Son
39j. Daughter
39k. Uncle
39l. Aunt
39m. Niece
39n. Nephew
39o. Grandchild

39p. Friend
39q. Colleague
39r. Commonality of interest
39s. Stranger
39t. No sitter present

40. If Mediumistic Communication, Relation of
Medium to Decedent:
    40a. Prior contacts
    40b. Commonality of interest
    40c. Strangers, but linkage (through object, photograph,
        etc.)
    40d. Strangers with no linkage

41. If Mediumistic Communication, Language of Communication
(Whether Written or Spoken):
    41a. English
    41b. French
    41c. Italian
    41d. German
    41e. Spanish
    41f. Russian
    41g. Other

ANALYSIS OF CASE HISTORIES

In Chapter 7, after summarizing briefly the lives of 12 people, all effort was concentrated on evaluating their performances as posthumous communicators in order to test the "equal ability" assumption.

Now the case histories of these people have been subjected to an in-depth analysis in order to see if there is any inter-relationship between good communicators and their histories. The analysis took into account all three lines of inquiry and their special factors. To make this analysis a biography has been prepared for each person. The biographies of six people in the general sample and of six in the special sample follow. To note the appearance of the special factors in their lives numbers in parentheses keyed to the special factors enumerated in the List of Special Factors have been inserted at appropriate places in the biographies: i.e., "She herself firmly believed in survival (15a)." In the list, "15a" describes someone with a strong belief in survival after bodily death. In addition, to pursue the third line of inquiry, as we have seen, numbers in parentheses keyed to the special factors appear in the analyses of posthumous performances in Chapter 7 ("Saints and Scoundrels").

Biographies of the General Population Sample

Case 1. John Jacob Astor IV

John Jacob Astor IV (4a, 5a) was born on July 13, 1864 (1j), at Rhinebeck, New York (2). His great-grandfather was the tycoon John Jacob Astor; his parents were William Blackhouse Astor, Jr., who preferred his race horses to business, and Caroline Webster Schermerhorn, a capable woman and a leader of society. John Jacob was one of five children; he was the only son. He lived at Ferndale, the Astor estate at Rhinebeck, and was educated at St. Paul's and Harvard from which he received a B.S. degree in 1888 (9b).

Having inherited a fortune, millionaire Jack rubbed elbows with the Morgans, Vanderbilts, Whitneys and Belmonts. He had huge real estate interests in New York City, ranging from hotels and tenements to offices and brownstones, which in the 1890's were valued at $200,000,000. He built several hotels, including the Knickerbocker, the luxurious St. Regis and, with his cousin William Waldorf Astor, one of the great luxury hotels in the world, the Waldorf-Astoria, which opened in 1897 (8g).

At Ferndale, his estate at Rhinebeck on the Hudson in New York, his garage contained 18 expensive racing cars (12k). He raced his yacht, *Nourmahal*, against those of the other millionaires like J.P. Morgan, and he also cruised the Caribbean (12k).

He purchased an artillery battery for $75,000 which, along with the men to man it, he gave to the government to use in the Philippines during the Spanish-American War. His subsequent appointment to the rank of lieutenant-colonel was severely criticized at the time as an instance of money buying anything. After the war he entered politics (12h) and might have become a congressman but for strong opposition from Tammany Hall.

In 1891 he married beautiful Ava Willing (6a) in the fairytale romance of the year, but this marriage, which produced two children, William Vincent Astor and Ava Alice Astor, ended in divorce in 1909. In 1911 he married young Madeleine Force whom New York society rejected because she was the daughter of a shipping clerk from Brooklyn. His son by this marriage, John Jacob Astor VI, was born in 1912 after his father's death.

Colonel Astor is pictured as a tall, slim man with a black moustache and sharp features. Although an officer during the Spanish-American War, he was not much in command in campaigns with his family. He was "hen-pecked" by his strong first wife, Ava, and dominated by his equally strong mother. The extent of his authority seems to have been the right to insist on punctuality at dinner. He was humorless and could be merciless. In 1894, despite adverse public opinion, he insisted on prosecuting a tramp who slept one night in the bedroom of his mother's laundress while she was away. The unfortunate man was sentenced to a year in prison (13j).

He had little affection for people and they little for him. One author described him as "a man who cared for nothing . . . cold-hearted, weak-minded, he was distinguished by an almost complete absence of personality, a being no one would have noticed had it not been for his millions."[1]

Jack Astor spoke only of cars and yachts and of whether his chef was better than someone else's. In matters of religion, politics or business, he was conventional, even dull (13c).

The extent of his religious beliefs is not known. He was, however, a vestryman of Trinity Church in New York City and attended an Episcopalian Church in Rhinebeck. It may be, therefore, that, instead of belonging to a church because it was conventional and appropriate for a person in high society to do so, he had some religious beliefs (11b).

Above the level of the conventional and of everyday affairs, however, Astor had strong interests and drives (13a) and greater abilities than people suspected. They entitle him to a much higher rating for intellectual capacity than the author above quoted allows him (10b). He was mechanically-minded. At Ferndale he set up experimental laboratories. Among his inventions was a bicycle brake, a marine turbine engine, a vibratory disintegrator to extract gas from peat and a pneumatic road improver which blew dust from roads. He also designed an air conditioning system for his Hotel St. Regis.

Astor was also a man of imagination and a writer. He published *Journey in Other Worlds*, a science-fiction book à la H.G. Wells, set in the year 2000 in which television, subways and automobiles racing at 40 miles per hour were forecast (13j).

But there is no indication that Astor's horizons extended further than his millions, his hotels, cars, inventions and science fiction. The question of survival does not seem to have interested him (14c). If he had any belief about it, it is not clear what it was (15b). The material available does not suggest whether he did or did not wish to survive death (16c) or to identify himself after it (17i). His son John Jacob Astor VI, with whom I spoke, refused to answer questions about these or any other matters.

Madeleine's rejection by New York's high society led her husband to take her on a trip to Egypt and France. In March 1912 Madeleine's pregnancy and Astor's business affairs, which required some decisions on his part and his return (22a), prompted him to arrange to return with her to New York on the maiden voyage of the luxury liner *Titanic*. Near Newfoundland the *Titanic* struck an iceberg at 2:20 A.M. on April 15, 1912 (18b, 18f, 19, 20g). Making 21 knots at the time of the impact, the vessel's bottom was torn out. Astor was among the first of the passengers to be told by Captain Smith of the grave situation.

According to the *New York Times* of April 19, 1912,[2] witnesses described Astor's conduct as "noble" during the crisis and as the end approached. He was seen with his arms about his wife, tenderly helping her into a lifeboat. One witness, Hilda Slater, said he asked an officer if he might go with her. When refused permission, Astor stepped back and calmly took a cigarette from his cigarette case. "Good-bye, dearie," he said gaily, as he lighted the cigarette and leaned over the rail. "I'll join you later." Another witness, Margaret Hays, said Colonel Astor stepped into the boat because there were no women waiting to get in. The boat was about to be lowered when women came running out on deck. Astor stopped the preparations to lower the boat, stepped out of it and helped the women board it.

Astor seemed very calm and accepting of the inevitable. Someone told him to put on a life preserver. But he refused. With Captain Smith and others (27g), Astor waited for the end as prayers were said and the orchestra played on (23a, 24a).

On April 30, 1912, the cable ship *McKay-Bennett* docked at Halifax, Nova Scotia. She had searched for bodies through miles of wreckage, pillows, tables and chairs. She found 306 dead. Of these, 116 were buried at sea and 190 were brought back to Halifax. The first to be claimed was John Jacob Astor IV, and for his death was issued the first death certificate stating "accidental drowning" (21, 15b, 28b), the same certificate thereafter issued for the hundreds who had perished. It was said that, when his body was recovered, on his person were $2500 and a gold watch that was still running. Astor was 47 years old (26c).

On May 4, 1912, 60 bodies were buried in Halifax because of their deteriorated condition. The weather was warm and it was difficult to preserve them.[3] Astor's body, however, was removed to Ferndale in Rhinebeck where funeral services were held in the Church of the Messiah in which Astor had been a warden. His body was contained in a coffin but its composition is unknown. Nor do we know whether Astor's body was embalmed.

From Rhinebeck the body was taken by special train to New York City to be placed in the Astor family vault (29d) in the north end of the west division of Trinity Cemetery at 153rd Street bordering the North River (31). The crowd around the cemetery numbered 5000; others watched from the roofs of adjoining houses. Only those with special cards were admitted. Astor's coffin was placed in the vault above his father's. In the immediate vicinity were the bodies of the first John Jacob Astor and Mrs. Waldorf Astor.[4]

Case 2. Samuel Langhorne Clemens (Mark Twain)

On November 30, 1835 (1m), with the return of Halley's Comet, Samuel Langhorne Clemens (4a, 5a) was born in the log village of Florida, Missouri (2), the third son of John Marshall Clemens and Jane Lampton. His father, formerly of Tennessee, polished, a businessman and lawyer, was called "Judge Clemens."

Sam Clemens was four years old when the family left the small village of his birth to move to the town of Hannibal, Missouri, where "Judge Clemens" became a leading citizen. With the death of his father in 1847 Sam Clemens' brief education at common schools run by a schoolmaster stopped (9c). He went to work for local printers (8g) and helped his older brother Orion run the *Hannibal Journal*. Clemens also wrote articles for it.

He was 18 when his wanderings by rail and steamboat began. Leaving Hannibal, he travelled to St. Louis, then to Chicago, Buffalo and New York, and back to rejoin his family, now living in Keokuk, Iowa, where he wrote reports of his travels for the *Evening Post*.

In 1856–1857 his wandering spirit led him to think of going to Brazil. After plying his trade as a printer in Cincinnati, he took a steamer for New Orleans to find a ship there heading for the Amazon. En route he met Horace Bixley, the steamboat pilot, and decided to follow that profession, which he did for over two years (8g), in his own words, "the happiest period of my life."

When the Civil War intervened, he served for a few weeks with the Confederacy, then struck out for California and Nevada where he staked out timber and mining claims and began doing freelance writing. He wrote increasingly successful articles for the *Enterprise*, a newspaper in Virginia City, Nevada. It was then that he adopted his *nom de plume,* based on the language of the Mississippi River boatmen who tested the depth of the river with a sounding line—"mark twain" means two fathoms deep.

The story of the "Notorious Jumping Frog" made him famous, and his fame spread soon not only as a writer but as a lecturer (13a). His books *Tom Sawyer, Huckleberry Finn, Life on the Mississippi* and *Roughing It* were extremely successful. He himself was not cultivated, and he did not write for the cultivated classes, "the thin top crust of humanity." He wrote for "the mighty mass of the uncultivated people who are underneath"[5] (10b), and they liked what they read (8i, 12j).

In 1870 he married beautiful, black-haired Olivia Langdon (6a) whom he had met in 1867 on a steamboat and to whom he wrote 200 love letters. They had one son and three daughters: Langdon, Olivia Susan (called Susy), Clara and Jean (7c). The family lived in Buffalo for a while where Twain edited the *Buffalo Express*, moved to Hartford and spent summers in Elmira, New York, Olivia's home town.

Olivia set out to cure Twain of excessive smoking and drinking and to turn him from a vagabond and roughneck into a good Christian. She succeeded in part. He swore off hard liquor, became a gentleman, read the Bible and said grace at meals during the first years of their marriage. But he still smoked 40 cigars a day and never became a Christian (11b). Christian Science, however, interested him (12e). Although he wrote a humorous article about it, he, Olivia, Susy and Clara believed in "mind cure."

Psychic phenomena were of interest to him as well. He was a member of the Society for Psychical Research from 1885 to 1903 and read its publications (12a). He himself had many experiences of what he called "mental telegraphy." He once had a vivid precognitive dream: He dreamed that his brother Henry was a corpse resting in a metal casket. On the basket was a bouquet of white flowers with a red flower in the center. The following morning Henry was killed in the explosion of the steamboat *Pennsylvania* near Memphis. Clemens went there and found that his brother had been placed by the people of Memphis in a metal casket, and, as Clemens watched, a woman placed on the casket the bouquet he had seen in his dream. There were also other examples of Clemens' paranormal abilities.[6]

He did not, however, seem to be interested in Spiritualism, nor did he entertain any special interest or belief in survival after death (14e, 15b). In 1902 when Olivia, who suffered from heart disease and breathed with great difficulty, told her husband that she did not want to die, Clemens assured her, "I more believe in the immortality of the soul than misbelieve in it" (15b). But his biographer Kaplan says this was an "heroic ruse" and that Clemens had said it only for Olivia's sake.[7] If Clemens ever expressed the wish to survive death or not to survive, or to identify himself after death, the material available does not indicate it (16c, 17i).

He was small-boned, had sloping shoulders and was about 5 feet 8 inches in height. His bushy hair, once red, became white. During his old age he dressed in white both winter and summer.

Samuel Clemens was two people. One was Mark Twain, the funny man, the roughneck, the showman, the charming and lovable platform and after-dinner speaker (13b); the other was Samuel L. Clemens, the poet, the dreamer (13c), the man of letters (13h, 13i). It is believed that Mark Twain was a rehearsed character, a controlled mask, behind which lived Samuel Clemens. But whether it is Mark Twain speaking or Sam Clemens speaking is at times difficult to determine.[8] Humorous, direct, bawdy, profane and admired (13d), he was highly successful and wealthy (8g). As poetic, pessimistic Clemens, he was moody (12f, 13f). Clara, who survived him, said that she and her sisters were afraid to be alone with him because his moods changed rapidly and he could be angry, stern and harsh with them.

After his early wealth and fame came difficulties to cloud the rest of Clemens' days. Langdon, sickly from birth, died in 1872. Then in 1890 Clemens had great financial troubles. He had invested heavily in the Paige typesetting machine, which was to make him millions, but he could not market it. In 1894 his publishing house was a failure. He was deeply in debt to the extent of $100,000 (an enormous sum then) and his friends advised bankruptcy. But he vowed he would repay every dollar.

In 1895 he went on a highly successful world lecture tour with Olivia and Clara. From Capetown he went to England where he waited for Susy to join him. A letter came that she was ill. Olivia and Clara sailed for home at once. Clemens remained in England, where he learned by cable that Susy had died of spinal meningitis. He had admired her grace and quick mind. At her death he said it was hard to think that one could receive a thunderstroke like that and live. He thought and grieved constantly after her death. Thereafter he lived in Chelsea, England, with Olivia, Clara and Jean. He succeeded in paying all his debts but was disillusioned and melancholy during those years. He finished few manuscripts, among them *The Mysterious Stranger* in which Satan says, "There is no God, no universe, no human race, no earthly life, no heaven, no hell. It is all a dream — a grotesque and foolish dream. Nothing exists but you. And you are but a thought, a vagrant thought, a useless thought, a hopeless thought, wandering forlorn among the empty eternities!" Observers think that all his misfortunes, all of meaningless life, was placed in the perspective of a dream in order to be examined at a distance to escape from it. *The Mysterious Stranger* reveals Clemens' pessimistic view of life.

In 1891 Clemens suffered from rheumatism in his right hand and shoulder which made writing difficult. In the winter of 1891–1892 one lung was damaged from a terrible case of influenza and from then on he had a chronic cough. The misfortunes he suffered in the 1890's were followed by Olivia's death in 1904 in Florence, Italy, where he had taken her on the advice of doctors. Her death was a calamity for him. He returned to New York with Clara and Jean but a few years later established a home called Stormfield in Redding, Connecticut.

In 1908 Clemens began to suffer from heart trouble which injections tended to relieve. Thinking it was a "tobacco heart," he smoked only four cigars a day instead of forty. A year later his daughter Jean, an epileptic, died, and he said, "I shall never write any more."

In December 1909 he went to Bermuda. When he returned he called the manager of the Associated Press. "I hear the newspapers say I am dying. The charge is not true. I could not do such a thing at my time of life. I am behaving as good as I can. Merry Christmas to everybody!"

In 1910, sick, he travelled once more to Bermuda but did not want to die there. He came back to die and, on his return, said, "Isn't there something I can resign and be out of all this?" (23a, 24a) There was nothing left for him (22b). Near the end he talked about split personalities and Jekyll and Hyde.

At 74 years of age (26f), on April 21, 1910 (18f), he died of angina pectoris (21a) at Stormfield, his estate in Redding (1, 20a). An autopsy was probably not performed (28b). With him when he died were his daughter Clara (27c), his biographer and editor Albert Bigelow Paine (27b) and two doctors, Cunard and Halsey (27d). He died at 6:22 P.M. (18b) at sunset at the close of a lovely spring day (18o). It was, says his biographer, "a peaceful falling asleep".[9] The day before he died Halley's Comet, which had been present at his birth, was observed again at its perihelion.

Clemens was laid in a wooden casket of either mahogany or rosewood (reports are conflicting) (29g). He was dressed in a white suit. He lay in state at Brick Presbyterian Church in New York where thousands viewed him. Then, two days after his death (30a), he was buried on April 23 in a grave (29e) in the family plot at the Woodlawn Cemetery in Elmira, New York (31).

Case 3. Hannah Wild

Hannah Wild (4b, 5a) was born in 1835 in England. Her parents, both English, were James S. Wild and Alice Wild. She had one sister, Bessie, with whom she was very close.

Exactly when Hannah came to America is not known, but we do know that the family settled in Holyoke, Massachusetts, where her father worked in a factory which manufactured cotton, yarns and twine. She fell in love but, because of undisclosed circumstances, did not marry (6b, 7a), "the one sorrow of her life," as her sister declared.

Probably because of her father's trade Hannah Wild became a milliner (8g). Her customers noted that she always wore black, had good teeth and light brown hair unmixed with gray which she wore parted in the middle and combed down on each side with a "French twist" behind. Her favorite pastime was the making of tidies.

No material is available to tell us very much about her. We assume that she had a moderate education (9b) and a moderate intellectual level (10b). She was known as an "ardent and indefatigable champion and head of the women's rights movement." She had the reputation of being courageous, outspoken and undaunted. Her letters on the subject of women's rights were printed in the magazine *Woman's Journal*. From Hannah Wild came many petitions for legislation to correct injustices to women. When a law finally was passed allowing women to vote in school elections, she was the only woman to vote in her ward for many years (12g, 13a, 13e, 13g).

She belonged to the Baptist Church. Bessie described her as a "strong Baptist" who never missed church (11a). The subject of survival after death seemed to upset her at first because, when a Boston paper published what was supposed to be a message from her dead mother, she was said to have been "very much wrought up about it." Yet her discussions with her sister and especially her willingness to write and seal a letter to put her survival after death to the test suggest that she was interested in the subject (14a). Her statement that it would be like ringing the City Hall bell if she communicated the contents of her sealed letter implies that she was not at all certain of survival

(15b) and clearly suggests the mode she had chosen to identify herself after death (17b). It is not clear from the available material whether she did or did not wish to survive death (16c).

When she was 51 years old, Hannah Wild died of cancer of the stomach (21a). She was ill for 17 months before she died. There is no doubt that her death was painful (25b). Bessie reported that her sister suffered frequent "bad spells" and that (Bessie's) husband, Dr. Blodgett, a noted physician, injected Hannah with morphia every few hours during the last days because "her pain was so great." Bessie did what she could to comfort her sister. Every morning, when she rubbed Hannah to make her feel better, Hannah would throw her arms around Bessie and say how good she was.

We assume, but do not know, that the circumstances of her illness made Hannah accept death (24a). For many years prior to her death she was deaf which made it difficult for her to do her work. But she pursued her life undaunted. She seems to have shown the same courage when faced with impending death from cancer. Bessie said that her sister did not think it hard to die. In addition, we have her calm determination to write and seal her letter a week before she died and the fact that she made her own funeral arrangements and selected the verse for her funeral sermon. Hannah was a brave woman who was ready to die (23a).

She died in her father's house in Holyoke (19, 20a) on July 2, 1886 (18i). It is probable that, when she died, her father (who survived her by five years) and sister were with her (27c). At her death, according to her sister, she left no work unfinished (22b). It is unlikely that an autopsy was performed (28b).

On July 30, two days after her death, after services at the Second Baptist Church, she was buried in the ground, unembalmed, in a wooden coffin (29c, 29e, 29g) in the Forestdale Cemetery in Holyoke.

Case 4. *Carroll Davidson Wright*

The son of Nathan R. Wright, a New England minister, and Elizabeth Wright, Carroll Davidson Wright (4a, 5a) was born on July 25, 1840 (1i), in Dunbarton, New Hampshire (2). The family moved to Washington where Wright was educated at public schools and at the Washington Academy. He attended high schools in Reading, Massachusetts, and academies in New England but did not attend college (9b). He studied law, however, and was admitted to the New Hampshire bar in 1865 (8h). Ill health suffered in the Civil War campaigns prevented his practicing law, however. He had enlisted in 1862 in the 14th New Hampshire Volunteers and rose to the rank of colonel.

Of a tall build and a soldierly and erect bearing, with shaggy eyebrows and searching eyes, he was considered patient, persevering, kind and tactful, with the ability to act as moderator between rival interests (13a, 13j). These qualities, plus a penchant for figures and statistics, allowed him in later years to achieve fame in political and educational circles (10a).

He received a Ph.D. from Dartmouth College and LL.D.'s from Tufts and Clark universities. He served in the Massachusetts Senate and became chief of the Massachusetts bureau of statistics of labor. During the great coal strike President Theodore Roosevelt appointed him to the Anthracite Strike Commission. There were other presidential appointments: President Grover Cleveland appointed him to complete the 11th United States Census (1893–1897) and President Chester A. Arthur appointed him Labor Commissioner of the U.S. (8g). He was also professor of social economics and jurisprudence at Columbia University (8c). When Senator George F. Hoar asked him to become president of Clark College in Worcester, Massachusetts, he resigned from government service to accept the invitation. He was its president from 1902 to 1909 (8c).

In addition, he was the author of hundreds of lectures and articles and received such international fame that he was decorated by France, Russia and Italy.

He had strong religious beliefs (11a). He was a Unitarian, the president of the National Conference of Free Christian Churches, and was a regular church-goer. He recognized a spiritual element in the human being but did not seem to be interested in survival (14c). Nor did he believe in spirit communication (15c). As a young man he had observed table tipping and thought it interesting but not much else. There is no indication whether or not he wished to survive (16c), and, since he did not believe in spirit communication, we conclude that he had no idea of giving evidence of his identity after death (1j).

Social and economic issues absorbed him (12g, 12i) as did music and singing. One of his pleasures was singing in the church choir (12f).

Wright was married (6a) and had daughters (7b). The names of his wife and children are not given in the material available. The family lived at 96 Woodland Street in Worcester from the time Wright became president of Clark College until his death.

Wright suffered from stomach trouble for which he took lithia tablets. For ten years before he died he also suffered from diabetes which, with the help of his doctor, F.H. Baker, was controlled so that he was able to perform his college duties and to give his lectures, which the students and faculty (who came in cap and gown) applauded and cheered as he walked down the hall to his office. But the diabetes gradually weakened him and, in combination with heart trouble (21a), forced him to stay at home around Christmas-time of 1908.

He was sick for weeks. During this period he continued to write letters and to work on his *Century Book of Facts*. But he was not forgotten by the students of Clark College who, in those wonderful, romantic days, would assemble outside his sick room and let him know by college yells that they missed their beloved "prexy." These demonstrations made him weep.

A month prior to his death, and probably in full expectation and acceptance of it, he finished his *Century Book of Facts* (23a, 24a). Two days before he died his family and doctor announced that death was imminent. Telegrams expressing sorrow poured in. On the morning of the day he died he slipped into a coma. His wife and daughters (27c) were with him when he died in their home in Worcester (19, 20a). Death came to him gently (25a). His life just ebbed away at 6:30 P.M. (18b) on February 20, 1909. He was 68 years old (26e).

Funeral services were held at noon at the Church of the Unity in Worcester. (The exact date could not be ascertained despite examination of newspaper clippings and correspondence with Clark University.) Wright's body lay in a casket before the church pulpit draped in the flag with other flags suspended on both sides on spear-pointed sticks. Behind the body, and on both sides of it, were a large number of floral wreaths, among them Mrs. Wright's Galax wreath of red leaves on the casket.

Following the service the body was removed by hearse and train to Boston to be cremated (29a) at the Forest Hills Cemetery (31). The ashes were placed in the family plot in Wright's former home in Reading.

Case 5. Isaac Kauffman Funk

Isaac Kauffman Funk was born at Clifton, Ohio (2), on September 10, 1839 (1k). His parents were John Funk and Martha Kauffman, both of Dutch and Swiss ancestry. Isaac had one brother, Benjamin. In 1863, Isaac Funk married Elizabeth Thompson (6a) and, after she died in 1868 (6e), married her sister Helen. Isaac and Helen had two children, Wilfred and Lida (7b).

Funk's father was a Universalist, his mother a Lutheran. In this atmosphere Funk was educated for the Lutheran ministry and was graduated from Wittenberg College in Springfield, Ohio (9b). He entered the college's Theological Seminary and was ordained in 1861. In that same year he held a pastorate in a Lutheran Church in Indiana. Subsequent pastorates included one in Carey, Ohio, and another, from 1865 to 1872, at St. Matthews Evangelical Lutheran Church in Brooklyn, New York (8d, 11a). He resigned in 1872 to leave America for trips through Europe, Egypt and Palestine.

In 1873 he returned to Pittsburgh to become associate editor of *The Christian Radical*. In 1876 he decided to go into the business of supplying books, pictures and other items of a religious nature to clergymen. At that time he had a desk at 11 Barclay Street in New York City (8g). In the same year he established the *Metropolitan Pulpit* which helped the clergy prepare sermons. In 1877 the name of this publication was changed to *The Complete Preacher* which, in turn, was merged into *The Homiletic Monthly*. The latter, in 1885, became *The Homiletic Review* (8i).

In 1877 Adam Willis established the I.K. Funk Co., later Funk Wagnalls and, still later, in 1891, the publishing house of Funk and Wagnalls of which Funk was the president and editor-in-chief. From this house, in addition to inexpensive books of high quality called "Standard Series," came several publications, including Spurgeon's *The Treasury of David* (seven volumes), *The Literary Digest* and *The Standard Dictionary of the English Language* (8i).

Following the publication of the *Standard Dictionary* in 1893, he was supported by Andrew Carnegie in his effort to simplify spelling and make it phonetic. The result was the simplified *Spelling Board*. Funk also produced *The Jewish Encyclopedia* in 12 volumes. Funk's other contributions to the literary world included several books: *The Next Step in Evolution*, *The Widow's Mite* and *The Psychic Riddle*. He also edited G. Croly's *Salathiel* under the title *Tarry Thou Until I Come* (8j, 10a, 12j).

Outside the literary world he had two interests. He was an ardent believer in the temperance movement (12h). In 1880 he founded *The Voice*, an organ of the Prohibitionist Party, which by 1888 had a circulation of 700,000. In the 1880's he persuaded others to join him in founding the Eastern Tennessee Land Co., a prohibition center in Harriman. It was a fiasco and great sums of money were lost. Later he set up another center in Staten Island known as Prohibition Park. Funk seems to have been a man determined to fight for what he believed both in literary and social areas (13a, 13e, 13j).

His second chief interest was psychic phenomena of the Spiritualist type which he investigated (12a, 14a). His reputation as a psychic investigator became generally known through his two books *The Widow's Mite* and *The Psychic Riddle*. Funk was thought by many "to be swallowing everything that came along." In fact, he was far from naive. "[H]e was quite willing for the public to think that he was deceived, if only he could get at the bottom of a case".[10] He was quoted in the *New York Times* as believing that living persons might receive communications from outside intelligences but as not accepting that these intelligences were necessarily people who once lived on earth (15c). This quotation contradicts an assertion that Funk "was converted to a belief in spiritualism."[11] Moreover, we have the statement of Hyslop on the point: "Dr. Funk was generally supposed to be a credulous spiritualist. He was nothing of the kind. The reviewer [Hyslop] knew him personally and he was not only a keenly critical man and sceptical about the phenomena in psychical research, but he was not at all convinced that the spiritistic theory was true."[12] (15c) We conclude that Funk was not a Spiritualist and was extremely sceptical about survival evidence. There is no suggestion from the material whether he did or did not wish to survive (16c). If he did survive, however, he intended to try to identify himself by revealing posthumously the contents of a letter he had left (1b).[13]

Funk was at his home in Montclair, New Jersey, when he became ill. After two weeks he seemed to be recovering well enough to go for an automobile ride. He could not therefore have been expecting to die (23b). But the ride tired him. At the age of 72 (26e), he died on April 4, 1912 (18f) in his home (19, 20a) of heart disease complicated by acute indigestion (21a). We do not know whether death was peaceful or painful, if he accepted it or who, if anyone, was with him when he died.

On April 8, four days subsequent to death (30b), funeral services were held at the First Congregational Church in Montclair with about 75 employees of Funk and Wagnalls in attendance. On April 8, Funk was buried in the Greenwood Cemetery in Brooklyn (31). Further details of the disposition of his body are not available.

Funk had made plans for *The Standard Dictionary* of which he was editor-in-chief and to which he intended to make editorial contributions. He was engaged in working on a manuscript of a later edition and, specifically, on the letter "S" when he died (22a).

Case 6. Emma Fischer

Emma "Fischer" is a pseudonym for a real woman. She was born in 1845. The material available about her does not supply the day, month or exact place of birth. Her parents were German. She was one of 11 children. Her father was of a very strong constitution. (He lived to be 92 years of age.) He was also a man of strict Puritanical standards, a teetotaller, a Methodist church-going man of considerable wealth who owned a mill. Emma's mother, also a Methodist, was strong physically, as well, but died by accident at the age of 65. Unlike her husband, she was very gentle and forgiving.

As a girl, Emma was educated at a local school and probably had a very limited education (9c). Her comforts, however, were not limited. She lived in a beautiful home, loved pretty things and had them to enjoy.

While on a trip her father met John "Fischer," a ragamuffin, apparently took both pity on him and a liking to him and brought him home. He gave John employment in his mill and put him in school. John, of course, met Emma. She was an intelligent girl (10b) and trustful and affectionate (13i). In 1861, when she was 16 years old, she eloped with John. Her father, angered because she had married (6a) without his blessing, disowned her and never forgave her.

From the time of the marriage her husband forced Emma to wash clothes on Sunday which, for her, was a sinful act. Soon Sundays had little significance. Nor did her life. During John's four years of service in the Civil War, Emma was on her own, scratching out a life for herself by whatever work she could get. After her husband returned their fortunes rose for a while when he got and held a responsible job. But, after a few years, he lost his job, neglected her, drank heavily and sometimes beat her.

She bore him 13 children (7d). Two or three died in infancy. Those who lived could barely be clothed by their parents. The family lived near Pittsburgh in squalor in a house not far from the Allegheny River which could be reached by climbing a nearby hill leading to the river. There was an old canal running out of the Allegheny where Emma worried about the children swimming.

Emma's photographs show her aging rapidly during this period. She not only cared for her children and performed her duties around the home but took in washing to help support the family (8k).

Of all Emma's children Doris, the youngest, was her favorite. Never did she whip Doris or show any authority over her. She loved this girl. For her part, Doris adored her "Mama." Doris would start each morning by caressing Emma, would want her to come home when she was away and would greet Emma as if she had been absent for a long time. In 1892, when Doris was three, she was thrown violently to the floor by her drunken father which produced not only a great fear of the father but a condition of multiple personality in the child as well. From that time until Emma's death, Doris alternated between her original personality (whom Prince called "Real Doris") and a secondary personality (whom he called "Margaret"). Sometimes they would talk to one another or exchange notes.

Doris's anxious mother saw her child's odd behavior and took special care of and gave special love to Doris. But Emma never seems to have suspected that Doris's moods and strange behavior and lapses into the appearance and ideas of a young and irresponsible child were due to a dual personality: Margaret childish, mischievous, forgetful; the Real Doris the opposite. Emma simply worried over Doris, thought her "odd" and hoped and prayed that she would mature eventually.

Real Doris might be playing with other children when Margaret would take control and try to force the others to play the fairy games and whispering games that she wanted to play. The result was that the original Doris either played by herself or, more usually, with Emma when Emma's other duties allowed. Sometimes she would sit on her back step peeling vegetables while Doris played in a nearby swing. Sometimes they would play croquet in the back yard. They would make up secrets, they would sing, they would walk together, they would play at pretending wonderful scenes and events. In their games Emma would imagine all the pretty things she loved but could not possess, would imagine a husband who was kind and gallant — the only way such a man could come to her (12k). Despite the poverty, the toil, the cruelty of her husband, Emma continued to show courage and love to her family and to retain her sense of humor and enjoyment of such a life as she had (13e).

Although brought up by strict Methodist parents, after her marriage Emma no longer went to church and even spoke of it bitterly. Her stern religious father having disowned her was no doubt a factor in her attitude. But she did not give up her faith altogether. She read her Bible often, an indication that her belief probably remained strong (11a). From the material available about Emma, we cannot say that, apart from her religious beliefs, she had any interest in or belief in survival (14c, 15b). There is no indication either way of her wish to survive (16c) or of any wish to identify herself after death (17i).

Emma had been endowed with the same strong constitution as her parents. She gave birth to and cared for many children, tolerated squalor, did her washing and housecleaning and cooking and endured occasional beatings from her drunken husband, all with no illness. On May 5, 1906, Emma was entirely well. She carried on as usual in the family home near Pittsburgh (19, 20a) until about 6 P.M. on that day when she began to feel ill and lay down.

On the same day, Doris, who was employed at the house of Mrs. M to do serving and housework, had an extrasensory experience in which she saw, reflected in a glass panel on a door, her mother lying down. Emma's face was turned toward the wall. The ESP image was repeated. Then it returned. On the third occasion Doris saw her mother turned to face her. Emma's face was flushed and her lips were white. Doris rushed home to find Emma looking exactly as she had seen her in her vision. Emma was sick.

Doris helped her mother upstairs and put her to bed. Emma complained about being cold. Then she lapsed into unconsciousness. A doctor came and said that Emma had pleuro-pneumonia (21a) and that it was fatal; then he left. This medical opinion of the cause of death has been accepted. But, given hastily, it may not have been correct because, when the symptoms were described later to five doctors, only one concurred in this diagnosis. Three disagreed. One would have concurred with the diagnosis if Emma had been an alcoholic which she was not. One of Doris's personalities thought Emma had died from a violent blow on the back, and all the doctors admitted this possibility.[14]

Doris was grief-stricken and stayed with Emma as she lay dying and breathing hoarsely (25b, 27c). Soon Emma's husband came in drunk. Advised that his wife was dying, he simply lay down on the bed next to her and fell into a drunken, snoring sleep.

About 2 A.M. on Saturday, May 6, 1906 (18b, 18g), Emma returned to consciousness for a few moments. She looked at Doris, said, "My baby," and closed her eyes for the last time. She was then about 61 years of age (26e).

Doris, then 16 years old, bathed Emma's body, combed Emma's hair and covered the body with a sheet. She stayed with Emma the entire night, kissing her on the lips and placing her cheek next to Emma's. It was at this time that a new, third personality, "Sick Doris," developed. Two more personalities were to follow.

The following day, Sunday, members of the family came as did an undertaker. He prepared Emma for a charge of $20.00. There was no autopsy (28b). When he asked Doris if she wanted Emma embalmed, Doris did not answer; the assumption is that, in the absence of permission, Emma was not embalmed (29c). Emma was placed in a coffin or "box" — probably of wood (29g). On Monday, May 8, a clergyman came to speak with the family. The wake continued through Tuesday when Doris, sitting by her mother's coffin, noticed Emma's favorite flowers, violets, in a dish on a mantel in the room. Roses were placed in Emma's hands as she lay in the coffin. On Wednesday, May 10, four days after her death (3b), she was buried in a grave (29e) in a nearby cemetery (31).

Did Emma wish to die? Was her life finished? "Her temperament was such that she probably did not want to die, she was fond of planning for and dreaming of the future, and there was a peculiar need for her on account of her daughter. . ." (22a).[15] Death came to her unexpectedly, "almost like a bolt from the blue sky" (23b).[16] Well and full of life and with a beloved daughter dependent on her, Emma probably did not accept death (24b).

Biographies of the Special Population Sample

Case 7. Eleanor Mildred Sidgwick

The eldest daughter of James Maitland Balfour and Lady Blanche Balfour, Eleanor Mildred Sidgwick (4b, 5a) was born on March 11, 1845 (1e) in Wittinghame, East Lothian, Scotland (2). She had two sisters and five brothers, one of whom was Arthur J. Balfour, later prime minister of England. In 1876 she married Henry Sidgwick (6a). There were no children of their union (7a). Although it is not clear from the record, it is probable that she shared her husband's doubts about Christianity and may have been, as he was, a theist (11b).

In the course of her long life she became the first principal of Newnham College in 1892. She was also the secretary and treasurer of the Society for Psychical Research of which her husband was the first president. She herself became its president in 1908 and, in 1922, its president of honor. She was a member of its Council until she died.

A woman of outstanding intellectual qualities (10a), she belonged to the group of highly educated people (9a) who founded the S.P.R. She commanded the highest esteem for her methodical and meticulous work in psychical research extending over a period of 50 years (8a, 12a, 13a). A small, gentle woman (13i), she is described as quiet, calm, reserved, not given to demonstration.

To the *Proceedings* and *Journals* of the S.P.R. she contributed important papers on phantasms of the dead, on the physical phenomena of Spiritualism, on premonitions and clairvoyance. She also did almost all the editing for the *Journal* of the S.P.R. when her husband was its editor. She analyzed Gilbert Murray's experiments on telepathy, carried out her own experiments at Brighton and, with others of the S.P.R., was a member of the committee that made the famous "Census of Hallucinations."

The subject of survival was one that interested her very much (14a). She studied the evidence for it carefully and authored many papers on the subject. As part of her study, she held seances with the physical medium Eusapia Palladino and with Catherine Fox, one of the sisters who inspired the Spiritualist movement. She investigated spirit photography. She examined the book tests that came through the medium Mrs. Leonard and analyzed the mediumship of Mrs. Leonore Piper from which she concluded that the medium's controls were elements of her consciousness which allowed her to impersonate them. When she considered the cross-correspondences among the scripts of various automatists, Mrs. Sidgwick felt that they afforded considerable ground for supposing the intervention behind the automatists of another mind independent of them. If this mind were not still in the body but should be one which had survived bodily death, this fact "would mean that intelligent co-operation between other than embodied human minds and our own, in experiments of a new kind intended to prove continued existence, has become possible...."[16]

When she was president of honor of the S.P.R. in 1932, her brother Lord Balfour delivered her paper, at which time he told the S.P.R. members that "I have Mrs Sidgwick's assurance—an assurance which I am permitted to convey to the meeting—that, upon the evidence before her, she herself is a firm believer both in survival and in the reality of communication between the living and the dead" (15a).[17] But there is no clear indication from anything available that she did or did not wish to survive death (16c) or that she wished to communicate in any special way in order to identify herself (17i).

Other than survival, her interests included mathematics, which she had studied and for which she had an outstanding talent. She helped her brother-in-law, the distinguished physicist Lord Rayleigh, in his research on electrical measurements and in his experiments with the Latimer Clark Cell and Solver Voltameter. He wrote three scientific papers with Mrs. Sidgwick (8b, 9a, 12b).[18] In addition to mathematics and science, she was active in the movement for the higher education of women (12c, 12g).

Eleanor Sidgwick died on February 10, 1936 (18b), at home (20a) at Fisher's Hill, Woking, Surrey (19), where she had lived from about 1912 on.

Her last paper, written when she was 87 years old, had been written for the jubilee of the S.P.R. in 1932. Although her intellect remained active, she had grown steadily more feeble and had no work in progress at the time of her death (22b). Probably expecting death (23a), she died a month before her 91st birthday (26g) of "old age" (21e) on a cloudy, windy, cold day (18p). It is likely that Mrs. Sidgwick accepted death (24a) not only because she was old and courageous but also because "she was by nature one who took things as they came."[19] At the time of her death she was probably in the company of a member of her family (27c). She suffered no pain and her death was peaceful (25a).

Her funeral took place at Terling Place, Essex, on February 14, 1936, four days after she died (30b). There were memorial services for her at the Presbyterian Church in London, at Trinity College in Cambridge and at the Balfours' home in Wittinghame. There was no autopsy (28b). Her body was not cremated or embalmed (29c). She was placed in a plain wooden coffin (29g) which may have had a metal lining. On a sunny winter afternoon she was interred in a double grave next to Henry Sidgwick in the churchyard at Terling Place (29e).

Case 8. Henry Sidgwick

One of four children of the Rev. William Sidgwick and Mary Crofts, Henry Sidgwick (4a, 5a) was born on May 31, 1838 (1g), at Skipton in the West Riding of Yorkshire, England (2). His father died when the boy was three years old. He was educated at preparatory school in Bristol and later at Rugby and Trinity College, Cambridge, where he studied the classics and mathematics (9a). In 1876 he married Eleanor Balfour (6a). They had no children (7a). Sidgwick's cousin E.W. Benson became archbishop of Canterbury, and his brother-in-law Arthur Balfour, England's prime minister.

Henry Sidgwick was elected to a fellowship at Trinity and became a professor of moral philosophy at Cambridge (8c, 8d, 10a). He was one of the founders and the first president of the Society for Psychical Research and, later, editor of its *Journal* (8a). As president he sought to encourage a systematic investigation of paranormal phenomena, for he believed that, if even one-tenth of them were true, they would have the greatest scientific importance.

A slight, bearded man who spoke with a stammer, he was candid, fair, conscientious, able and persistent despite failures (13a, 13j). His spirit encouraged confidence in others; his integrity gave psychical research status.

William James said that Sidgwick had the most critical mind in England. He carried this critical attitude into his work. He collaborated with Frederic W.H. Myers to investigate mediumship, carried out experiments in hypnosis and telepathy with his wife, helped in the "Census of Halucinations" and held seances with mediums such as Henry Slade and Mrs. Piper. He rejected Eusapio Palladino, and his interview with Mme. Blavatsky set the stage for Richard Hodgson's later exposure of her.

Early in life he intended to enter the Church of England as his cousin Benson did, but gradually he came to entertain grave doubts about Christianity. He had been elected to a fellowship at Trinity but, when it was required that the holder of a fellowship affirm himself a member of the Church of England, he could not do so and, in 1869, resigned his fellowship. He declared himself a theist—he thought there might be a Mind or Heart behind all phenomena (11b). But he was not a Christian because he could not see any reason for treating the marvels of the Gospels any differently from other marvels.

He was hopeful about establishing evidence for telepathy but not for survival of death. Originally, he did not believe in survival of death. While the question interested him (14a) and he came to accept grudgingly that there might be some *prima facie* evidence for it, Sidgwick retained strong doubts. In 1887 he stated that his conclusion was that there was no empirical evidence for it and that none was likely to be obtained. In the same year he said, "It is best to forget the blackness at the end," so that clearly he did not believe in survival (13f, 15c). He gave no indication of wishing or not wishing to survive (16c) or how he might want to identify himself posthumously (17i).

Outside of psychical research (12a) and philosophy (12d), Henry Sidgwick's other main interest, which he shared with his wife, was to press for higher education for women (12c, 12g). He was also interested in reforming the constitution of his university at Cambridge and of making financial and educational changes there (12c).

Sidgwick discovered that he had a terminal cancer of the bowel and that an operation was necessary, but, as Lord Rayleigh who came to see him after the news had been received said, "There was not one shade of difference from his usual cheery manner." A month later, when Rayleigh saw him again, the physical change that had taken place was "terrible." Yet Sidgwick inquired only how Rayleigh's scientific work was going and then wished him good-bye. If Sidgwick was troubled by impending death, it was caused by his having so much literary work to be finished (22a). He expected (23a) and accepted (24a) death. He wrote to Myers that he would try to meet death "like a man" with his wife helping him (27c).

As the end approached he grew weaker. Myers, who went to see him at Terling Place to say good-bye, said Sidgwick was quite peaceful. He was not in pain but was very uncomfortable (25b) and hoped for death. It came on August 28, 1900 (18j), at the age of 62 (26e) as he lay in the Rayleigh house in Terling Place, Essex (19), his second home—his "Garden of Eden" as he once called it and where he had spent much time during his engagement to Eleanor Balfour (20a).

At the time he died the weather was dull, warm and windy (18a). Three days later, on August 31 (30b), he was buried in the village churchyard at Terling (29e). To promote the rapid dissolution of his body he wanted his coffin to be of wicker or basketwork (29g). He was not embalmed (29c).[19] It is unlikely that an autopsy was performed (28b).

He did not want a Church of England service. He wished these words only to be said over his grave:

> Let us commend to the love of God with silent prayer the soul of a scornful man who partly tried to do his duty. It is by his wish that I say over his grave these words and no more.

Case 9. Frederic William Henry Myers

Born on February (1d) 6, 1843, at Keswick, England (2), Frederic William Henry Myers (4a, 5a) was one of three sons of the Rev. Frederic Myers, the curate of St. John's there, and his wife, Susan Harriet Marshau. Following the Rev. Myers' death in 1851, the family moved to Cheltenham where Myers attended Cheltenham College. Subsequently, he was educated at Trinity College, Cambridge, where he achieved some fame as a poet (12f) and classical scholar (9a, 10a).

Death intrigued and at the same time terrified him. When, in early childhood, he saw a dead mole and his mother told him that it had no soul and so could not live again, he said that "[t]he first horror of a death without resurrection rose in my bursting heart." In later years, while swimming the river below Niagara Falls, he had a vision of death. "May death," he exclaimed, "be such a transit, terrifying but easy and leading to nothing new."

He fell in love with a married woman, Annie Marshall. She responded to him and inspired him, but they could not marry or enjoy any relationship. When she drowned herself in 1876 he was deeply stricken, but in 1880 he married Evelyn Tennant (6a). Two daughters and a son were born to them (7c). They remained married to the end of Myers' life.

Tall, handsome, bearded, Myers was a poet (8f, 12f, 13c), author (8i), classical scholar and philosopher (8d, 12d), sensitive, emotional, able to imbue matters of interest to him with strong feelings and novel insights. In *Human Personality and Its Survival of Bodily Death*[20] he produced one of the classics not only of psychical research but of literature (12j, 13j). In it he advanced an original psychological theory of the subliminal region and also tried to do what he attempted to do all his life (13a): to relate life and the facts of psychical research to the cosmos and the riddle of human life. In this endeavor he became the optimist (13e) and took a positive stand. But he was socially arrogant, his style tended to be florid and he was not generally liked.

At first he was an ardent Christian and, in 1867 and 1868, even wrote religious poetry. But doubts mounted and, by 1869, he had become an agnostic (11c). A pupil of Henry Sidgwick, he studied the classics with a man who became his close friend. He worked with Sidgwick in the movement to improve women's education and, together with Sidgwick, Sidgwick's wife, Eleanor, and Edmund Gurney, formed a group to investigate psychic phenomena.

Myers agreed to join the Society for Psychical Research only if Sidgwick became its president. Myers was appointed the honorary secretary of the S.P.R. and, in 1900, became its president (8a, 12a). Another colleague, besides the Sidgwicks and Gurney, was Frank Podmore. With Gurney and Podmore, Myers coauthored the classic *Phantasms of the Living*.[21]

In the course of his investigations his intrigue with death led him to sittings with various mediums (14a). His initial faith in them, however, was generally followed by disappointment. Along with his friends William James and Richard Hodgson, he investigated Mrs. Piper's mediumship. He had a number of sittings with her as well as with Mrs. Thompson. The evidence he sought for the survival of death did not come from any of the mediums with whom he sat early in his investigations. But when he received through Mrs. Piper communications from Annie Marshall, his first love, and further communications through Mrs. Thompson, his belief in survival was given a firmer footing. These communications combined with his philosophy made him certain that there was an afterlife (15a). Death was no longer terrifying to Myers. It was something that happened to the physical body but would not change the subliminal self, the soul. Death was a freeing of, an enlarging of, the soul and its opportunities and of its chance to reunite with other souls (16a).

Myers placed a letter in a sealed envelope which he delivered to Sir Oliver Lodge. He intended after death to communicate the contents of the envelope through a medium to prove his survival and identity (17b).

Myers had Bright's disease which caused his heart to be enlarged and his arteries to degenerate. A few months before his death he developed Cheyne-Stokes breathing, a condition characterized by great difficulty in breathing (21a). On the recommendation of his friend William James who had been treated there, Myers went to a clinic in Rome (19) to receive injections. Within a few days he worsened. Suffering terribly, he struggled for breath (25b). But, as he faced death, he told Dr. Alex Munthe who had been called in for consultation, "I am glad, I am ready, I have no fear. I am going to know at last. . . . I am very tired and very happy." His indifference and courage at this time were so great (23a, 24a) that the doctor in attendance called his dying "a spectacle for the Gods" and said that it was "edifying to see how a genuine conviction of immorality can make a man indifferent to what to ordinary people is so horrible."[22]

Leaving unfinished two massive volumes on *Human Personality* (22a), Myers died in the Hotel Hassler (20d) in Rome at 9:30 in the evening (18b) on January 17, 1901 (18c), attended by his wife, Evie (27c) and a doctor (27d). He was 58.

No information is available as to whether an autopsy was performed. His body was embalmed (29b) and returned to England. He was placed in a lead coffin (29f) and entombed (29a) in the churchyard at Keswick, the place of his birth, on February 13, 1901, 27 days after his death (30e).

Case 10. Edmund Gurney

The son of John Hampden Gurney, a clergyman, Edmund Gurney (4a, 5a), one of eight children, was born at Horsham, near Walton-on-Thames (2) on March 23 (1e) in 1847. He received a private education and then attended Trinity College, Cambridge, where he studied the classics and mathematics. During his college days music was a strong interest which preoccupied him (9a, 10a).[23]

He was a tall man (over six feet in height), good-looking and athletic. A picture of him shows that he had a moustache and thick hair parted down the middle. He was considered witty, was a good conversationalist and very well-liked, even admired, although some thought him sarcastic. Like his colleague Myers he was a classical scholar but, in addition, he had artisitic gifts, perhaps inherited from his mother who had been a musician, which financial security allowed him to develop. He studied, played and composed music and trained hard to become a composer and pianist (12f). This ambition, however, was thwarted by an absence of manual dexterity, and, when compelled to surrender the idea of becoming a composer or pianist, he became quite unhappy and frustrated. He is said to have had moods of congenital melancholy which sometimes were replaced by periods of great happiness. His melancholy increased, however, in 1875 when three of his sisters were drowned when their boat capsized in a storm.

Married in 1877 to Kate Sara Sibley (6a), he had one child, Helen May, by her. They lived in London. Happy though it was, the marriage did not satisfy his restlessness. A few months after his wedding he began a course in medicine (12b) to replace his lost musical ambitions. By 1880, however, he had to give up medicine because he could not stand the sight of blood or the suffering of the pained and sick.

He thereupon proceeded to study law (12g) which, by 1882, he abandoned as well. On what did his thoughts dwell? On human misery (13f). Religion did not comfort him; in fact, he was antagonistic toward it (11c). Hall, perhaps unfairly, describes Gurney's personality as "a manic depressive type."[24] In any case it is true that nothing he chose to do was successful, so that he kept searching for something to balance the frustration and unhappiness he must have felt. He wanted to succeed at something (13a).

The door now opened to psychical research (12a), which had not interested Gurney before 1882. Other things appealed to him. But mainly
because of his friendship with Myers and Myers' influence, he became one of
the group which Sidgwick and Myers formed to investigate Spiritualism and
psychic phenomena. Along with Myers, he consented to join the Society for
Psychical Research if Sidgwick became its president. Gurney became its first
honorary secretary in 1883, and from that date to his life's end was one of its
most industrious, energetic, persistent and competent workers (8a, 13j).

He both studied and experimented with hypnosis, accompanied Myers
in investigating mediums, worked with the physicist Sir William Barrett, the
guiding force behind the formation of the S.P.R., in telepathic experiments.
He called William James his friend. Although Gurney was its main author,
Myers and Frank Podmore joined with him in producing the classic *Phantasms
of the Living*, in which Gurney expressed the then original theory that apparitions were created in the minds of percipients by telepathic impulses from the
minds of the subjects of the apparitions.

Human suffering continued his concern. He believed that relief from it
might come only by offering people, not religious creed, but hope based on
facts which showed that there might be survival of physical death. In Myers'
Presidential address[25] he said that Gurney was interested in the survival question (14a) also because it was the only test for the existence of God—for how
could a God be loved or worshipped if human beings were foredoomed? As
for himself, Gurney did not believe in or have any wish or hope for, and little
preoccupation with, a life after death (15c). It is evident that none of the
evidence he considered ever convinced him of survival so that he would have
had no basis for saying that he wished to survive or wished to identify himself
after death (16c, 17i).

On June 23, 1888 (18h), Gurney died a death shrouded in mystery. After
leaving his London home and checking in at the Royal Albion Hotel (20d) in
the resort town of Brighton (19) on Friday evening, June 22, he had dinner
in its restaurant and retired about 10 P.M. A waiter gave him a glass of water
at about that time and Gurney seemed in good health. The next day he did
not come downstairs. Nor did he respond to the maid's knocking on his locked
door. On orders of the hotel manageress the door was broken in at about 2
P.M. Gurney was discovered dead in his bed. Apparently he had died alone
in his room (27a) several hours before and probably during the night (18b).
Pressed by his right hand over his mouth and nose was a small sponge-bag.
A bottle, empty except for a small amount of clear liquid, was near the
bed.

According to the *Brighton Gazette* and *Sussex Telegraph* of June 28,
1888, an inquest was held at the Brighton Town Hall by Mr. A. Freeman Gill,
the Deputy Borough Coroner, on the Monday (June 25) following Gurney's
death. Dr. Arthur T. Myers, a friend of Gurney's and brother of his colleague

Myers, testified that Gurney had suffered from acute neuralgic pains and had been accustomed to take anaesthesia, which his medical education had taught him how to use, to reduce his pain. Dr. Myers was of the opinion that the death was accidental. A surgeon, Dr. C. Burland, said that he had made an autopsy of the body (28a) and found no clear cause of death. But he also opined that Gurney had taken an overdose — apparently of the chloroform that was supposed to have been in the bottle — and that this overdose was the cause of death. The testimony of Gurney's brother Alan corroborated Dr. Myers.

This testimony seems doubtful, however, first, because neither Gurney's wife nor Henry Sidgwick nor Gurney's secretary, George A. Smith, seemed to know that Gurney suffered from neuralgia or took drugs. For some reason, they did not testify at the inquest. Further doubt arises because some of Gurney's closest friends suspected that he had really committed suicide. Myers noted in his diary that Gurney frequently expressed the desire to end things. Sidgwick wrote in his diary that he had "painful doubts" about the cause of Gurney's death.

What might have been the sources of these doubts or for Gurney's statements that he wanted to end his life? One might have been that he was fearful of being blackmailed or revealed as a homosexual. That homosexuality was practiced by some members of the early S.P.R., including J.A. Symonds and Raden Noel, as it was among many aesthetes of the period including Oscar Wilde, seems to be accepted by some writers.[26] The homosexual center for the S.P.R. group seems to have been in Brighton where Gurney died and where Smith, his secretary, was associated with young men who were used by Gurney and others in experiments with hypnosis. But there is no evidence that Gurney was a homosexual. Even Hall, no friend of the S.P.R. group, dismisses homosexuality.

More probable causes of Gurney's wish to take his own life, if he did, were that his major work, *Phantasms of the Living*, had been subjected to penetrating criticism and that he might have discovered that Smith, whom Gurney had used in his hypnosis experiments, had tricked him by using a secret code. Then there was also a mysterious letter that had brought Gurney to Brighton. Neither its contents nor the writer's identity was disclosed, which suggests that it either contained information or a threat to disclose information which caused Gurney to commit suicide.

Some believe that Gurney took his own life.[27] Although, as indicated, there might be reason to doubt that his death was accidental, the conclusion of suicide seems unwarranted for three other reasons. Despite Sidgwick's doubts, he did make the following entry in his diary: "[B]ut the evidence is very strong that he (Gurney) was making plans vigorously for the future up to almost the very day of his death."[28] Renée Haynes tells us: "Many Victorians as a matter of course used dangerous chemicals such as ether, morphine and opium to relieve pain (my own great-great-grandmother's recipe book contains a powerful home brew of laudanum, nutmeg and warm brandy and water for 'a complaint in the bowels'."[29] The general attitude of the day was probably shared by Gurney who used chloroform. Finally, the possibility of suicide was raised at the inquest, but the testimony of witnesses tended to contradict it. The jury there decided nothing hastily. On the contrary, "after a long consultation they determined that Gurney had died accidently from an overdose of chloroform to relieve pain." (21c)

We conclude therefore that death was a peaceful (25a) but unexpected event (25b) that Gurney was not ready to accept (24b), especially because he had unfinished business (22a).

Like Gurney's death, the disposition of his body was also shrouded in uncertainty. Questioning of numerous people who should have known brought no information or misinformation. At last, through personal investigation, the information was obtained. Gurney was buried on June 29, 1888, six days after his death (30c), in a brick grave in consecrated ground (29e) in the Brighton Extramural Cemetery (31). His body was placed in a lead coffin (29f), probably for health reasons because it had not been embalmed (29c) and he had been dead for days. At the time the weather was hot and clear (18o).

Case 11. Frank Podmore

The Rev. Thompson Podmore, at one time headmaster of Eastbourne College, had three sons. One, Frank Podmore (4a, 5a), was born at Elstree, Hertfordshire, on February 5, 1856 (1d) (Kunwitz and Haycroft's *Twentieth Century Authors* gives 1855). Although Podmore won a classical scholarship to Pembroke College, Oxford, in 1874, and took second class in classical moderations (9a), he was not drawn to scholarly pursuits. In 1879 he entered the higher division clerkship in the secretary's department in the General Post Office (8g). Married in 1891 to Eleanor Bromwell, Podmore lived for a while in Wellwalk, Hampstead. The marriage produced no children (7a) but, as will be seen, much discord.

His photograph shows that Podmore had dark hair, a beard and a grave face. He is described as unimaginative, yet Ernest Rhys and others who knew him well considered him cultured and full of intellectual curiosity. Dingwall[30] says that Podmore had a "keen analytical mind." (10a) His interests were varied. He loved to play cards (12m). He founded the Fabian Society, a socialist organization whose members included G.B. Shaw, and he was drawn to "social reconstruction." He wrote a biography of the socialist Robert Owen (12g). In his earlier years he had an interest in Spiritualism and contributed to Spiritualist publications (12d). His interest in psychic phenomena and in the survival question which Spiritualism inculcated in its teachings (14a) was the same as Myers'. Although he and Henry Sidgwick seem to have been friends, no such relationship existed with Myers or Gurney although he worked with them.

He joined the Society for Psychical Research after its founding in 1882 and became a Council Member in 1883. After Gurney died he became joint honorary secretary of the S.P.R. with Myers (8a, 12a). With Gurney and Myers he investigated and collected spontaneous cases and, jointly with them, produced *Phantasms of the Living* (although, as already stated, Gurney was its chief author). Following Gurney's death, Podmore collaborated with Alice Johnson and Henry and Eleanor Sidgwick to conduct a "Census of Hallucinations" (13a, 13j).

Although Podmore began as a Spiritualist, with the years his belief diminished and his scepticism grew. In 1902 he published his *Modern Spiritualism* in which he forcibly expressed the greatest scepticism about the physical phenomena of Spiritualism. Nor did his sceptical mind confine itself to these phenomena. As "the prosecuting attorney of the S.P.R.," as William James called him, Podmore assailed poltergeist cases, apparition cases and the cross-correspondences, which he investigated as well to show up defects in research wherever possible. Unlike Myers, whose view of the relation between psychic phenomena and the riddle of life and the cosmos was optimistic, Podmore was pessimistic (13f). For him, psychic phenomena could be attributed to mistake, misinterpretations, fraud or credulity. Rarely would he allow another possible cause. The only phenomenon he acknowledged was telepathy.

In a letter to Sidgwick[31] written just before the latter died, Podmore made two revealing comments to which we must turn because there is otherwise pathetically little material about him. He wrote, first, "I am not sure now that I very much care whether or not there is a personal, individual immortality." At this stage he therefore had little, if any, interest in the survival question (14c), no particular wish to survive (16b) or to give evidence of postmortem identity (17j), a singular betrayal of the holonic need for such evidence. He also said, "I have at bottom some kind of inarticulate assurance that there is a unity or purpose in the Cosmos: that our lives, our own conscious force, have some permanent value — and persist in some form after death." This statement implies some belief in a form of survival. He was a cautious and severe critic of survival who had not found the evidence persuasive. Although he was critical of the cross-correspondences, they may have given him some evidence to support the "inarticulate assurance" he felt because, in his *Newer Spiritualism*, published posthumously, he seems to have considered this evidence a "promising form of inquiry." Podmore's letter to Sidgwick is also significant because it makes no reference to a deity or to any religious belief. From this one can infer that he had none (11c).

After Frank Podmore and his wife moved from Wellwalk to another home at 6 Holly Place, Hampstead, his friends noticed that Eleanor Podmore saw him less and less frequently. He never came home before midnight. She became quarrelsome, severed many friendships and went for a visit to her family in Scotland. In 1907 they became estranged (6d). Podmore moved from Holly Place to the office of the secretary at the General Post Office in London. Shortly thereafter, after 28 years of employment in a respected position, Podmore suddenly retired from the Post Office without a pension. He did not try to explain this abrupt departure even to his friends. Rhys conjectured that he had been dismissed from the Post Office because of "his sadistic tendencies,"[32] a provocative phrase left totally unexplained.

If we knew what these tendencies were, they might shed light on the real nature of his death. Was he a practicing homosexual? Some,[33] citing Hall's *The Strange Case of Edmund Gurney*, say that perhaps he was. As we have seen, some members of the S.P.R., and, in particular the young men at Brighton, seem to have been homosexual. From our limited sources of information about Podmore, however, we have no reason to think seriously that he was homosexual. Hall's work does not suggest the possibility; on the contrary, it counters it. Dr. Dingwall pictures Podmore as a straitlaced Victorian in terms of sex. Podmore is said to have condemned "perverted or unnatural desires" and masturbation. Whatever Podmore's sadism, we have no reason to believe that it had anything to do with sexual practices.

What were the circumstances of his death? Prior to August 10, 1910, he had been staying in the country with his brother. On that date, a Wednesday, he went to stay for a few days at a rooming house owned by one Henry Cross at 2 Ivy Cottages, Lower Wyche, Malvern. Podmore was no stranger to Cross. He had stayed at Cross's lodging the previous year. On Sunday, August 14, Podmore went out, came back, and went out again about 6:30 P.M. This time he came back with a young man and had supper with him. Following supper they left together for a walk. Soon thereafter Podmore returned alone. It was then raining hard. About 10 P.M. Cross bade Podmore good night and went to bed. Podmore seemed cheerful. It had by now stopped raining. Podmore remained in his room and started to write a letter to his mother. About 10:30 P.M. he went out again for a short walk. He was never again seen alive.

When he did not come back a search was made for him by police, boy scouts and friends. His body was found in a large sheet of water known as New Pool which adjoined the Malvern Golf Links about a half mile from Cross's rooming house (19, 20g). In his pocket were 24 pounds and a gold watch which had stopped at 11:23 P.M. when, in all probability he had died (18b). He was 54 years of age (26d). On the evening of Podmore's death the weather was inclement. It had been raining just before his last walk. Lightning had been seen, and, around midnight, very close to the time of Podmore's death, there had been a thunderstorm (18p).

Was the death accidental? An inspection of the bank of the pool showed no marks which might have been left by someone falling in at the end of the pool where the bank was bricked and the water deep. The police found Podmore's cane a yard from the edge of the pool where the water was shallow. If he had been walking at that edge and slipped in, he would have had no difficulty in getting out of the shallow water.

Was it suicide? At the inquest Podmore's brother George testified that Podmore was of a cheerful disposition and would have been the last person in the world to commit suicide and that he had always upheld the sacredness of human life. But, in spite of this testimony, Podmore's break with his wife and the loss of his pension suggest suicide. One author even asserts that Podmore might have committed suicide because he was afraid that "his scandalous private life" would be exposed,[35] and Hall thinks that the "mysterious circumstances" are "suggestive of suicide." To these suggestive circumstances we might add that Podmore's *Newer Spiritualism* had been completed though not yet published. This accomplishment and the ruin that seems to have been Podmore's life after 1907 make it easy to think that when he died he had little hope and no plans for the future (22b). Yet one fact keeps us from concluding that he committed suicide. He left open his letter to his mother. She always wrote to him on Saturday. It is thought that he left his letter unfinished in the expectation of hearing from her the next day, Monday.

If his death was not an accident or suicide, was Podmore killed deliberately? If he was, the motive was not robbery because his gold watch and money were found on his person. If he was, no violence was used because his body was free of any such signs. Yet the position of his cane and the fact that he must have been drowned in the center of the pond where the water was deep suggests that foul play was used to cause his death for what motive we cannot say—except that it could have had something to do with Podmore's "sadistic tendencies."

At the inquest the coroner called the attention of the jury to the absence of any motive for suicide, and the verdict was simply "Found drowned" (21i). The people who had every opportunity to consider all the evidence at the time left the cause of death undetermined, and we must leave it that way, too (21h). Because of this finding it is, unfortunately, not possible to classify Podmore's death as expected, accepted, peaceful or painful, or whether he died alone or in the company of others, murderers or otherwise.

There is also an odd silence about the disposition of Podmore's body. A determined inquiry has turned up the fact that, without an autopsy (28b), Podmore was buried in a six foot deep grave in unconsecrated ground (29e) in Malvern Wells Cemetery (31) on August 20, 1910, six days (30c) after his body was discovered. He was not embalmed (29c) or cremated and, from an opinion hazarded by the park and cemetery superintendent, was buried in a wooden casket (29g).

Case 12. *William James*

On of the five children of a contemplative Swedenborgian father, William James (4a, 5a) was born in New York City (2) in the famous Astor House (3e) on January 11, (1c) 1842. Of a privileged family, he travelled to Paris, Geneva and London, attended schools in France, Switzerland and Germany and, after his return to the United States, received an M.D. degree in 1869 (8b) from Harvard where he taught anatomy, physiology, psychology and philosophy (8c, 8d, 9a, 10a). In 1878 he married Alice Gibbens (6a). There were five children of the marriage (7c); one, a boy of 18 months, died in 1885. The family home, except for a summer cottage in Chocurua, New Hampshire, was at 95 Irving Street in Cambridge, Massachusetts.

James was a physician, psychologist (12b), philosopher (12d). He had a vital and inquiring intellect (13j) whose interests ranged over religion, philosophy and psychology. His books — *The Varieties of Religious Experiences, Pragmatism and Principles of Psychology* — reflect these interests (13a). His *Varieties*, especially the final chapter and conclusion, summarize his own religious beliefs: that this world is part of a more spiritual world and that one ought to feel a union with the higher order (11a).

He shared the interests of his friends F.W.H. Myers and Edmund Gurney in psychical research and was a founder and leader in the creation of the American Society for Psychical Research (8a, 12a). He was an admirer of Henry Sidgwick and was president of the S.P.R. in 1894–1895. He felt that psychical research would lead to great scientific conquests of the secrets of the universe (13e). Reviewing Myers' *Human Personality*, he said that the phenomena with which it dealt — apparitions, hauntings, trances, telepathy — ought to be followed with scientific curiosity. James himself investigated a variety of psychic phenomena, especially the mediumship of Leonore E. Piper whom he met in 1885 and came to call his "white crow." Myers' idea about the subliminal regions impressed James as well. In his *Varieties* he specifically and frequently refers to and quotes Myers.

The question of survival after death was of the greatest importance to him, as shown by his Ingersoll Lectures delivered at Harvard in 1898 (and later published as *Human Immortality: Two Supposed Objections to the Doctrine*) in which he advances the transmission theory to support "immortality . . . one of the great spiritual needs of man." (14a) He analyzed with greatest care the communications that allegedly came through Mrs. Piper from the Richard Hodgson personality. His position regarding the survival question was well summarized at the end of his report: "I remain uncertain (15b) and await more facts."[36] There is no evidence that he did or did not wish to survive (16c) or that he did or did not wish to identify himself posthumously (17i).

In 1870 James had a nervous collapse apparently provoked when he was experimenting "for the fun of it" with the drug chlored and had taken an overdose. His real problem began in 1898 after the battleship *Maine* was blown up and, after a speaking tour against imperialism and "barbaric patriotism," he camped in the Adirondack Mountains to improve his health. Instead of improving his health, he damaged his heart permanently by overexerting himself climbing Mount Marcy. In the next years he went to Bad Nauheim in Germany for its mineral baths and, though not cured, he was able to resume his work and travel extensively.

He was outside Myers' hotel room in Rome when Myers died there in 1901. From there he went to London and Edinburgh where he delivered the Gifford Lectures on natural religion. He felt his health improving by 1910 so that he travelled to Nauheim and Switzerland. But in Geneva James became ill. With his brother Henry and Alice he travelled to Paris and London and, by way of Quebec, to the summer cottage in Chocurua, New Hampshire (19) which James longed to see again (20a).

Back at the cottage James knew he was dying (23a). He died there in his wife's arms (27c) on Friday, August 26, 1910 (18j), at about 2:30 A.M. "without pain or struggle." (24a, 25a) He was 68. Information concerning the weather is not available.

An autopsy was performed (23a), and the finding was acute enlargement of the heart (21a). His body was placed in a casket of unknown material. On Tuesday morning, August 30, 1910, four days following his death (30b), a funeral service was held in Appleton Chapel in Cambridge on the grounds of Harvard Yard. After the service the body of one of America's foremost philosophers was cremated (29a) at Mount Ashburn Cemetery. The ashes were removed to Chocurua and dropped into a small stream in which James liked to bathe.

William James left a widow and four children and, as the possessor of an active and inquiring intellect, much unfinished business (22a).

9
COMPARISONS AND FINDINGS

As an integral part of this exploration, a technique of cross-referencing was employed. In addition, a statistical test of significance was made to determine which preliminary findings might be explained on a purely chance basis and which seemed to be nonchance. This methodology will be found in tables of comparison for each line of inquiry.

As a first step in the cross-referencing process, the investigation here began with the cases of Sidgwick, Gurney and Myers (cases 8, 9 and 10) in the special sample. They were taken as exemplars of the "star" communicator because they were the chief performers in famous "cross-correspondences" (see Chapter 7), which seemed to have been planned by dead communicators after Myers's death. The "cross-correspondences" were made up of fragments of messages, a part being sent at about the same time to a different medium. Separately, the fragments were meaningless; together they showed a connected plan. The "cross-correspondences" are considered by many, including the undecided Gardner Murphy,[1] to be perhaps the best evidence of discarnate intelligences originating, willing and planning communications. These intelligences are therefore entitled to the status of "stars."

Sidgwick, Gurney and Myers belonged, of course, to a homogeneous group — a *holon* — consisting of people of similar social class, education and intellect, all of whom had common interests and aims and among whom there were ties of friendship. This group was hardly typical of the general population.

The research then turned to the sample consisting of people with differing values and backgrounds, with no interests in common and who were strangers to one another. This group — the nonholons — is representative of the general population and was used as a cross-reference so that the data obtained from a study of the "stars" could be compared with the data obtained from a study of the good communicators in the general sample, i.e., Astor, Wright, Funk and Fischer (cases 1, 4, 5 and 6). Factor after factor in each line of inquiry was scrutinized to see if the data clashed or whether the factors which seemed to contribute to the making of the "stars" in the special sample meshed with and recurred in the cases of these other good communicators. If they coincided and were repeated, there would be justification for thinking that a basic pattern of factors characteristic of the good communicator had emerged.

The approach was a demanding one and extended over a year. The analysis of the 12 case histories required not only a reading of the literature but extensive correspondence with relatives, friends and colleagues of the 12 people studied and with societies for psychical research, libraries and government offices. To fill in gaps left by the literature and correspondence detective work had to be done, such as personal and telephone interviews, the inspection of newspapers yellow with age and old burial registers and even visits to gravesites. At last, the data were collected so that the three lines of inquiry could be pursued.

First Line of Inquiry:
Analysis of Personal Factors Among Good Communicators

Did personal data of the sort described as numbers 1–17 in the List of Special Factors go into the making of a good communicator? Did factors that appeared in the cases of the "stars" in the special sample also show up in the cases of the good communicators in the general sample? If so, there might be an interrelationship between these features and good communication.

BIRTH OF DECEDENT (1)*

Lack of sufficient information concerning hours, or weather at the time, of birth of "stars" in the special sample and of good communicators in the general sample made it impossible to inquire into these factors. There was no commonality of days, months or years of birth among the stars in the special sample. For the good communicators in the general sample birth dates, birth months and birth years all varied, also, and there was no recurrence of any of the days, months or years of birth of the stars among the good communicators in the general sample.

GEOGRAPHICAL LOCATION OF BIRTH (2)

All of the stars were born in England, although this is an artifact of the research. Their places of birth in England are all different, however: Skipton, Yorkshire (Case 8); Keswick, Cumbria (Case 9); Hersham (Case 10). These places of birth did not recur among the good communicators in the general sample, one of whom was born either in Germany or in the United States (the information is not sufficient to be more precise) (Case 6), and three others of whom were born in the United States: Rhinebeck, New York (Case 1); Dunbarton, New Hampshire (Case 4); and Clifton, Ohio (Case 5).

*Numbers in parentheses are keyed to the List of Special Factors.

PLACE OF BIRTH (3)

No information about this factor was available for either the stars or the good communicators.

SEX (4)

The masculine sex emerges strongly in both samples. All the stars were male as were three of the good communicators in the general sample, the fourth being a female.

RACE (5)

All the stars and all the good communicators were Caucasian.

MARITAL STATUS (6)

All the stars and all the good communicators in the general sample were married.

CHILDREN (7)

Is having children connected to good communication? Two stars in the special sample had children; one did not. All the good communicators in the general sample were parents.

OCCUPATION (8)

Is occupation a factor? The stars were all psychical researchers, but none of the good communicators were. Two stars were also interested in philosophy, however, as was one good communicator. One star was connected with education as was one good communicator. Literature absorbed one star and one good communicator, also, but the art or science of music which appealed to one star does not appear among the good communicators. There is likewise no appearance among the stars of the business or mercantile interests which engaged two of the good communicators. Neither does being a housewife as one good communicator was nor a professional man as was another.

EDUCATIONAL LEVEL (9)

All stars were highly educated, which contrasts with the moderate education of three good communicators and the very limited education of a fourth in the general sample.

INTELLECTUAL LEVEL (10)

The same advanced intellectual level enjoyed by all the stars in the special sample was shared by two of the good communicators. The other two good communicators were of a moderate intellectual level.

RELIGIOUS BELIEFS (11)

No meshing of religious beliefs (or disbeliefs) among the stars is evident. One had a weak religious belief; the others had none at all. In the general sample, one good communicator also had a weak belief in religious teachings, but three good communicators had strong beliefs which was not true of any of the stars.

SPECIAL INTERESTS (12)

Psychical research was a special interest (as well as an occupation) of all the stars. This same interest, however, recurs only in the case of one good communicator in the general sample. Science (medicine), which was of interest to one star does not recur among the good communicators nor does education, which interested one star, nor philosophy, which interested two stars. On the other hand, the interest in literature or belles-lettres of one star is repeated by two of the good communicators in the general sample. There is also a recurrence of an interest in music and poetry shared by two of the stars since one good communicator was also interested in music. The legal and social issues that appealed to one star appealed also to one good communicator.

PERSONALITY (13)*

All the stars seem to have been people to whom achievement was important and seem to have been of a persistent nature. Two were pessimists, one an optimist. The importance of achievement appears also among three of the four good communicators as does persistence in carrying through endeavors. The introspection of one star is repeated by one good communicator and the optimism of one star is repeated in the cases of two good communicators. The pessimism of two of the stars, however, is not repeated. The gentleness of one good communicator is not a factor found among any of the stars.

All observations made here concerning the factor of personality are subject to reclassification and reevaluation of the persons in the samples by qualified psychologists.

INTEREST IN SURVIVAL AFTER DEATH (14)

The interest in the survival question shared by all three stars in the first sample was shared by only one of the good communicators in the general sample.

BELIEF IN SURVIVAL AFTER DEATH (15)

Although one star believed strongly in the survival of the human personality after death, two others did not, and not one good communicator in the general sample believed strongly in surval after death. Two good communicators shared disbelief with two stars. Two other good communicators had weak or uncertain beliefs that do not coincide with the beliefs of any of the stars.

WISH TO SURVIVE DEATH (16)

Only one star is known to have wished to survive death. The information available does not allow a judgment to be made about whether the other two stars may have wished to do so. Nor is any information on this point available concerning the good communicators.

HOW WISHED TO IDENTIFY SELF (17)

One star communicator intended and planned to identify himself after death by a specific message through a medium. This factor was repeated in the case of one good communicator in the general sample. The other two stars and two good communicators gave no indication of how (or if) they might try to identify themselves. A fourth good communicator had no wish to identify himself.

First Line of Inquiry:
Resume of Analysis of Good Communicators

After examining the recurrence of personal factors among the stars and the good communicators, we proceeded cautiously to make some findings.

POSSIBLY RELATED FACTORS

It would seem that there may be factors in the lives of people that make for the ability to communicate after death and mark off good communicators from poor ones.

The masculine sex of the three stars meshed with that of three of the four good communicators. The figures are extremely fragmentary, but they may imply that the male sex and good communication are causally related.

When marital status was examined for its connection with the problem, the data tell us that the marital status of the three stars was confirmed by the four good communicators so that there is a possible relation between marriage and good communication.

With respect to the factor of parenting, two of the stars and all four good communicators had children which allows the inference that children may have a possible correspondence with good communication.

What data we have allow us to think also that intellect may be a related factor because five good communicators, three in the special sample and two in the general, were of high intellectual quality.

With respect to special interests, political and economic issues interested good communicators, so that these interests deserve some consideration as correlates. Even more consideration should be given to poetry and music, which attracted several good communicators, and to literature, which did, also.

Persistence and the importance of achievement came to the fore as potentially bearing on good communication as six of the seven good communicators had these characteristics.

FACTORS THAT SEEM UNRELATED

On the other hand, it is difficult to perceive any similarity among stars and good communicators when we examine the days, months and years when they were born. The geographical birthplaces of the stars are not repeated since the good communicators for whom we have information were born outside the British Isles.

Occupation seemed unrelated to the ability to communicate. Psychical research, the occupation of the members of the holon, does not appear as such among the good communicators in the general sample. Other doubtful occupations include science, education, religion, business and government, the professions and architecture.

Family as an occupation seems of no importance. As distinguished from simple special interests, art, music, poetry and literature, too, are doubtful occupations. Philosophy was the occupation of less than half the stars and good communicators and must be discarded.

The inference made from data showing that less than half the stars and good communicators were highly educated or even moderately educated people is that there is no correspondence between these factors and good communication. A meager education, however, is not a mark of the good communicator, either, since only one was poorly educated.

Noted above as a possible related factor was high intellect. A moderate intellect does not seem to be a significant item, however, since fewer than half the good communicators were of moderate intellect.

The evidence shows that of the seven good communicators, only three were strongly religious while two had weak religious beliefs and two had none at all. Religious belief may encourage during life the hope of immortality and postmortem rewards according to Judeo-Christian teachings, but it does not seem to play any role in the make-up of the good communicator.

As to special interests, most seem to have no correspondence with the good communicator. Psychical research, the burning interest of the stars in the special sample, is not repeated as an interest among three-quarters of the good communicators in the general sample. Other interests excluded as factors include science, education, philosophy, religion, legal and social issues, political and economic issues, family, sports and other interests. Less than half the stars and good communicators showed any of these interests.

With the exception of persistence and the importance of achievement, other personality characteristics, such as showmanship, introversion, extroversion, optimism, pessimism, gentleness or being easily discouraged, do not appear to merit further consideration.

An interest in survival does not seem related to good communication because this interest, so strongly manifested among the stars, does not show up as an interest of three of the four good communicators.

If an affirmative belief in the survival of the human personality after death has anything to do with good communication, it is not apparent from the examination just made. Only one star had a strong belief that an element of the human personality continues after death. This belief, however, did not recur among the good communicators or other stars. Equally, the weak or uncertain belief of two of the stars does not appear to be a factor since none of the good communicators shared it.

QUESTION MARKS

Whether or not where a person is born — family home, home of another, hospital, etc. — contributes to producing a good communicator could not be determined because information was lacking. It therefore remains a question.

The importance of race could not be assessed. Mediumistic and other survival research projects have not been reported from the perspective of racial background and records of racial types do not exist in regard to communications or the absence of them from nearly all people. Even if they had and comparisons could have been made, we did not seriously expect to find good communicators only in one or some races. Nevertheless, whether race has anything to do with good communication requires further investigation.

The question of whether a wish to survive, or not to survive, death is an operative factor also remains undecided. It is of interest that the one person who wished positively to survive made a good communicator (Case 9) and the one person who did not wish to survive did not make a good communicator (Case 11). It is a question that also ought to be pursued. But, at the moment, it is impossible to make any comparisons with other good and poor communicators because of the absence of pertinent information.

The wish to identify oneself after death cannot be considered and must be left out of account because we lack information concerning six out of seven good communicators. No judgment can therefore be made about this factor.

First Line of Inquiry: Personal Factors Indicated

From the cross-referencing, eight personal factors seem indicated as entering into the constitution of the good communicator. These are:

1. masculine sex
2. high intellect
3. persistence and importance of achievement
4. married
5. children
6. aptitude for art, music, poetry
7. interest in literature
8. scepticism toward survival

TABLES OF COMPARISON

To test all preliminary findings made after cross-referencing, and to arrive at a more precise evaluation of whether any factors thought to be part of a pattern of factors related to the good communicator were so related or whether they were factors that might be expected on a chance basis, two-by-two tables were set up to show and compare the frequency of the factors among good and poor communicators in the two samples. This was done to enable us to see if what were operating were nonchance factors typical of the good communicator. A low enough probability value ("p") for any factor specified (or for any other not detected by a preliminary analysis) would justify saying that nonchance elements were in operation and that such elements bore some positive causal relationship to the good communicator.

Certain criteria were used here to serve as bases for judgments of whether factors were "significant," "suggestive" or "interesting" and therefore not likely to have occurred solely on the basis of chance among the general population. (For the benefit of the statistically-minded reader these terms are defined more precisely in Appendix A.)

First Line of Inquiry:
Tables of Comparison

As stated above, to see if these factors would have been likely to be produced in the general population solely on the basis of chance, two-by-two
tables were used. For this first line of inquiry, three tables were prepared. The
first showed the distribution of factors among three good and three poor communicators in the special sample. A second table made a comparison of such
factors among four good and two poor communicators in the general sample,
and, finally, in a third table, evaluations were made concerning the factors
among seven good and five poor communicators in both samples. For readers
not overly concerned with statistical tables, a nontechnical explanation of
them is that they provide mathematical results of the comparisons made and
showed whether any factor was unlikely to be a chance event. If the chance
probability (p) was low enough for a factor, the factor might have a positive
relationship with good communication.

First Line of Inquiry:
Statistical Investigation of Eight Personal Factors
Among Three Good and Three Poor Communicators
in the Special Sample

After judging in the first table the eight factors just enumerated in relation to three good and three poor communicators in the special sample, five
of the factors were found to have no statistical interest. We therefore concluded that these five factors bear no positive relationship to good communication.
These factors are high intellect, persistence and importance of achievement,
marriage, children and interest in literature. No statistical significance could
be found for a sixth—masculinity—but we are not entitled to think it
unrelated to good communication because this result could have been produced by the selection of a virtually all male group made up of five male
psychical researchers and one female. An equal division between the sexes
should have been a fairer comparison for a resolution of the sex question,
which deserves further study.

No effort was made in the first table to test the days, months or years or
geographical locations of birth because, on the face of them, there was no con-
sistency among "star" and good communicators so that these factors were entirely omitted from this table. Also excluded were weather conditions at birth
and hour and place of birth because not enough information was available
concerning these matters.

The table showed that, of the eight factors listed, only two were suggestive (p = .2): a special interest in art, poetry and music (12f), and a disbelief in survival after death (15c). Another factor that was suggestive was one not indicated before: a weak or uncertain belief in survival (15b) (p = .2). No other factors of importance were revealed.

First Line of Inquiry:
Statistical Investigation of Eight Personal Factors
Among Four Good and Two Poor Communicators
in the General Sample

According to the next table, six of the personal factors seemingly indicated did not achieve levels of significance. But two merit attention. One, not shown important by the first table, was children (7b). This factor was interesting at the level of p = .2. More specifically, to be the parent of one to three children has a possible positive relation to good communication. Besides this, persistence was shown to have a higher than chance expectation and was interesting (p = .2). But no other factors showed any statistical importance.

First Line of Inquiry:
Statistical Investigation of Eight Personal Factors
Among Seven Good and Five Poor Communicators
in Both Samples

The third table showed that, out of the eight factors listed, three had a possible bearing on good communication. Once again the factor of having one to three children (7b) appeared, this time as highly suggestive (p = .07). Consistent with this statistic was the interesting negative result of p = .14 for the factor of childlessness (7a). "Negative" is used in the sense that a factor is not found to be present among good communicators. Here the absence of childlessness makes for the good communicator. Another p was low enough to point to persistence (13j) as another factor that may bear on the good communicator. It was interesting at the level of p = .14. Also a negative belief in survival (15c) was now shown as a highly suggestive factor (p = .07). A factor which the first table showed as suggestive but which the second table did not appeared in the third table: A special interest in art, poetry and music (12f) was shown to be interesting with a p value of p = .14.

Second Line of Inquiry:
Analysis of Death-Related Factors Among Good Communicators

Do factors touching on a person's death — time, place, cause, kind of death, the attitude of that person toward death, what was done with the body, etc. — play any significant part in the production of the good communicator? Here, we see what factors and circumstances related to death recur in two samples of good communicators.

HOUR OF DEATH (18)

In the special sample, information about one star was incomplete. We know, however, that the other two stars died between 6 P.M. and 6 A.M. Three of the good communicators died in this same time period. For the fourth good communicator information was absent.

MONTH OF DEATH (18)

The death-month not only varies among the stars in the special sample but does not coincide with the months of death of the good communicators in the general sample, either. Nor is there any pattern in this factor among the latter.

DATE OF MONTH (18)

The three stars in the special sample all died on different days of the month. The days of death were different as well among the good communicators in the general sample.

YEAR OF DEATH (18)

All three stars in the special sample died in different years. Among the good communicators in the general sample, none died in any year in which a star died, but two of the good communicators died in the same year (1912).

WEATHER AT THE TIME (18)

The two stars in the special sample about whom we have information died in clement weather. But an absence of weather information prevents our seeing if any of the good communicators in the general sample died in clement weather, also.

GEOGRAPHICAL LOCATION OF DEATH (19)

Geographical locations of death were mixed for the stars. Two died in England, one in Italy. The good communicators in the general sample did not die in either of these locations. Three of them died in the United States and one near Newfoundland in the Atlantic Ocean.

PLACE OF DEATH (20)

Two of the stars in the special sample died in hotels; one died in a home which, although not his own, he loved dearly. Hotels are not repeated in the general sample. Three of the good communicators also died in the family home; however, one perished at sea.

CAUSE OF DEATH (21)

Disease claimed two of the stars, accident a third. In the general sample, disease as a cause of death recurs for three of the good communicators and accident for the fourth.

UNFINISHED BUSINESS AT DEATH (22)

All three stars died with unfinished business. In three of the four cases of good communicators in the general sample, this factor repeats itself. The fourth died with his work done.

DEATH EXPECTED (23)

Among the stars, two had reason to anticipate death; one did not. When we turn to the good communicators in the general sample, there is an even split. Two expected death and two did not.

ACCEPTANCE OF DEATH (24)

The acceptance of death? Two of the three stars did. Of three good communicators, two also accepted death, but the third did not. There was no information about the fourth.

KIND OF DEATH (25)

A peaceful or painful death as a correlate? Two stars died painful deaths; one died peacefully. In the second sample, two also died painfully and one peacefully. No information could be obtained about the fourth communicator.

AGE AT TIME OF DEATH (26)

The stars were all of different age groups when they died, i.e., one was between 40 and 50, one was between 50 and 60 and one was between 60 and 70. Three of the good communicators died in the 60–70 age group; one was between 40 and 50.

WITH WHOM DECEDENT WAS AT TIME OF DEATH (27)

One star died alone; the other two died in the presence of their families. One of the latter also died with a doctor in attendance. We do not have information about one of the good communicators in the general sample. Two of the three others, however, also died with families present. The third died in the company of strangers doomed with him.

AUTOPSY PERFORMED (28)

An autopsy is known to have been performed on one star. No autopsy was performed on another. We have no information about the third star. With respect to the general sample, we have no information either for two of the good communicators. The two others, however, were not autopsied.

DISPOSITION OF BODY (29)

Are the procedures followed in the disposition of the body important to good communication? One star was embalmed. One was buried in the ground in a wicker coffin but two were placed in metal (lead) coffins. One of the latter was entombed. When we look at the general sample we discover that some of these procedures were repeated. Two good communicators were also buried in the ground. One was unembalmed and laid in a wooden casket. As to the other, information concerning embalming and the nature of the casket was not available. A third communicator was entombed, whether his casket was of wood or metal not being ascertainable. A fourth good communicator was cremated.

LAPSE OF TIME BETWEEN DEATH
AND DISPOSITION OF BODY (30)

Does the length of time between death and the funeral matter? One star was entombed 27 days after death (Case 9) and one good communicator in the general sample 19 days after dying (Case 1). One star was buried within 3 to 4 days after death, one within 5 to 7 days. We find the same 3 to 4 day period recurring for two of the good communicators. This factor could not be determined for a fourth for whom we lack information.

GEOGRAPHICAL LOCATION OF DISPOSITION OF BODY (31)

England was the locus of the funerals of all the stars: Terling Place, Essex (Case 8); Keswick, Cumbria (Case 9); Brighton (Case 10). Final disposition of all bodies of the good communicators took place in the United States: New York (Case 1); Boston (Case 4); Brooklyn, New York (Case 5); Pittsburgh (Case 6).

Second Line of Inquiry:
Resume of Results of Analysis of Good Communicators

We were in a position to put forth gingerly some findings concerning whether any of the "Circumstances Relating to Death" were interrelated with good communication.

POSSIBLY RELATED FACTORS

Several factors appear to have had a positive relationship. The hour and the cause of death may be a pair of them. Dying before morning and because of a disease may be typical of the communicator since five of those we examined died in those circumstances. Unfinished business at the time of death seems to have been strongly connected to good communication as it appeared in six of seven cases of good communicators. Expecting death may also contribute to the good communicator because expectancy on the part of two stars meshed with a similar expectancy on the part of two good communicators. The same was true of accepting death, which appeared among the stars and was repeated among the good communicators. Painful or unpleasant death could have been important since it can be seen in both groups.

There is no doubt that the family of people about to die can serve them well. Thanatologists tell us that a terminally ill patient's responses to dying are greatly helped if the family can share the feelings of the patient and confront the reality of death with him or her. Although a good communicator can die alone (Case 10) or with perfect strangers (Case 1), the data provided by this analysis make it seem that the family may also have contributed to the good communicator because a member of the family was present both when two stars died and when two good communicators died. Dying at home as did one star and three good communicators may have been another possibly related factor.

The best age group for the good communicator seems to have been the 60 to 70 year old age bracket which was repeated several times among good communicators.

The lapse of time between death and the disposition of the body may also have had some bearing. None of the stars or good communicators were entombed or cremated within one or two days of death which may signify that burial or cremation too soon after death may inhibit good communication. The best time for disposing of a body seems to be within three to four days of death, for one star was buried within this period as were two good communicators. Burial in a grave may also be a possible correlate since two stars and two good communicators were so buried.

UNRELATED FACTORS

Crookall thought that procedures followed in disposing of the body had a postmortem significance.[2] Metal coffins, embalming, and cremation were, he thought, undesirable. Burial in a wooden box was the best procedure. With regard to postmortem communication, the data suggest that Crookall's anxiety was not justified insofar as embalming is concerned since one star was embalmed. Yet, since no good communicators were embalmed, this factor seems to have nothing to do with good communication. Crookall's anxiety about metal coffins may not have been justified, either, insofar as postmortem communication is concerned because two "stars" were placed in such coffins. However, we cannot consider metal coffins as a factor because one good communicator was buried in a wooden casket and because information concerning the caskets of three of the good communicators is lacking.

It does not appear, either, that the day, the month or the year that a person dies are important for postmortem communication. The geographical locations where death took place varies from one good communicator to the other and so was not regarded as significant. Equally, the geographical locations of the dispositions of the bodies of stars and good communicators were too widely distributed to be of importance.

Although two stars died in hotels, this place of death was not a recurring factor in the cases of the other good communicators.

Autopsies are encouraged as a means of finding out what caused a death and of helping medical science prevent future deaths from similar causes. Autopsies, however, seem to have no bearing on good posthumous communication since only one star was autopsied.

Crookall thought that cremation was undesirable, and it does seem to be questionable because six of the seven good communicators were not cremated.

A prolonged delay in a funeral of over 11 days had no effect on one good communicator (Case 1). But is burial or entombment five to seven days after death important? Apparently it is not, for only one star was buried during this period after death.

Nor did it seem of any consequence whether funerals were conducted in England or in the United States since the bodies of good communicators were disposed of in both places.

QUESTION MARKS

It was not possible to make judgments about some factors for lack of data. Among these was the weather at the time of death.

Second Line of Inquiry: Death-Related Factors Indicated

A comparison of the information supplied by the stars with that supplied by the good communicators indicated that the following death-related factors seem to recur and to have a positive relation to good communication:

1. Death is expected.
2. Death is accepted.
3. Death takes place between the ages of 60 and 70.
4. Disease is the cause of death.
5. At the time of death, decedent is with the family.
6. Death occurs at home.
7. Death takes place prior to 6 A.M.
8. Death is painful or unpleasant.
9. The decedent has unfinished business at the time of death.
10. The body is disposed of at least two days after death and within three to four days of death.
11. The body is buried in a grave.

Second Line of Inquiry: Tables of Comparison

As was done with respect to the First Line of Inquiry, an investigation was conducted to test from a statistical standpoint the death-related factors indicated when "stars" and good communicators were studied. Are they real correspondences with good communication or are they the result of chance? Are there any other factors with a positive relation to the good communicator?

Three tables were prepared to try to arrive at estimates of the true significance of the 11 factors. One showed the frequencies and results for three good and three poor communicators in the special sample, a second table those for the general sample and the last table for all communicators, good and poor, in both samples.

Second Line of Inquiry: Statistical Investigation of Eleven Death-Related Factors Among Three Good and Three Poor Communicators in the Special Sample

Days, months, years and geographical location of death were too variable to be set out. Nor were weather conditions because of insufficient data.

The first table showed that the findings relating to nine of the factors were not supported statistically. Those evaluated as without significance were death at home, disease as a cause of death, the expectation of death, the acceptance of it, death in the 60–70 year old age bracket, family with a decedent at the time of death, death prior to 6 A.M., disposition of the body after or during certain periods of time and burial in the ground.

One factor not considered important previously was death in a hotel. But, since no poor communicators died there and two of the stars did, this factor was evaluated as suggestive (p = .2). It should be looked at more closely. Another factor that had been discarded as unimportant was placement in metal coffins. When the poor communicators who were not in such coffins were taken into account, this factor also became suggestive at the level of p = .2.

Only two of the 11 factors listed were determined to have statistical support. Unfinished business at death with a value of p = .2 was suggestive. Another factor, painful or unpleasant death, was shown by the table as marginally interesting (p = .2).

Second Line of Inquiry:
Statistical Investigation of Eleven Death-Related Factors Among Four Good and Two Poor Communicators in the General Sample

A factor shown before as causally related continued of importance as the second table showed unfinished business at death (22a) at a higher than chance expectation level of p = .2. Another factor indicated as having a positive relationship with the good communicator was death in the 60 to 70 year old age bracket (26e) which this table showed to be of interest (p = .2).

Metal coffins were given no statistical significance by the second table because of the lack of enough data. As indicated previously, information concerning the nature of the casket used for three of the four good communicators was not available.

This table gave disposition of the body within one to two days after death a significant negative result (p. = .067) which is to say that this is not the best time for good communication. On the other hand, disposition of the body within three to four days continued to be a possible related factor as it was shown by the table to be of statistical interest (p. = .2).

No other factors are revealed by this table to be beyond chance expectation.

Second Line of Inquiry:
Statistical Evaluation of Eleven Death-Related Factors
Among Seven Good and Five Poor Communicators
in Both Samples

Except for four factors listed earlier as being related to the good communicator, none of the others were given statistical support by the third table.
The first of the four factors was painful or unpleasant death which was suggestive with a value of p = .05 although information about two of the subjects
was not available. A pleasant death had a negative value so that the absence
of such a death among good communicators may have been important. A
negative value was given once more to disposing of the body within one to
two days.

A second exception was, once again, unfinished business at death (22a)
which was determined highly significant (p = .035). Another factor of
marginal interest (p = .22) was a lapse of one to two days between death and
the body's disposition. Another factor of marginal interest (p = .22) was death
between the ages of 60 and 70 which was of interest in Table 2.

Third Line of Inquiry:
Analysis of Factors Touching on Communication

Do circumstances relating to communication have anything to do with
the ability of a good communicator? This line of inquiry obviously is concerned only with those who, in the special and general samples and from the
critical study and evaluations made of mediumistic records, were classified as
"star" or good communicators. We dealt here with data concerning factors
that attended postmortem communication in both samples of good
communicators:

LAPSE OF TIME BETWEEN DEATH AND COMMUNICATION
OR MANIFESTATION (32)

Did the amount of time that elapsed between death and communication
matter? With respect to the stars in the special sample, one communication
began within a week (Case 8), one within two weeks (Case 9), another more
than a year later (Case 10) and, in two cases, more than eight years subsequent
to death (again cases 9 and 10). Each of the good communicators in the general
sample communicated after a different interval of time: one before six months
had passed, one after a year, one after two years, one after eight years.
Some of the same time lapses found in the cases of stars recurred in the

cases of good communicators. A star had communicated after an interval of from two to six months; so did one good communicator. In the case of another good communicator, the interval of from one to two years was repeated. In a third case, a good communicator communicated after an interval of two to four years as had two stars. In a fourth case, a good communicator communicated after a lapse of over eight years to repeat what two stars had done.

GEOGRAPHICAL LOCATION OF COMMUNICATION OR MANIFESTATION (33)

Did the location where the communication was received matter? While all stars communicated through mediums sitting in England, each also succeeded in doing so in France, Algeria and India. Not one place in which a star communicated, however, is repeated in any of the cases of good communicators in the general sample. All communicated in Boston, Massachusetts, but not one in England, France, Algeria or India.

PLACE WHERE COMMUNICATION OR MANIFESTATION OCCURRED (34)

All three stars communicated through a medium when she was sitting in her home. On one occasion, a communication was received when a medium was in the office of a society for psychical research and, on another occasion, when a medium was in the office of a society for psychical research and, on another occasion, when a medium was in the home of an experimenter. But one factor recurred in every case in the general sample. All messages were received from the good communicators in the home of the medium.

DISTANCE BETWEEN LOCATION OF COMMUNICATION OR MANIFESTATION AND WHERE DECEDENT LIVED (35)

Did the distance between the place where the communication was received and where the decedent had lived matter? In all cases, the stars communicated not only within 200 miles but also when there were more than 1000 miles between the two points. One communicated when the distance was more than 200 miles but less than 500. As did the stars, the good communicators were able to communicate without regard to the distance separating their former homes from the locations where their communications were received. One communicated when the distance was 30 miles, one when it was between 500 and 1000 miles and, repeating what one star had done, two when the distance was between 200 and 500 miles.

DISTANCE BETWEEN LOCATION OF COMMUNICATION OR MANIFESTATION AND WHERE DECEDENT DIED (36)

Was there any relationship to the distance between the place where the communication was received and the location of decedent's death? All stars communicated when the distance was over 1000 miles, two when it was less than 200 miles and one between 200 and 500 miles. Two of the good communicators, like one of the stars, communicated within 200 to 500 miles of their places of death. One communicated within a range of less than 50 miles, and the other when it was between 500 and 1000 miles.

WEATHER CONDITIONS AT THE TIME OF COMMUNICATION OR MANIFESTATION (37)

This factor could not be determined because of a lack of information.

FORM OF MANIFESTATION OR CHANNEL OF COMMUNICATION (38)

What form or channel of communication seemed to correspond best to good communication? This study was limited to mediumistic communications. In the special sample, all stars were able to communicate through the medium when she was doing automatic writing, and two were able to do so when she was in trance. As with the stars, each good communicator communicated through the automatic scripts of the medium. Three good communicators did so also during the trance states of the medium.

RELATIONSHIP TO DECEDENT OF SITTER RECEIVING COMMUNICATION OR PERSON WITNESSING MANIFESTATION (39)

The relationship of the sitter to the communicator was tested for its relationship to good communication. A friend sat when two stars communicated, and, on other occasions, a colleague sat when the same two communicated. One star was able to communicate, however, when no one sat and the medium was alone. Only in the case of one good communicator in the general sample is there a recurrence of the factor of friendship between sitter and communicator. Two others communicated when strangers sat and two when a daughter sat. There were more differences than similarities here.

RELATION OF MEDIUM TO DECEDENT (40)

Did it matter if the medium had some linkage with the communicator? All the stars communicated when the mediums had had prior contacts with them, but they also managed to communicate when the mediums were strangers to them. In only one case did the medium use an object as a link. Showing a strong similarity to the "stars," all the good communicators in the general sample were able to communicate with mediums who had no linkages with them while they lived.

LANGUAGE OF COMMUNICATION (41)

All stars and good communicators who were themselves English-speaking communicated in English with English-speaking mediums.

Third Line of Inquiry: Resume of Analysis of Good Communicators

Based on the foregoing, it was possible to advance a few findings concerning the postmortem factors which had been examined for their correspondence with good communication. There were two factors that, in every case, seemed to fit in with good communication.

The first was that good communication was related in all cases to its receipt in the home of the medium.

The second was the use of English by the communicators. Of course, the mediums through whom they purported to communicate were all English-speaking people. It is possible that communicators were conveying impressions and not words, but that these impressions were framed in English words by the mediums. But it is also possible that the communicators were communicating verbally. If they were, they used a language native to them or a language they had learned while they were alive in order to effect their communications. They did not speak Spiritese or whatever tongue may be used by the inhabitants of their other world, and they did not speak or write any other earth language. Every good communicator who once used English appeared willing and able to remember and preserve it. Since it is a possibility that poor communicators may not be able to preserve their original language and are unable to communicate, the original speaking and the preserving of English for mediums who speak only English may be related to the good communicator.

No other factors seem related to good communication.

It is sometimes argued that there is a "seven year rule" which communicators obey and beyond which period they do not communicate. But the data obtained from this analysis do not support the argument since three communicators (cases 6, 9 and 10) gave excellent evidence after more than eight years had gone by after death. It does not seem possible to put a limit on the lapse of time. Nor does it seem to make a difference how little time has passed since death. An apparition of a deceased person, for example, has been seen on the day, and within 12 hours, of death.[3] In one of our cases (Case 7) postmortem communication began within one week after death.

It is also of interest to see that good communication could take place anywhere in the world that a mediumistic experiment was being conducted. It did not matter whether the distances from where a decedent had lived or died were small or great.

Nor could it be said that the method used by a medium, whether automatic writing or trance, contributed to good communication. The slight difference registered in favor of automatic writing (7–6) hardly justifies a claim that it is superior to the trance state.

The data also showed that no prior contact between medium and communicator was needed to produce good communication. It was also difficult to discern any important connection between good communicators and the persons who sat with mediums because successful communications took place whether friends, colleagues, daughters, strangers or, in fact, no sitters at all were present.

Third Line of Inquiry:
Communication Factors Indicated

The analysis made of the factors touching on postmortem communication indicated that there might have been two postmortem factors related to good communication. These factors were: (1) mediumistic experiments conducted in the homes of the mediums, and (2) English-speaking communicators and mediums.

Third Line of Inquiry:
Table of Comparison

To examine these findings more precisely and to determine whether the two factors specified were merely products of chance, a final two-by-two table was prepared to show the number of times these particular factors as well as other factors touching on communication were present or absent among the good communicators in both the special and general population samples. These factors were considered to have been absent in the cases of the poor communicators who were assumed not to have communicated at all.

Third Line of Inquiry:
Statistical Investigation of Two Communication Factors
Among Six Good and Six Poor Communicators
in Both Samples

The table indicated that the home of the medium could be of the highest significance (p = .00176). The lowest possible p value for a communication in English warranted the conclusion that this factor was also of the highest significance (p = .00176).

The table showed that other factors were involved in good communication, some more than others. A medium's having had prior contact with a decedent (40a) was judged interesting (p = .15), but a medium's being a complete stranger with whom a decedent had had no prior contact (40d) was judged highly significant (p = .00176). It was significant (p = .0076) both when the medium was in a trance and speaking (38b) and when the medium was an automatist.

According to the table several other factors were interesting (p = .15). One appeared in the cases in which two to four years had elapsed since death and the first communication (32h), and another in those in which over eight years had elapsed since death (32j). In other words, no significant correspondences were established when the time lapse was four to eight years after death (32i) or when it was measured in days (32a–d), months (32d–f) or was less than two years (32g). Distances were also interesting. Where the distance between where the decedent had lived and the locus of the first communication was 50 to 250 miles (35b) or over 1000 miles (35e), there was more than chance expectation with a value of p = .15. Distances of from one to 50 miles (35a), 200 to 500 miles (35c) and 500 to 1000 miles (35d) were nonsignificant. But the distances of between 200 and 500 miles (36c) or over 1000 miles (36e) between the location of the first communication and where decedent had died were significant. No significance was attached to other distances.

A friend as the sitter receiving a communication (39p) proved to be interesting (p = .15). But none of the other relationships indicated in the List of Special Factors, such as grandfather, grandmother, parent, sibling, spouse, child, or others, were of interest.

FACTORS POSSIBLY INTERRELATED
WITH THE GOOD COMMUNICATOR

Based on the analyses and statistical tests which have gone before, tentative findings can be made concerning 23 specific factors which possibly have positive relationships with the good communicator.

Like ducks in a shooting gallery, many factors that seemed positive from the cross-referencing fell before a cross-fire of high p values. The likelihood that these factors had occurred by chance was too great to consider them further as correlates. But some survived the statistical battle and others not perceived as important at first also came through as factors that might have a causal relation with good communication. They are:

1. Sex of the communicator
2. Persistence
3. Children
4. Interest in art, music, poetry
5. Scepticism toward survival after death (including a very uncertain belief about it)
6. Painful or unpleasant death
7. Unfinished business at death
8. Death in the 60–70 year old age bracket
9. Death in a hotel
10. Disposition of the body more than 1–2 days after death
11. Mediumistic experiments conducted in the home of the medium
12. Communication in English
13. Prior contact between medium and decedent
14. (Opposite to the last) Where the medium was a stranger with no linkage with the decedent
15. Communication where the decedent was in trance and speaking
16. (Different from the last) Communication where the medium was doing automatic writing in or out of trance
17. Sitter was a friend of the decedent
18. Lapse of 2–4 years between death and the first communication
19. Lapse of over 8 years between death and the first communication
20. Distance of 50–200 miles between where the decedent lived and the location of the first communication
21. Distance of over 1000 miles between where the decedent lived and the location of the first communication
22. Distance of 20–500 miles between where the decedent died and the location of the first communication
23. Distance of over 1000 miles between where the decedent died and the location of the first communication

Now that a small group of cases had been examined carefully and much detail gathered about them in an effort to get some insights into what makes the "star" or "good" communicator, these 23 factors seemed to emerge as the common property of such communicators. But one more step needed to be taken to see if these factors could be verified or falsified.

10

A THUMBNAIL SKETCH

In order to verify or falsify the statistically significant factors enumerated at the conclusion of the last chapter, a mass of cases was examined. A systematic survey was conducted to discover every case that seemed to point to a good mediumistic communicator. The survey covered the first 90 years of the existence of the Society for Psychical Research, the first half of which witnessed the heyday of mediumship and experiments with mediums to test the question of human survival after physical death. The Society's *Proceedings* from 1882 to 1972 were all examined and 97 cases were found that met a single criterion: In the judgment of the experimenter, reporter, sitter or myself, the case presented *prima facie* evidence of postmortem identity. To round out the number of cases to an even 100 over and above the seven cases of good communicators previously examined, three additional cases were taken from an early *Proceedings* of the American Society for Psychical Research. Any cases in the *Proceedings* of either society that could be explained on nonsurvivalist grounds were rejected; for example, where an observer said that the evidence did not support a claim that a discarnate entity had communicated.[1] Appendix B contains citations of the publications from which the 100 cases were selected for examination.

Tables were also prepared, one for each apparently significant factor, to show the proportion of "yeses" to "nos." "NI" (no information) indicates those instances in which information is lacking.

THE TABLES

Table M1*. Sex of the Communicators

Male	78
Female	22
Total	100

This table shows a heavy preponderance of male communicators (78 percent) over female (22 percent).

*The letter "M" for the first three numbered tables distinguishes them from tables 1, 2 and 3 in Appendix A.

Table M2. Persistence of the Communicator

Yes	5
No	0
NI	95
	100

The data provided by this table show that 5 communicators were persistent. Unfortunately, there was no information concerning the other 95.

Table M3. Communicators with Children

Yes	18
No	15
NI	67
	100

As shown, 18 percent of the communicators had children, 15 percent did not, and in 67 percent of the cases we cannot say.

Table 4. Aptitude for Art, Music or Poetry

Yes	10
No	4
NI	86
	100

Ten percent of the communicators had an aptitude for art, music or poetry; 4 percent did not. In 86 percent of the cases insufficient information was furnished.

Table 5. Scepticism Towards Survival After Death

Yes	3
No	3
NI	94
	100

The smaller group of cases suggested scepticism towards survival of death as a correlate. In the mass study we see that three communicators were sceptical and three were not, while 94 of the cases could not be judged.

Table 6. Painful or Unpleasant Death

Yes	41
No	3
NI	58
	100

The number of cases reported in which the fact that death was painful or unpleasant was given or from which the fact could be inferred (41) was considerably greater than those in which death was not painful or unpleasant (3).

In 58 cases it was not possible to determine the nature of the death.

Table 7. Unfinished Business at Time of Death

Yes	5
No	-
NI	95
	100

Five communicators had unfinished business when they died. In 95 cases there was not enough information to make any finding.

Table 8. Death in the 60–70 Year Old Age Bracket

Yes	8
No	27
NI	65
	100

Twenty-seven communicators were not within the 60–70 year old age bracket while eight were. The remaining 65 communicators could not be classified for lack of information.

Table 9. Death in a Hotel

Yes	
No	30
NI	70
	100

We know that 30 communicators did not die in a hotel. We do not know about the other 70 cases because this information was not given.

Table 10. Disposition of Body More than 1 or 2 Days After Death

Yes	2
No	1
NI	97
	100

Two communicators were buried after two days had elapsed since death, one was buried within that time and there was no information for the remaining 97 communicators.

Table 11. Mediumistic Experiments in the Medium's Home

Yes	57
No	21
NI	22
	100

In the cases of 57 communicators, mediumistic experiments were conducted in the medium's home. In 21 cases they were not and in 22 we do not know.

Table 12. Language of the Communicators

English	97
French	-
Italian	1
German	-
Spanish	-
Other	2
	100

Table 12 gives the data concerning the language used by the communicators whether the medium was in trance or doing automatic writing. In 97 percent of the cases the communicators used the English language. In one case (Case 13), Italian was spoken, in another (Case 14) Hawaiian was written and in another (Case 35) Dutch was spoken.

Table 14. Prior Contacts Between Medium and Decedent

Yes	7
No	92
NI	1
	100

From Table 14 we see that, while 7 of the good communicators had prior contacts with the mediums, 92 did not. In one case there was no information.

Table 15. Medium Was a Stranger with No Linkage to Decedent

Yes	92
No	7
NI	1
	100

This table is a mirror image of the last table. Where the medium was unknown to decedent, there was communication in 97 cases as opposed to 7 cases in which there had been prior contacts. One case gave no data.

Table 16. Communication Where Medium Entranced and Speaking

Yes	47
No	45
NI	8
	100

Table 16 shows that 47 of the mediums were in a state of trance and communicating orally while 45 were not. Of the remaining cases in the "no information" column, 3 of the 8 really provided no information. The remaining 5 cases (93, 94, 95, 96, 97) did not clearly use a medium. A "home circle" used a Ouija board.

Table 16. Communication Where Medium Did Automatic Writing

Yes	42
No	50
NI	8
	100

This table indicates that 42 mediums were automatists as opposed to 50 who were not at the time of the communications. In 5 of the 8 "no information" cases, there were no mediums. In cases 93–97 a Ouija board was used.

Table 17. Friendship Between Sitter and Decedent

Yes	12
No	88
NI	-
	100

Table 17 indicates that in 88 cases no friendship existed between the sitter and the decedent communicating. In 12 cases it did.

Table 18. Lapse of Two to Four Years Between Death and First Communication

Yes	11
No	46
NI	43
	100

In 43 of the cases there was no information concerning the time that had gone by between death and the first communication. In 46 of the 57 known cases 2–4 years had not elapsed.

Table 19. Lapse of More than Eight Years Between Death and First Communication

Yes	13
No	47
NI	40
	100

This Table shows that 13 decedents communicated for the first time after more than 8 years had gone by since their deaths while 47 did not. No determination could be made in 40 other cases.

Table 20. Distance of 50–200 Miles Between Where Decedent Lived and the Location of First Communication

Yes	16
No	19
NI	65
	100

While in 16 cases there was a distance of from 50 to 200 miles between the places where decedent had resided and where the first communications were received, in 19 cases there was not. In 65 cases the distance was not known.

Table 21. Distance of Over 1000 Miles Between Where Decedent Lived and the Location of the First Communication

Yes	8
No	26
NI	66
	100

Table 21 indicates in 8 cases a distance of more than 1000 miles between the decedent's residence and the location of the first communication. In 26 cases no such distance existed and in 66 cases we do not know.

Table 22. Distance of 200–500 Miles Between Where Decedent Died and the Location of the First Communication

Yes	14
No	19
NI	67
	100

This table shows the number of cases (14) in which there was a distance of 200 to 500 miles between the places of decedent's death and his or her first communication, and the number of cases (19) in which there was no such distance. In 67 cases we do not know.

Table 23. Distance of Over 1000 Miles Between Where Decedent Died and the Location of the First Communication

Yes	10
No	24
NI	66
	100

The table reveals that in 66 cases no determination of distance could be made. In 10 cases the distance was that indicated in the table, but in 24 it was not.

The factors which seemed in the analyses and statistical tests to be significant, suggestive or interesting were those not likely to have occurred among the general population by chance. Still, the findings were guarded and received gingerly because of a keen awareness that they had resulted from a very small number of cases. The strategy was to test these findings by the mass study.

It seemed reasonable to suppose that, having arrived at 23 factors, we could easily examine the mass of good communicators to determine if positive or negative results would verify or falsify the findings and factors. They would be verified if they were present in an impressive preponderance of the cases for which information was supplied. They would be falsified if a preponderance showed them absent.

But the data produced by the mass survey did not turn out exactly that way. Although the data verify five of the factors put forward at the end of the analyses and tests and falsify 13, the data neither verify nor falsify the remaining five.

VERIFIED FACTORS

The data suggest that there may be some ties between the small group of good communicators studied earlier and the large series of good communicators just studied. These links make it appear that the good communicators in each of the small samples may be part of a natural category of good communicators. It is these links which good communicators may have that distinguish them from poor ones. Which factors seem verified as having positive relationships with good communicators?

1. Sex. In every case studied, no matter how sparse other details may have been or other information ignored, the sex of the communicators or of persons for whom a communicator might be speaking, was always described with utmost clarity by the communicators themselves or by the experimenters or sitters as "he" or "she." It is, then, extremely interesting and important to note that good communicators retain their sexual differences. Their masculinity or femininity is never forgotten, concealed or ignored.

The much greater preponderance of males (78) over females (22) verifies that masculinity plays a definite role in good communication. In reaching this conclusion consideration was given to the fact that the period studied saw the eruption of two great wars (1914–1918 and 1939–1945) in which the killings were almost exclusively of men and which might have explained the high percentage of male communicators included in the survey. Offsetting this consideration, however, were other facts. The period studied extended over 90 years and not simply the period of the two wars. Moreover, during a portion of this period the death rate due to childbirth was not only exclusive to women but was extremely high and did not decline until the 1930s or 1940s as medical procedures improved. Yet the numbers of female communicators was not nearly so great as the numbers of male communicators. Nevertheless, because of the possibility of an unusually large percentage of male communicators resulting from two wars, the cases were reviewed from this angle. It was found that of the 100 cases 17 communicators had died of battlefield wounds, airplane crashes and, in one case, from having been torpedoed. Even subtracting these cases, there remained a heavy preponderance of male communicators over females which clearly confirmed the masculine factor.

2. *Painful or unpleasant death.* Since 41 of the 44 cases that give data about the nature of death demonstrate the presence of this factor, it is considered confirmed.

3. *Mediumistic experiments in the home of the nedium.* In 57 of the 78 cases supplying information on the locus of the communication, the medium's home was the place.

4. *The medium is a stranger with no linkage with the decedent.* This factor coincided with 92 of the 100 cases examined and seems overwhelmingly supported.

5. *Language of the communicator.* In 97 out of 100 cases, a good communicator who had spoken English during life communicated through an English-speaking medium which suggests that, to ensure good communication, the medium ought to speak the same language as the communicator. But is this factor of language just an artifact of the research? Wouldn't the use of English be natural to English-speaking mediums regardless of the language of the communicator? If communicators are not speaking but conveying telepathic impressions instead, wouldn't an English-speaking medium be expected to frame these impressions in her native tongue? Not necessarily. It is a fact that English-speaking mediums do not always use their own language. They have used Latin and Greek. In three of our cases they used the unfamiliar tongues of the communicators during the communication: Hawaiian, Italian and Dutch. It may therefore be the communicator who plays the decisive role in determining the language in which a communication will be couched. At the same time, in none of the cases examined here was there a non–English-speaking medium. Would the 97 good English-speaking communicators have been able to communicate at all if the medium had not spoken their language? We cannot know. But from their success it seems best to assume that there may have been a language correspondence between medium and communicator which should be maintained.

FALSIFIED FACTORS

On the other hand, many factors were falsified. They either hovered near the halfway mark or fell below it and so are considered merely representative of the general population. In this class were:

1. *Having children.* This factor recurred in 18 of the 33 known cases and does not seem higher than chance expectation.

2. *Death in the 60–70 year old age bracket.* In 65 of the 82 cases the decedents were not in this age bracket.

3. *Death in a hotel.* It was clear from every case in which the circumstances attendant on death were more or less indicated that the decedent had not died in a hotel. For example: Case 13, death in a sailor's bethel; Case

30, in a railway accident; Case 40, playing handball; Case 46, on a boat; Case 84, in a bicycle accident; Case 87, in an auto accident; Case 91, mountain climbing; Case 94, drowned in a river. In addition, 17 other cases involved people killed during a war. In all there were 30 cases from which it could be inferred that the hotel factor was unimportant. In 70 other cases no information was given from which any inference could be made, and while, as will be indicated later, the absence of information is usually considered neutral, this factor cannot be saved when it is absent every time pertinent data are given.

4. *Prior contacts between medium and decedent.* The appearance of this factor in only 7 of 99 cases falsifies it.

5. *Medium speaking in trance.* Of the 92 of the cases in which the state of the medium could be determined, this factor appeared in 47 and falls within chance expectation.

6. *Medium doing automatic writing.* This factor was present in a minority of the cases (50–42).

7. *Friendship between sitter and decedent.* In the great majority of the cases this factor did not recur (88–12).

8. *Lapse of two to four years between death and first communication.* This factor failed to appear in 46 of 57 cases in which the time could be judged.

9. *Lapse of more than eight years between death and first communication.* There is an absence of this factor in 47 of the 60 cases which supply adequate data.

10. *Distance of 50–200 miles between where decedent lived and the location of the first communication.* Only a minority of the 35 cases that gave this kind of information contained this factor (19–16).

11. *Distance of over 1000 miles between where decedent lived and the location of the first communication.* This factor seems negated by 26 of the 34 cases giving necessary data.

12. *Distance of 200–500 miles between where decedent died and the location of the first communication.* There was a recurrence of this factor in only 14 of the 33 cases supplying information.

13. *Distance of over 1000 miles between where decedent died and the location of the first communication.* No confirmation was given this factor because of its nonappearance in 24 of 34 cases providing information.

FACTORS NOT VERIFIED OR FALSIFIED

1. *Persistence.* There is some very fragmentary evidence for this factor in that 5 percent of the communication had this trait. But, lacking data from 95 percent of the cases, we cannot say that this factor was either confirmed or falsified.

2. *Aptitude for art, music and poetry.* Some support for this factor is

found since it appeared in 10 of the 14 cases where sufficient facts were provided. But, with no data on this factor obtainable from the remaining 86 cases, the number of cases is not great enough to allow any conclusion to be drawn about it.

3. *Scepticism toward survival after death* (including uncertainty about it). With 94 percent of the cases saying nothing about this factor, any judgment concerning it was impossible. Where six cases spoke to it, the communicators were evenly divided.

4. *Unfinished business at the time of death.* Null data from 95 percent of the cases prevented any evaluation of this factor, even though 5 percent of the cases where data were given made a positive showing of this factor.

5. *Disposition of the body after 1 or 2 days elapsed.* This factor could not be verified or falsified when only 3 percent of the cases could be examined for it and 97 percent could not be.

There are two possible ways of looking at the frustrating failure of the data to produce negative or positive results with respect to these five factors: either that the absence of figures confirming them destroys their validity as correlates or that the high percentage of "NI"'s in the tables was due to the reports of the cases which, for reasons of privacy, neglect or ignorance, simply did not furnish adequate information about many of the points being studied. Thus a legitimate way of viewing the result is that the failure to confirm was due entirely to the absence of sufficient details in the reports. The failure of the data is merely inconclusive but does not destroy the possible positive relationship of the five factors to the good communicator. The only judgment we can make with regard to them now is "not proved" one way or the other.

This lack of detail was immediately observed when, at the start of this research, a preliminary, random and brief glance was given to case reports. The scantiness of detail made it difficult to detect what might make communicators different or the same. I therefore decided to begin with the study of a small number of cases for which details might be accumulated. At that time, however, I did not know that scantiness of information would be characteristic of all the cases reported and with respect to so many features. In other words, the frustrating result was unexpected.

The five factors about which no conclusion can now be drawn can be tested and falsified or verified as efforts are made by future researchers to ferret out and provide more details about good communicators. We hope that these factors will act as a magnet towards which research thought and design will be turned for the purpose of confirmation or invalidation. Meanwhile, we can look upon these factors the way some religionists view their deity: Some facts have appeared, such as an order in nature, which seem to them to justify a belief in a being while none have been shown to undermine the deity. Similarly, the study of the 12 cases brought forward some facts to support the factors while, so far, none has been produced to contradict them. Their validity as correlates might have been confirmed by the mass study had enough information been supplied. So they remain provocative and interesting.

THE "IDEAL" COMMUNICATOR

Idealizing or making a composite pattern of an experience is not a novel idea. Ian Stevenson took features from his investigations of cases of the reincarnation-type to describe a "perfect" reincarnation case with features which could not be explained away by the extrasensory abilities of the living.[2] Tyrrell set up his "perfect apparition" by taking characteristics from his collection of narratives.[3] Moody constructed the "ideal" near-death experience based on elements he found recurring in his collection.[4] But a composite of all the factors and conditions that may be interrelated with and contribute to the "ideal" communicator who may be able to supply excellent evidence of postmortem survival and identity had never been made.

From the analyses that were made covering three areas of inquiry and two population samples it became possible to make tentative findings concerning factors thought related and those believed unrelated to good communication. A mass study thereafter confirmed, falsified and left up in the air many of the related factors. All these results may now be taken into account and the various factors related, verified, falsified and still remaining to be checked may now be collected and composited into the following thumbnail sketch of the ideal communicator:

A male who persists in the pursuit of his interests and endeavors, he is an artist or has an aptitude for poetry or music. His attitude toward the possibility of human survival after death will be heavily tinged with scepticism or doubt. When he dies his death will be painful or unpleasant, and he will die leaving work unfinished.

No disposition should be made of his body until at least two days have elapsed after his death.

Any efforts at communication with him should be made in the home of a medium who speaks the language he spoke and who had been a stranger to him.

11
A STORY OF SURVIVAL

If this composite of the features of the "ideal" communicator and of the atmosphere in which this communicator performs best were confirmed by future research, increased production of high quality evidence might be achieved. We would drop the egalitarian assumption that the capacity to communicate posthumously is possessed by every deceased person and would understand the good communicator. We would be able to predict which people would make good communicators. We would approach our research differently.

There should be greater assurance of success in the outcome of an investigation if we select those people for our research projects who replicate as many as possible of the factors that the model communicator exhibited. This assurance will be strengthened if we also take pains to see that all the circumstances that seemed conducive to good communication are reproduced.

As a case in point, after completing the research reported so far in this book, the author conducted a mediumistic experiment with a deceased subject who closely corresponded to the "ideal." Never before reported, the experiment is as new as this research and is offered to suggest what might be done when a selective eye is trained on the communicator angle of the mediumistic triangle.

William Lee Petty III was killed at the age of 25 on Friday, March 24, 1978, on Interstate 10, near Baton Rouge, Louisiana, when the small car he was driving crashed into the rear of a parked truck. Two dogs in the car were killed with him. The description of "Lee" which his mother Catherine gave me fitted that of the model communicator. Lee became the subject of an experiment that deserves attention because of the great care taken to prevent leakage of information to any of those involved in it.

Let us suppose that A makes a proposition to X to perform a certain contract. Thereafter B and C who have never heard of A receive unexpected letters from X which have no significance for them but which offer to perform part of the contract A proposed. It would be supposed that X intended the letters for A but somehow misaddressed them or that the Post Office simply delivered the mail to the wrong addresses. From the legal point of view X's letters, since they had not accepted A's offer exactly, would not constitute a legal contract. But if, in a similar situation, X is a deceased person, A, B and C are mediums and the proposition and letters are mediumistic communications, the situation becomes more interesting.

At the time of Lee's death, according to Mrs. Petty, Lee's older sister, then at a state university in Commerce, Texas, dreamt that Lee was dead and told her husband so. She had seen her brother smiling and not unhappy. Subsequent to Lee's death, Mrs. Petty had sittings with several mediums during which data was purportedly received that persuaded Mrs. Petty that Lee had survived death. She was particularly impressed by readings given her in England by the English medium Donald Galloway who seemed to have obtained evidential information about a monkey that had belonged to one of Lee's friends and with which Lee had played. This medium also gave persuasive information about Lee's accident and the fact that Lee's two dogs had died with him.

In addition to this anecdotal material, Catherine Petty made this statement to me:

> Over and over again Lee predicts from the spirit world that the story of his survival will be told to the world.

Anecdotal material like this either can be shrugged off and forgotten as lacking evidential value or, because it involved an apparently good communicator, can stimulate a researcher to follow in the direction in which it seems to be pointing: the framing of experiments to try to produce more evidential material under controlled conditions. It seemed to me that the latter course should be followed to give Lee, the ostensible communicator, the opportunity to tell "the story of his survival" in a way that might be more convincing to the scientific community.

Critics of mediumistic communications generally have maintained that survival is not the only explanation for them. Theoretically, mediums could have derived their information from the sitter's mind or from the mind of some other living person who knew the information. To make this view less tenable and any information obtained more likely to have come from a deceased mind, I devised an experiment along the lines of the "cross-correspondences" of 100 years ago. Alice Johnson, research officer of the Society for Psychical Research and editor of its *Proceedings* in the early part of this century, described a cross-correspondence in these words:

> What we get is a fragmentary utterance in one script, which seems to have no particular point or meaning, and another fragmentary utterance in the other, of an equally pointless character; but when we put the two together, we see that they supplement one another, and that there is apparently one coherent idea underlying both, but only partially expressed in each.[1]

Through this kind of evidence she believed, as did many of the early researchers, strong evidence might be obtained of a mind outside the minds of the mediums who were making the oral or written statements. An experiment along this line was designed to see if Lee Petty could tell his story. Basically, it consisted of two parts.

First, I had to initiate it. There was ample precedent for my doing so. Many cross-correspondence experiments were begun by experimenters. Sir Oliver Lodge, for example, asked the purported communicator, Hodgson, through one medium to send a message to another,[2] and the "Lethe" case began when the experimenters Dorr and Lodge asked the dead Myers, "What does the word Lethe suggest to you?"[3,4]

If there were reason to believe that Lee Petty was communicating at any mediumistic session with Mrs. Petty as sitter, a question would be put to him to ask him if he would agree to take part in an experiment. If he agreed, I would proceed to the second phase. Mrs. Petty would be excused from the session and the experiment would be described to the communicator. The experiment was to consist of three numbers, one of which was to be the sum of the other two. The communicator was to select these three numbers and not to reveal them to me at the time the experiment was proposed. At a later time, however, he would take the initiative to convey one number to another medium with whom those who loved him might be sitting, a second number to still another medium with whom they might be sitting and the third number to a third medium under similar circumstances. Neither the sitters nor the mediums knew anything about the nature of the experiment. They did not know that the experiment had anything to do with numbers so that the meaning of the numbers would not be understood by any of them. But when the communications were connected, they would be seen to be relevant to the experiment. If the third number received by a medium was the sum of the two smaller numbers received by each of two other mediums, the experiment would be a success. The actual numbers would be left to the ingenuity and plan of the communicator. I would not be present at any of the sittings but at the end would see if the results could be tied in.

Mrs. Petty, who lives in Baton Rouge, Louisiana, arrived in Florida in February 1983. I had made two appointments with mediums in the Hollywood, Florida, area who were strangers to Mrs. Petty and knew nothing of her or her family. At no time were the identities of these mediums disclosed to Mrs. Petty. A sitting was held on February 23 with one of these mediums. Mrs. Petty, coexperimenter Joyce Berger (JB) and I were the sitters. But, as Mrs. Petty was not satisfied that her son had communicated in this sitting, the experiment never went forward. No further sittings were held with this medium.

To keep the appointment with the second medium on February 24, Mrs. Petty drove from her motel in Pompano Beach to Hollywood (about 30 miles), where JB and I rendezvoused with her. Although it was already dark, she was blindfolded and driven through strange streets for a time to ensure that she would not know where she was going. At the appointed hour we reached the home of the medium, Serraine Diane Newman (SDN). Leaving Mrs. Petty and JB in the car, I entered SDN's home to arrange for proper seating. Then I returned to the car and led Mrs. Petty, still blindfolded so that she could not see the address or the name of the medium, up the walk and into the house. The blindfold was removed only when Mrs. Petty was inside. When it was removed, SDN was seated with her back to Mrs. Petty who sat behind the medium. Mrs. Petty remained there during the entire sitting. At no time during the sitting did the medium see Mrs. Petty nor did Mrs. Petty see the medium's face. I sat facing the medium and Mrs. Petty. JB sat next to Mrs. Petty.

During the sitting, and following my instructions, Mrs. Petty remained absolutely silent. She was to nod to me if material that seemed right was expressed or to shake her head if it was wrong. She was to write notes to me to clarify matters or to ask questions. The statements made by the medium in the course of this sitting meant little to me. I left the evidential weight of the medium's statements to Mrs. Petty. If she thought that the medium was getting a number of successful hits, she was to nod to me or to write me a note so that I would know there were reasonable grounds for going on with the next part of the experiment. If that had occurred, my plan had been to have Mrs. Petty leave the sitting while I remained with the medium.

But it did not occur during this sitting. Precautions were taken again at the end of the sitting. The medium remained seated. JB escorted Mrs. Petty to the door. Before leaving the house, the blindfold was replaced and Mrs. Petty taken back to the car where JB remained with her. When I got back to the car after a few minutes, we returned to the original rendezvous point. From there Mrs. Petty returned to her motel.

The following day, February 25, Mrs. Petty reported to us that she felt that there had been some evidential statements made by the medium but she was not sure that Lee had communicated. Another sitting was arranged for that night with the same precautions taken as for the first sitting. This second sitting ended as had the first with Mrs. Petty giving no sign to JB or to me that Lee had appeared. On the next day, however, after Mrs. Petty had had the opportunity of reflecting on the notes she had made in the course of the sitting with SDN, she told me that she now realized that many true statements had been made by the medium and that she was convinced that Lee had communicated after all. I was therefore encouraged to go on to another sitting with SDN.

By the time another sitting could be arranged, however, Mrs. Petty had left Florida to return to her home. I determined nevertheless to proceed with the experiment. JB, accompanied by an observer, Mrs. Daisy Zeitlin, went to SDN's home on March 3, 1983. Providing the medium with some objects that had belonged to Lee Petty, such as his wrist watch and bracelet, she asked SDN to try to establish communication with Lee Petty. When JB felt that the communicator might be Lee, although she was not sure, she proposed the experiment to the communicator and he agreed to it.

To reassure ourselves that the communicator had made an appearance in this sitting, a record of it, with all references to the experiment expunged, was sent on March 15 to Mrs. Petty in Baton Rouge. She was asked to evaluate the material. On March 26 she replied, "I believe Lee was present in the March 3rd sitting." Her answer gave me reason to believe that perhaps the experiment was under way.

Mrs. Petty then made arrangements with mediums of her choice to hold sittings to try to reach her dead son. If they were willing, the sitters were to be herself, Lee's sisters, his father and Lee's girl friend. Mrs. Petty selected seven mediums, all unknown to me and JB. Prior to the conclusion of the experiment we never had any dealings of any kind with any of them.

Two were English mediums. RH gave absent readings to Mrs. Petty from England in April 1983. NR gave her a reading in the United States in November of that year. Mrs. Petty sent tape of their material to me but none of it was significant and will not be discussed. For the same reason none of the material provided by two other mediums with whom Mrs. Petty sat in May and November 1983, and by a person who gave a tea leaf reading in June 1983 to Lee's sister, Cay Petty, will be discussed.

There were, however, sittings with two other mediums chosen by Mrs. Petty. One was the English medium Donald Galloway (DG), who had impressed Mrs. Petty before. Mrs. Petty and Lee's girl friend, Mary Ann Parish, sat with him in Baton Rouge, Louisiana, in March 1983. Another medium was Vera Long (VL), with whom Mrs. Petty sat in Pensacola, Florida, in August and September 1983.

Tapes were made of all the mediumistic sessions with Mrs. Petty and Ms. Parish and of the session with coexperimenter Joyce Berger. They provide the record which follows. Only those parts of the sittings pertinent to the experiment are given.

Record of Five Sittings

SITTING NO. 1

March 3, 1983
Place: Medium's home, Ft. Lauderdale, Florida
Sitter: Joyce Berger, coexperimenter
Observer: Daisy Zeitlin

Joyce Berger arranged this sitting with Mrs. Newman after Catherine Petty had returned to her home in Baton Rouge, Louisiana. Psychometric objects which had belonged to Lee Petty, including his watch and bracelet, were used as aids during the sitting. A cassette recorder was used to record the sitting. After the medium purported to be in communication with the communicator, remarks passed between the communicator and coexperimenter relating to his family and matters not important to the purpose of this experiment. Then:

JB: "What we would like you to do is to take two numbers, any numbers, two numbers, big, little, it doesn't matter."

SDN: "2,3; 2,3."

JB: "No, don't tell me what they are. Take anything you want. And we would like you to tell one of these people, one of these mediums, one of the numbers, another medium the second number and the third medium the sum of those two . . . three . . . TWO numbers. That simply. It isn't that easy, I know. But your mother, your father and your sisters are going to be having sittings with other people, and, if you could tell them anything like that, then they would know really they were talking to you. So if you can try that, if you can remember that, I think even next week, maybe, if time means anything to you. Do you think you could try to do that?"

SDN: "Of course I could."

JB: "All right, that's wonderful. I hope you will, that's wonderful. . ."

SDN: "You don't want to know the numbers?"

JB: "I don't want to know them. No, No. I don't want to know them."

SITTING NO. 2

March 25, 1983
Place: Louisiana Society for Psychical Research, Baton Rouge, Louisiana
Present: Medium: Donald Galloway
        Sitter: Mary Ann Parish

Ms. Parish sat alone with Mr. Galloway in the offices of the L.S.P.R. The sitting was taped. Much material was discussed to the effect that Lee was aware of her and was watching her. He described himself as a shepherd to care for her and others. He didn't want a flock but he had it. References were made to St. Francis of Assisi. Then there was a pause and this followed:

DG: "I'm also getting a strange thing here. [Pause. Then half-whispering] One, two, button my shoe. One, two button my shoe. . . [something inaudible] One, two, button my shoe. One, two, button my shoe. I don't know what sense there is to it. But Lee's saying very audibly 'One, two, button my shoe.' I think that when I was a kid there was a poem—a popular song called that. One, two, button my shoe. What's he doing with his shoes? He's trying to make a play on [inaudible]. One, two, button my shoe. I really don't know what that means."

SITTING NO. 3

March 25, 1983
Place: Louisiana Society for Psychical Research, Baton Rouge, Louisiana
Present: Medium: Donald Galloway
        Sitter: Catherine Petty

After the sitting with Ms. Parish, Catherine Petty sat alone with the medium. The medium told the sitter that Lee was placing an image over her and that he wanted her to know that he was doing so with love because he knew the strains under which she had been working. After material not relevant to this experiment, this passage followed:

DG: "Now, also, a very strange thing here because he's . . . [talking under his breath] Just a minute . . . [Now, in a low whisper] 1, 2, 3; 1, 2, 3; 1, 2, 3; 1, 2, 3; 1, 2, 3; I don't know. He's not beating time. 1, 2, 3; 1, 2, 3; 1, 2, 3; 1, 2, 3; 1, 2, 3; 1, 2, 3."

CP: "There are three other people that own the farm."

DG: "Are there? Oh, all right. 1, 2, 3; 1, 2, 3. Just like that."

SITTING NO. 4

August 12, 1983
Place: Medium's home in Pensacola, Florida
Present: Medium: Vera Long
        Sitter: Mary Ann Parish

The medium gave the sitter a general reading concerning her character and some personal matters. The remarks then turned to Lee Petty:

VL: "I want to put this number down but I have no idea what it means that I got at the beginning: 58742. Now that was a number I don't know if that would be his driver's license. . . I don't know what it is. But the number came in, and I don't know what it is: 58742."

SITTING NO. 5

September 29, 1983
Place: Medium's home in Pensacola, Florida
Present: Medium: Vera Long
        Sitter: Catherine Petty

The medium, among other things, described some personal and family problems, and then:

VL: "Lee will appear to you in a vision or a dream and he will talk to you very briefly but he will say three sentences that you will not forget. I don't know what they are. Right after that you will notice a rainbow and when this rainbow appears in the sky three things regarding Lee will be tied together."

The experiment proposed, and to which the communicator supposedly agreed, was that he was to give a number to each of three mediums. He gave numbers to only two mediums. To one of them he gave not just one number but, on one occasion, two numbers, and, on another, three. The communicator did not perform all the terms of the proposition made to him so that, from a literal and legalistic view, the experiment was a failure.

But while the communicator did not literally perform the experiment, a liberal view of the situation would hold that the communicator (if it was indeed he) performed the agreement substantially because one medium was used in two separate sittings. DG in the March 25 sitting with Ms. Parish reported two small numbers, 1 and 2, and in the later sitting on that date with Mrs. Petty these same numbers were reiterated along with the number 3. Three numbers were wanted. Also wanted was that the third number be the sum of the other two numbers, and 3 is obviously the sum of 1 and 2. According to this view, the communicator came very close to performing the spirit and object of the experiment.

Yet we must retain a scientific attitude. It is truly said that "it is the most scientific course to press a normal explanation at all hazards, and in the face of every obstacle, before admitting anything else."[5] Following this course, we must ask how we are to explain this experiment. Are the results normal or paranormal?

We must reject any explanation based on normal knowledge. The experiment was proposed to the communicator in the sitting of March 3. We must assume that the medium, SDN, even though she was in trance when the proposal was made and says that she was not aware of what the coexperimenter said to the communicator, knew the terms of the experiment. Therefore, she, the experimenters and the observer, Mrs. Zeitlin, knew the nature of the experiment.

But did this knowledge reach the sitters or the mediums with whom they sat through any normal channels? The careful arrangements made precluded any such possibility. They prevented Mrs. Petty from obtaining any normal knowledge about SDN and from finding out anything about the experiment from her either personally, by telephone or correspondence. This medium had no opportunity to obtain normal knowledge about Mrs. Petty. She never knew Mrs. Petty's name, never saw her face or even heard her regional accent. SDN had no way of reaching Mrs. Petty or Ms. Parish, and, since the mediums selected by Mrs. Petty were equally unknown to SDN, she could not have been in touch with them, either.

Mrs. Petty probably told these mediums that she, JB and I were involved in some sort of experiment with Lee Petty. But since Catherine Petty was ignorant of the nature of the experiment, she could not have told the mediums anything more about it even if she had wished to do so. Sitting in Baton Rouge and Pensacola, DG and VL had little opportunity to acquire normal knowledge about the experiment from SDN or the two experimenters. As for Mrs. Zeitlin, Mrs. Petty did not know that she had any connection with the experiment and had no opportunity of communicating with her or she with Mrs. Petty or her mediums. The coexperimenter and I told no one about the nature of the experiment.

Another possible normal explanation for the numbers reported by the medium DG is that it might have been his usual method or stock in trade to present numbers to his clients as he did with Ms. Parish and Mrs. Petty. Ms. Parish had never sat before with DG, but Mrs. Petty had had several other sittings with him. To determine if numbers were given in other sittings with DG I asked Mrs. Petty to send me her tapes of all previous sittings with DG, the first of which took place in 1978. The tapes were examined and not one instance of this kind ever appeared in his half-dozen sittings with Mrs. Petty during the prior five years so that this explanation was rejected, also.

Did chance dictate the numbers which came through in the sittings with the medium DG? If it did, then how do we explain the appearance of numbers, especially the number 3, in different sittings with a different medium (VL) purporting to be in communication with the same communicator? Since numbers were the target of the experiment in all these sittings, their appearance seems more than chance.

If normal knowledge, a medium's usual technique of dealing with sitters and chance are eliminated as explanations, we are left with only two others: that the numbers were obtained either from the minds of living people or from the dead Lee.

Mediumistic communications usually refer to incidents about the past life of a dead person. These incidents are usually known to some living person so that any such communication can be explained as telepathy from the living. In this experiment the communications were to deal with material which would take form after Lee's death. Lee was to show his survival by selecting numbers none of us knew, two of which would add up to a third. The communication of these numbers which no one living knew would effectively sidestep the explanation that living people had been their sources.

In this case both Mrs. Petty and Ms. Parish were completely unaware that numbers were involved in the experiment and so could not have been the sources from whom the medium DG might have obtained the information telepathically. DG probably knew that an unidentified medium in the Hollywood, Florida, area and two experimenters named Arthur and Joyce Berger were doing an experiment with Mrs. Petty to reach Lee. But how did he obtain the numbers he gave? Since they were not known to his two sitters, could they have been obtained by telepathy from SDN or from the experimenters or the observer?

When the experiment was proposed by the coexperimenter, she asked the communicator to take any two numbers. The medium SDN immediately said, "2, 3; 2, 3." I was not present, but these numbers were heard by SDN, JB and the observer, Mrs. Zeitlin. Thus the medium DG was afforded the paranormal opportunity of obtaining these numbers from the minds of living persons so that the value of the evidence as having come from the communicator is weakened. We must assume that, if living persons know information later given by a medium such as DG, these persons, rather than a deceased person, are its source. "To do otherwise," wrote Alice Johnson, "would be to beg the whole question at issue, for the very thing to be proved is the existence of the dead person."[6]

Further reflection on the case, however, permits us to rebut this assumption and to restore a good deal of the evidence. After "2, 3; 2, 3," were spoken, JB explained that she did not want to know the numbers and the communicator gave no more. The numbers given by DG in Ms. Parish's sitting were not "2, 3." Indeed, "3" was not given in her reading at all while a number appeared not known to SDN, JB or the observer or anyone else. That number was "1," and the numbers given were "1, 2." In Mrs. Petty's sitting with DG the unknown number again appeared so that the numbers given were not "2, 3" but "1, 2, 3." The unknown number "1" could not have had its source in a living mind. Moreover, in both sittings, the combination of numbers is different from what it would have been in the minds of SDN, JB and Mrs. Zeitlin so that their being the telepathic agents is not a plausible explanation.

During the medium DG's sittings with both sitters, something out of the ordinary and striking seems to have been going on and impinging on the medium's mind. In Ms. Parish's sitting the medium said something strange was happening. He whispered and seemed baffled when the numbers one and two appeared. His mind formed these numbers into a child's rhyme, "One, two, button my shoe," but he recognized at once that no rhyme was intended and that it was a play on words. Something more was behind the numbers, but DG was unable to grasp what it was. "I don't know what sense there is to it," he said. The communicator was saying the numbers "very audibly" — as if to guard against mistakes and to impress the medium with the importance of the numbers. But the medium confessed, "I really don't know what that means."

In his next sitting with Mrs. Petty the numbers one and two reappear, are equally meaningless and the medium was baffled still. "I don't know," he said. "He's not beating time." The medium repeated "1, 2, 3" about a dozen times but stopped when the sitter suggested that the numbers referred to three owners of a farm. The circumstance carries with it the faint suggestion of the presence of an external deceased mind. The suggestion becomes stronger when the numbers "1, 2" given in Ms. Parish's sitting with DG are put together with the numbers "1, 2, 3" in Mrs. Petty's sitting with him. They are right in line with the experiment proposed to the communicator to show his survival. It may be inferred that the numbers were part of the experiment and referred to it.

The sittings with the medium VL reinforce even further the suggestion of the operation of a deceased mind. When Ms. Parish sat with VL the number 58742 was given by the medium. "I have no idea what it means. . . I don't know what it is," she said. Although it is either a five digit number or a series of five numbers and is therefore not what was requested of the communicator, nevertheless numbers coming through an independent medium at a different sitting fit into the theme of the experiment and give the sense of one mind behind the separate sittings. The presence of this mind can be detected once more in Mrs. Petty's September 29 sitting with VL. The medium stated that "three things regarding Lee will be tied together" — again reiterating the theme of the experiment which was based on three numbers in a certain cor- respondence with one another — and perhaps meant that the communicator had tied "1" to "2" to make "3."

Time and again we have been counselled that the scientific attitude is not to find a plausible or superficial explanation for a case like this, but the true one.[7] When we examine the whole of the evidence here, it is very hard to be satisfied with a normal explanation of the case or a paranormal one based on telepathy from the living. The whole of the evidence suggests that the truest hypothesis is that one mind, outside the minds of all the living people in this experiment, was operating to tell Lee Petty's story of survival after bodily death.

It also suggests, first, a confirmation of the findings of the "ideal" com- municator whom Lee Petty resembled. Second, it suggests that, when a person is selected who seems specially gifted as a communicator, the evidence resulting from his communications is of a quality high enough to resist alter- native explanations.

12
LOOKING TO THE FUTURE

The experiment with Lee Petty was basically no different from the mediumistic experiments that have crowded the pages of the proceedings and journals of the societies of psychical research. The evidence produced by them all had its inception after the deaths of Lee and other communicators. Yet this common feature starts a whole new train of thought for us. The perspective of researchers has been forever one of looking backwards from the experiment to a death—which may explain the unconvincing nature of most of the evidence and why it excites contradictory points of view.

A fresh perspective becomes possible if we lay the basis for the evidence before the death of a communicator. Why not have it come into existence from the moment of its planning and preparation by people who, anticipating death sooner or later and wishing to try to give evidence to establish their existence after death, had taken the time and pains to prepare the exact manner of doing so? Since their antemortem preparation would be undertaken in concert with researchers, investigation could begin effectively before the subjects of the experiments died. The perspective of the investigators would be reversed because now they would be looking forward from an antemortem groundwork to a postmortem fact which they would be ready to submit to a prearranged form of objective verification.

It is obviously too late for Lee Petty and others already dead to come within this perspective. It looks to the future; they are in the past. It is concerned with people who are living and can prepare the evidence of their postmortem survival to help future generations.

But do any of us reading these pages know what evidence of our own survival we can plan and prepare? The author incorporated such a question in a study dealing with the opinion of the general American population concerning death and the possibility of life after death. The question was, "How, in what exact ways, would you give evidence that you had personally survived death as a conscious, remembering personality?"

The questionnaires were distributed to two different samples of the general population. A small pilot study was conducted with students attending the author's course on survival after death given at Florida International

University and with students attending a course in philosophy at Louisiana State University. None of the respondents had the remotest idea of how to answer the question, but, of course, these students probably were extremely sceptical about a postmortem existence and were little disposed to think about the subject.

Questionnaires were then distributed to members of the Spiritual Frontiers Fellowship, a "metaphysical" organization in the United States consisting mainly of middle-class adults concerned with spiritual development and interested in psychic phenomena including those related to survival after death. This mature and special group was much more inclined to a belief in postmortem survival than the students and, it was thought, would not only have a greater interest in the subject but would have given it serious consideration. Altogether 3500 questionnaires were distributed to this group. The return rate was about 12 percent. The responses to other questions in the questionnaire, such as whether respondents believed in the survival of human consciousness after death, were expected. But the survey produced the following unexpected results to the question of what evidence would be given of postmortem survival:

Do not know	36%
Question left blank	35%
Vague or irrelevant answers	29%
Specific facts	0%

Even among people, such as SFF members, who have a strong interest in survival, therefore, there is a complete lack of knowledge of the sort of evidence they can give to try to establish their postmortem survival. Perhaps this lack explains the paucity of persuasive survival evidence. Among the many who have died, surely a good fraction were good communicators. Why didn't they supply more convincing evidence? Possibly because they did not know what to communicate. The trite and trivial mediumistic communications that have been received over the years should have revealed to us that death does not make people smarter or teach them what they did not know. If, while alive, people, even those keenly interested in the subject, are not taught the survival evidence they can try to communicate, there is no reason to expect them to know what to do after death.

Another new perspective emerges out of all this. It is not enough to discard the "equal ability" assumption and to recognize that certain people under certain circumstances are privileged to be good communicators and to select these people for experiments: They must also be shown what scientifically acceptable evidence to communicate.

A further question was therefore inserted in the questionnaire. People were asked if they would like to be shown the kinds of postmortem survival evidence to attempt to supply. To this question 97 percent of the respondents answered, "Yes."

An educational program has been started by the author and is described in the literature.[1] It turns on antemortem plans in which a living person arranges posthumous experiments with investigators with the intention of communicating after death specific, verifiable, but unrecorded, facts as a signal of postmortem survival and identity. These experiments consist of cipher and combination lock tests using key words or sentences known only to those arranging the tests who encipher a test message with a verbal key or set a lock with it. The test message or lock is left with the investigators. Without the key the message cannot be read or the lock cannot be opened. Participants intend to communicate after death these keys which are not disclosed to anyone or left in any recorded form. Psychics attempt by telepathy to obtain the keys from people while they are alive. If such attempts do not succeed during the lifetimes of these persons but, if after their deaths, keys are received in a telepathic communication or are communicated by another means (to be indicated), which keys are checked by investigators and verified as correct because they decipher the messages left behind by the participants or open their locks, reasonable people could interpret such a result as strongly suggesting the survival of such persons and their identity as the same persons who deposited the messages or locks and who alone knew the deciphering or lock-opening keys. Such a result might also raise the eyebrows of philosophers, like that redoubtable British sceptic, Antony Flew, who deny the logical possibility of discarnate survival because, up until now, they could not see how it would be possible to show that a disembodied postmortem being was identical with a particular premortem one.

The "By the Numbers" test designed by the author is an example of one of the tests used in the program. In this test a dictionary is opened at random and a word chosen as the key. This word becomes the starting point for a sequence of numbers in numerical order. The first letter in the key word and every letter thereafter both in the word and in the pronunciation, etymology and definition following it for an indeterminate length are counted. Parentheses, punctuation marks, phonetic symbols and other numbers are not counted.

If, for example, the word "builder" had been selected at random from *Merriam-Webster's New International Dictionary*, second edition, the word and what followed it would be numbered as shown in the accompanying illustration.

These numbered letters are now used to make up a test message, such as, "We have souls." This message is enciphered by replacing the letters in it with the digits corresponding to them in the numbering sequence. Thus:

Test message:	W	E	H	A	V	E	S	O	U	L	S
Encipherment:	98	6	18	106	29	12	32	26	21	39	53

(Note that different numbers have been used for the letter "E" which appears twice in the message and for the letter "S" which also appears twice to make breaking the encipherment without knowlege of the key exceedingly difficult.)

1	2	3	4	5	6	7	8	9	10	11	12	13
B	u	i	l	d	e	r	(b	i	l	d	e	r)

14	15	16	17	18	19	20	21	22	23	24	25	26
1. o	n	e	w	h	o	b	u	i	l	d	s	o

27	28	29	30	31	32	33	34	35	36	37	38	39
r	o	v	e	r	s	e	e	s	b	u	i	l

40	41	42	43	44	45	46	47	48	49	50	51	52
d	i	n	g	o	p	e	r	a	t	i	o	n

53	54	55	56	57	58	59	60	61	62	63	64	65
s;	o	n	e	w	h	o	s	e	o	c	c	u

66	67	68	69	70	71	72	73	74	75	76	77	78
p	a	t	i	o	n	i	s	t	o	b	u	i

79	80	81	82	83	84	85	86	87	88	89	90	91
l	d,	a	s	a	c	a	r	p	e	n	t	e

92	93	94	95	96	97	98	99	100	101	102	103	104
r,	a	s	h	i	p	w	r	i	g	h	t,	o

105	106
r	a

The enciphered message is left with investigators together with a notation that *Merriam-Webster's New International Dictionary*, second edition, had been used by the encipherer. Nothing else is revealed. The key is never disclosed to any living person and is not left in written or other recorded form. The encipherer plans to remember it and to try to communicate it after death.

Repeated attempts can be made to decipher the test message in this test as well as in the other tests used. Since only one word will decipher it, incorrect words will fail. The ability to make many attempts is essential because communication, at best, seems to be very difficult. As Myers, one of the "stars" we examined, said in a posthumous communication about trying to communicate through a medium:

> The nearest simile I can find to express the difficulties of sending a message — is that I appear to be standing behind a sheet of frosted glass — which blurs sight and deadens sounds — dictating feebly — to a reluctant and somewhat obtuse secretary. A feeling of terrible impotence burdens me — I am so powerless to tell what means so much — [2]

Communicators using the tests are now given many chances to get the right message through. Their tests remain uncompromised until they do. In the example given only the key word, "builder," will permit investigators, using the correct dictionary, to set up the sequence of numbers that will convert 98, 6, 18, 106, 29, 12, 32, 26, 21, 39, 53 into the letters assigned to them into the subject's message, "We have souls." "Builder" is therefore unquestionably the correct key. The result is simple and clear-cut. There can be no doubt about it.

Would this result suggest to reasonable people the postmortem survival and identity of the encipherer of the message? It should. There was no normal way that this positive result could have come about since neither investigators nor anyone else could have known the key, which the encipherer kept a carefully guarded secret. Could the result have come about by chance? Since the *Merriam-Webster's* used in the example is an unabridged dictionary which contains approximately 600,000 entries, the chance of finding the key "builder" by random guesses is 1 in 600,000, odds great enough to eliminate chance. Could psychics have obtained the key by clairvoyance or telepathy? They could not have used clairvoyance to "read" the key in any document prepared by the encipherer because the key was not left in writing. The test message itself, if read normally or by clairvoyance, would not reveal the key. Telepathy then? No, not from the mind of any living person anywhere because the encipherer, now dead, was the only one who knew it.

Telepathy from the encipherer's mind before death? As part of the test, and to rule out this very possibility, antemortem experiments are conducted with psychics in which they are asked to make repeated efforts to get the key during the encipherer's lifetime. Since one would expect it to be easier to obtain a key word by telepathy while an encipherer is alive rather than after death, failures of antemortem trials followed by a postmortem success would make the counter-explanation that a key had been obtained telepathically from a living encipherer unlikely. One could infer that success had been caused by new elements: the death of the encipherer and a willingness now to supply the secret key word. If "builder" deciphers the test message, such an inference could be made.

In other words, virtually every alternative theory used to explain away survival evidence will have been avoided by this antemortem pact and postmortem result. Here would be presented evidence of a formidable nature that does not yield easily to nonsurvivalist explanations. Is there hope of success for this type of evidence? There are cases on record which suggest that secret information can be conveyed to the living from the dead. Swedenborg's learning from a dead man that a receipt for a silver service was in a secret compartment of an upstairs bureau is one such case. In the Chaffin will case, a dead father appeared in the dreams of one of his sons to reveal the existence of an unknown will. The will was found and admitted to probate in 1928 in the Superior Court of Davie County, North Carolina.[3] In these cases, of course, no antemortem plans had been made. Neither the husband who communicated with Swedenborg nor Mr. Chaffin had prearranged matters in order to prove their survival.

But in other cases prearrangements for survival evidence had been made. In twelve of these, performance of antemortem agreements to appear as apparitions was claimed.[4] In another case a brother and sister devised an experiment in which a brick was marked with ink. The brick was then broken in two. One piece was given to the sister and the other was kept and secreted away by the brother who agreed to show his survival by revealing the hiding place after his death. Following his death his sister said that he had communicated to her where his piece of brick was hidden. When she found it, it fitted exactly the piece she had retained.[5]

To show his survival after death Myers also devised an experiment in which a message, not revealed to any living person, was to be communicated after death. In 1891 Myers sent a sealed envelope to his close friend, the physicist Sir Oliver Lodge, with the intention of posthumously communicating its contents to a medium. Myers died in 1901. In 1904 the script of the automatist Mrs. A.W. Verrall seemed to contain allusions to the envelope from the Myers personality. Her script of July 13, 1904, reported Myers saying, "I have long told you of the contents of the envelope. Myers' sealed envelope left with Lodge. You have not understood. It has in it the words from the Symposium — about love bridging the chasm." It was decided to retrieve the envelope from the bank and to open it in the presence of the Council of the Society for Psychical Research and a few of its members whom Lodge had invited to witness the event. In the envelope Myers had enclosed a paper on which he had written, "If I can revisit any earthly scene, I should choose the Valley in the grounds of Hallsteads, Cumberland." At Hallsteads Myers had fallen in love with Anne Marshall, his cousin's wife, whom he could not have but whom he never forgot.

Was the communication right or wrong? According to the *Journal* of the SPR, "[I]t was found that there was no resemblance between [the envelope's] actual contents and what was alleged by the script to be contained in it. It has, then, to be reported that this one experiment has completely failed...."[6] It has since been argued, however, by the noted authority Salter[7] that, if the meaning of the script is stretched and interpreted, although it is not a literal statement of the contents of the envelope, it will be seen to have a clear and definite connection with it and to Myers' love for Anne Marshall. Salter's argument is sufficiently persuasive to raise the possibility that the ostensible Myers may have communicated and may have partly succeeded in communicating the contents of his sealed envelope.

We have indicated that an indispensable condition of survival research is that communication with the dead be possible. One hypothesis we make is that mind-to-mind communication by dead people attempting to convey planned information might come through intermediaries between the living and the dead called mediums. Great mediums like Mrs. Piper and Eileen Garrett have existed in the past and, although the Golden Age of mediumship seems to have waned so that many persons claiming to be mediums today are little more than charlatans, there is no logical reason to suppose that trustworthy persons possessing genuine paranormal gifts through whom telepathic messages can be received will not be found in the future.

A new phenomenon has appeared in recent years, however, which makes the need for finding such persons less urgent and offers some basis for thinking that tests, like the "By the Numbers" test, can have successful outcomes. There have been mounting reports of postmortem communications through electronic instruments operated by people who claim and demonstrate no psychic abilities. By the time he had published *Breakthrough* in 1971,[8] Konstantin Raudive claimed that he had recorded over 70,000 strange, inaudible but human-sounding voices on his tape recorder. In the period following the book's publication, which stimulated interest in Great Britain, Europe and the United States, housewives, students and scientists who had never thought of themselves as mediums began to conduct their own experiments. Using microphones, diodes and interfrequency methods, they claimed to be recording the "Raudive voices" on tape, voices of people who had died and were now on the "other side."

Besides voices of the dead recorded on tape, claims have been made that they have been heard over the telephone. Over 100 reports of telephone calls from the dead were recently investigated.[9]

Are the dead trying to take advantage of modern electronic technology to communicate the evidence of their survival to the living? There are many counter-indications. A counter-theory for the "Raudive voices" is that, even if the voice phenomena are objective, the voices are produced by the experimenters themselves whose subconscious minds have generated electrical impulses which have been converted by psychokinesis into voices on the tapes. The phantom telephone calls can be explained away on the grounds that the reports are largely unsubstantiated and are usually made long after the event when memory has become weak and imagination strong.

But we cannot be dogmatic. The counter-theories are plausible but they may be wrong. There may be fire behind this smoke. One single voice detected on tape or heard on the telephone that provides the secret word to decipher a test message which cannot be deciphered without it would be a genuine breakthrough and would establish postmorten electronic communication.

In the early days of psychical research antemortem plans to provide postmortem evidence of survival were regarded with the highest favor. One of the founders of the S.P.R. wrote:

> I think it very desirable that as many persons as possible should provide a decisive test of their own identity, in case they should find themselves able to communicate through any sensitive after their bodily death.[10]

He also said:

> [S]mall as may be the chances of success, a few score of distinct successes would establish a presumption of man's survival which the common sense of mankind would refuse to explain away.[11]

To produce evidence of a superior quality and to establish this presumption, tests of survival remain highly desirable provided the phrase "as many persons as possible" in the above statement is amended to "as many good communicators as possible." The successful completion of the tests for survival depends upon people, such as the Lee Pettys of the future, who are capable of communicating key words which will decipher messages or open locks.

If the first and second of our new angles of vision — of the future good communicator who is trained — are combined, the outlook brightens and a model for empirical investigation comes into view. An approach through tests for survival that living people, selected for their ability to communicate, have prepared with the cooperation of investigators and intend to complete offers survival research a glowing opportunity for a fruitful and rapid advance.

13
THE RISING WAVE

Although serious inquiry into the question of survival after death was begun over 100 years ago by psychical researchers, the steadily increasing emphasis in the last decades on extrasensory perception and psychokinetic experiments in the laboratory and with computers has been matched by a steadily decreasing interest in traditional lines of research into the survival question, such as mediumship and spontaneous cases, and by a lack of imagination in designing new methodologies and doing experimental research.

At the same time, this erosion of interest on the part of the community of psychical researchers has been counterbalanced by a burgeoning interest in death and the possible postmortem state on the part of academics of religion, philosophy and humanistic disciplines, theologians and the clergy, and workers in the fields of thanatology, sociology, psychology, medicine and nursing. Concern with death is no longer limited to people facing death or to widowers or widows. This taboo topic has been uncovered and placed in the sunlight for examination by people in a wide range of disciplines. Thousands of courses on death and dying are offered in high schools, colleges and universities and professional schools such as law, medicine, nursing and theology. Elisabeth Kubler-Ross's book, *On Death and Dying* (1969), became a bestseller and was followed by such a flood of books and papers on these subjects that a bibliography of such materials put together in 1975 by the Center for Death Education and Research at the University of Minnesota showed that in excess of 3000 publications apart from sermons and lectures had come out.

Examples are not wanting, either, of the proliferation of interest in the issue of whether there is continuation beyond physical death. After Raymond A. Moody, Jr. wrote his best-selling *Life After Life* (1975) to describe the visions of dead relatives and friends in another dimension reported by patients who were dying or who recovered after being declared clinically dead, professional and public interest in these apparitional experiences was sparked and they became the center of studies by professionals working in several different areas—Sabom, the cardiologist; Ring, the psychologist; Greyson, the psychiatrist; even parapsychologists like Osis and Haraldsson. Organizations such as the International Association for Near-Death Studies sponsor research and conferences and publish journals containing these reports for professional audiences and the intelligent lay public.

A final illustration of the rising wave of interest in exploring the postmortem state are the recent conferences attended by university professors, scientists and theologians that have made this subject their exclusive theme. In 1987, for example, two noteworthy conferences on the afterlife were held, one by Louisiana State University in which Raymond Moody, noted philosopher John Hick, and I participated, and another by the Center for a Post-Modern World in the School of Theology at Claremont, California. Two years earlier, an International Congress on Life After Death was held in Basel, Switzerland, in which scientists, theologians and physicians took part. Also in 1985, a Symposium on Issues of Consciousness and Survival was held at Georgetown University in Washington, D.C., in which prominent figures in various fields, including theologian Bishop John Spong and philosophers John Hick and Antony Flew, psychologist Kenneth Ring, psychiatrist Stanislov Grof, and even a United States senator, Claiborne Pell, made presentations. The *Washington Post* reported that the symposium "was a landmark in the growing general recognition that life after death is worth serious attention and scientific study."[1] As if to underscore this mounting interest on the highest levels in life after death, the *Post* article, by unanimous vote of the United States Senate, was printed in the *Congressional Record*.[2]

This rising interest in and openness to new methods and data relating to postmortem survival make the waning years of the twentieth century opportune for a systematic attempt to study the question and suggest that the moment has come to pick up the fallen torch and to carry it forward in the quest for hard survival evidence.

We are helped and encouraged to do so by the new angles of vision discussed previously. The views of the neglected angle and of death as an unequalizer should point our thoughts in the direction of the communicator and should help us both to identify all the complex factors that may produce someone with the ability to give evidence of survival and to understand that people with this ability ought to be trained in what information to give following their deaths. Focus the new angles of vision on Job's familiar question, and new workers and a new model for investigation come into view.

The perspectives provide us with a compass to guide the investigation. But compasses by themselves have never achieved anything. Ships and ships' companies putting the compasses to use have always been needed to reach harbors and make voyages of discovery. What kinds of ships can be built now to explore the still uncharted survival question? Who among us would be asked to be shipmates? Where would our work be done and what might be the meaning of this reoriented and reorganized effort to penetrate the veil that has kept what happens to us at death an enigma?

We must attack the mystery of survival after death with courage and imagination. An experimental program can be launched against it based on local teams of determined volunteer investigators raised from the ranks of professionals in a broad spectrum of disciplines and from the intelligent lay public. Such an effort, in Myers' words, would befit "all 'men of good will' to help toward this knowing with what zeal they may."[3]

The principle of direct attack on the problem is a call for democratizing survival research. For good reason or bad, the societies for psychical research and the Parapsychological Association have often protested against what they believe are the worthless opinions of credulous enthusiasts whose entry into psychical research would destroy scientific standards in the field. But the protesters by and large have nearly abandoned survival research, as the last half-century bears witness, and it may be time to remove the subject from their charge and to encourage serious interest and study by the laity. The time has come to spread responsibility for the investigation of survival and to give all who wish the opportunity to do something about it.

Popularizing investigation within the confines of an experimental program hinged to tests for survival will not necessarily allow the expression of valueless opinions. It is true that average people generally are not competent to express opinions on whether psychic phenomena are or are not evidence of survival. Many religious people and Spiritualists are prone to interpret all phenomena as proof of life after death while most sceptics are inclined to reject all such interpretations as impossible and any such conclusions as wishful thinking. In tests for survival, however, there is no room for interpretations or expressions of conflicting opinions either by lay persons or professional researchers because the outcome of a test cannot be debated as the phenomena of a seance might be. A test for survival always produces a result that is definite: An enciphered message either is deciphered with the secret key or it is not. A posthumous communication is a hit or a miss; there is no in-between.

Popularization need not deviate from high scientific standards. In the first place, the special mission of the investigative teams is not silly or naive. It is a scientific mission: the systematic and critical testing of the survival hypothesis, which states that a person whose attributes and circumstances correspond to the "ideal" communicator and who prepares a test for survival with experimenters will provide strong evidence of postmortem survival and identity. Experiments will be conducted to validate the hypothesis or invalidate it. If results fit the prediction, the modern torch-bearers will have caused survival research to make its most fruitful advance.

Secondly, if we think of the investigative team as a triangle, at the first angle are competent experimenters whose makeup even the professional societies and associations find hard to define. But it should be possible for men and women to attain to a high level of competence by informing themselves about the rigorous investigations and experiments reported in detail in the parapsychological literature and by observing the methods used by the best investigators of the survival question in their efforts to collect evidence. Early experimenters such as Hodgson and Hyslop and present day investigators such as Stevenson and Karlis Osis serve as excellent examples of how to use scientific methods in survival research. These lessons plus a critical attitude, intellectual honesty and capacity and a love of truth should be credentials enough to qualify one as a volunteer experimenter for an investigative team. Membership in one of the societies or associations does not seem to be a requisite; in fact, judging from the record of the last fifty years during which scientific interest in survival plunged to new lows, it would be better for investigators not to be members of these groups.

Experimenters will want to make it unlikely that potential communicators can cheat before death through the deliberate disclosure of a secret key (which, of course, would not be secret any more). The creation of multiple blind conditions and the splitting of information among the different elements in the unit would accomplish this end.

Although Emma Fischer was a good communicator and, in our mass survey, many good female communicators were found, there was a great predominance of males (78 percent) so that, for best results, mainly those males now among us whose profiles, as it were, match the ideal communicators of the future should occupy the second and vitally important angle of the investigative team.

Since age was found not to be a factor, volunteers expecting to communicate can range, therefore, from those in the twilight of life (euphemistically called "senior citizens") to the middle-aged and young. They will arrange posthumous experiments by preparing tests for survival, by specifying the tests they have selected and by depositing with experimenters the test messages or test locks involved in the tests. After tests have been prepared, volunteers will practice remembering their keys. Their tasks will be to remember the keys during life and after death and to make the effort after their deaths to convey to the waiting experimenters their secret keys so that their messages can be deciphered or their locks opened. If these keys should be received and messages are in fact deciphered or locks left behind opened, the communicators' tasks will have been accomplished. Of course, there is no special hurry for them to die! Their task is not a "suicide mission." But when their times come, they may provide significant and cogent evidence.

It is hoped, however, that volunteers will come from the terminally ill and those choosing euthanasia or suicide. Their participation, of course, will increase the probability that members of the experimental teams will be able to see tests for survival completed before they themselves shuffle off this mortal coil. But through the knowledge that they may be rendering a service for their families, society and science, the terminally ill and others may rediscover meaning in their remaining lives and deaths.

In normal life you and I are able to talk directly to one another. Unless we speak different languages no third person, such as an interpreter, is needed. But in the abnormal environment surrounding the investigation of survival, communications from the dead to the living pass through a third living mind or through electronic instrumentation. It is by means of this human or mechanical interface that the dead interact with the living by using any of the forms of communication hypothesized earlier: telepathy, psychokinesis, possession, apparitions. The final angle of the investigative team, therefore, will be some form of interface that may operate as a channel for the reception of a communicator's key. The traditional form likely will be the mental medium. Mainly women, though sometimes men, they will work best by doing automatic writing, whether going into trance or maintaining their normal states. But several other forms of interface will be employed in postmortem experiments to reach volunteer communicators.

Sleep research conducted at the dream laboratory at Maimonides Medical Center suggests that living agents may be able to exert telepathic influence on the dreams of sleeping subjects. Dream telepathy attempts might be made to see if dead commands similarly can affect dream content and have sleeping subjects dream of their keys. Attempts also can be made to repeat what many individuals and groups have claimed to do: use tape recorders connected to radios or other devices to record the voices of the dead. Dying persons and those who meditate or claim to be able to induce out-of-body experiences may serve also as interfaces. Such people frequently assert the conviction that consciousness has separated from the physical body. During such experiences ESP of a postmortem reality may be increased sufficiently to facilitate the reception of communications from that world. Besides this group, those who have strong feelings of identification with deceased persons should be considered. In reincarnation cases subjects claiming memories of past lives often affirm a sense of identification with dead people of another era and place. If reincarnation theory is correct, adult subjects regressed hypnotically or young children whose memories have not yet been dimmed by time might show knowledge not only of diverse details of the life of a communicator with whom they have identified themselves but also of the key used by him to encipher a message or set a lock.

In addition, perhaps survival evidence remains unconvincing because, although good communicators have died and may have been waiting to provide evidence of their postmortem existence, no one knew of their deaths or, even worse, cared enough to try to obtain their evidence. To prevent a repetition of such ignorance or apathy in the future, registration procedures ought to be adopted by the teams that will enable the experimenters to know when volunteer communicators have died. All potential communicators should be asked to give the names and addresses of friends and family members who have agreed to dispose of their bodies and bury them in conformity with the procedures that seem related to good communication and to give the experimenters notice of the deaths of the volunteer communicators. In addition, volunteers should carry identification cards requesting that, upon their deaths, experimenters be notified. On the receipt of such notice, experimenters must begin at once to try to obtain the keys of the deceased volunteers.

Where might the experimental teams find hospitable homes? When J.B. Rhine referred to "the psychical research societies" that were virtually inactive on the survival question, he probably had in mind the American Society for Psychical Research in New York and its English cousin, the Society for Psychical Research in London. Although these are both highly respected and responsible societies run by competent councils and staffs, they are not suitable homes for the teams precisely because, as Rhine said, the survival issue is almost a dead one for them. There is also a profusion of small, lesser known societies for psychical research scattered everywhere. But their directors, members and programs evince interest in such topics as human auras, mysticism, astrology, unidentified flying objects, hypnosis, handwriting analysis, pyramid power, the Bermuda Triangle and the Abominable Snowman. These occult or esoteric groups are unsuitable for scientific research.

Similarly, churches provide no haven for our teams. Although a positive resolution of the survival question might help them by supporting the prospect of the future life that religion has promised, churches see no necessity for doing experimental research on the question. Faith has persuaded them of the reality of life after death. Why go further?

Although Spiritualist churches and camps which use mediumship to provide evidence of survival appear logical vehicles for the investigation the volunteer teams will be undertaking, it is not the case. One Spiritualist principle, taken from the Declaration of Principles published by the National Spiritualist Association, is "We never die." Another says, "We affirm that communications with the so-called dead is a fact, scientifically proven by the phenomena of Spiritualism." To Spiritualists the case is already closed. They accept readily the most nonsensical mediumistic messages as "scientific proof" of survival. Rarely do the Spiritualists exhibit any willingness to conduct the kinds of careful and critical experiments our investigative teams are meant to.

On the other hand, since the academic community has proved to be a major force in the current wave of interest in death, dying and eschatological issues, and since these issues have the greater relevance for religion and philosophy, university departments of religion and philosophy might consider establishing investigative teams with professors and students working with other volunteers. Advice from some of the centers still doing survival research, such as the Survival Research Foundation, could aid the teams in their work.

Research laboratories, perhaps funded by philanthropic individuals or charitable organizations, in which the teams will carry on their research can be created. These laboratories could either be independent or be affiliated with an academic institution offering a program in parapsychology.

A final possibility is the formation of membership organizations. Supported by its investigative teams, their object will be to carry on an empirical investigation of the survival problem with advisers from an established survival research center, if necessary, and to publish the results of their investigations. Membership units need not be limited to American or British teams. The matter of human survival after bodily death is obviously not peculiar to any one country or culture; investigations should be on an international basis.

Experimenters cannot expect to dial "C" for communicator whenever they wish and to receive a prompt answer, even from an "ideal" communicator who will supply a message-deciphering or lock-opening key. We suppose that it is the wish of the dead communicator that governs whether any communication will be effected and not the wish of the living experimenter. It seems essential, therefore, that besides making careful antemortem preparations with experimenters with respect to the evidence to be given, volunteers be strongly motivated to communicate after death. In the previous chapter, reference was made to antemortem pacts that were performed. But others have failed. The difference between the cases can perhaps be explained on the ground that the deceased party to the failed pact was not a good communicator to start with. But it is also possible that, although the decedent was a good communicator, he or she no longer wanted to communicate with the other party to the experiment. The importance of continuing motivation cannot be ignored.

Although volunteer communicators will include both older and younger people, the importance of motivation draws a distinction between the two groups. Those dying of old age usually do not die with unfinished business. They have fulfilled their obligations to people close to them and to society. When the time comes for them to communicate with the living to accomplish their experimental mission, therefore, they may lack the motivation to communicate. Nevertheless, the elderly ought not to be excluded from the investigative units; many should make excellent subjects. Emphasis should be placed, however, on inviting the middle-aged and young to volunteer for the teams. If cut off before they have had a chance to live or complete plans, work or obligations, they would not be done with earthly affairs. They might be really motivated to communicate and could increase the chances of the success of a given experiment to receive a crucial key.

Not only to effect large-scale enlistments of potential communicators, experimenters and interfaces in the investigative teams but also to ensure that the motivations of communicators will endure after death, it ought to be broadcast repeatedly, with skill and fervor, that the purpose of the experiments is to perform an important service for persons who are living after the would-be communicators have died. The experiments are prearranged with the intention of attempting to communicate after death valuable empirical evidence of conscious continuation after death, which, if it can be given—or even if not given—would bring the gift of precious knowledge to millions of people and make a significant contribution to science. In this way, the potential communicators in the experimental program will be donating their deaths to humanity and science just as other people donate their bodily organs to medicine.

Experimental resolution one way or another of the hypothesis that strong evidence of survival will come from an "ideal" communicator would have sweeping implications. A positive resolution suggestive of a postmortem existence would be of utmost importance to religion. Buddhism and Hinduism, on the one side, and Christianity, on the other, can be thought of as religions of death. The former, which despair of present human life and disclaim the reality of this world, emphasize escape into a higher reality. The latter, which looks to the hereafter, can survive only if the candle of belief in life after death is kept burning. For Judaism, a religion of both life and death, the question also is important; rabbinic sources show that the soul, reward and punishment, resurrection and transmigration are among its central doctrines.

If the resolution were positive, it might have great practical importance in medicine. The medical problem of how long to use medical technology to keep people alive who, for all practical purposes, are merely inert and unresponsive vegetables, would be clarified. Life support systems might be more easily turned off to let people make their transitions in dignity. A positive resolution would be of personal importance. The fear of death would be lessened and the present life made worth living for many people. As I wrote elsewhere, "[W]hat might be the effect on us if we had strong evidence for the belief that death was not a thief in the night that steals and the murderer that kills? If the weight of this belief could be removed, would life not bound forward joyously into new dimensions like the coiled spring that leaps up after a great weight has been lifted from it?"[4]

On the other hand, if there were no successful communications, if every experimental mission failed so that all the accumulated evidence was negative and did not confirm the hypothesis of strong survival evidence, one (but not the only) justifiable interpretation would be that constant failures to communicate on the part of volunteers determined to try to do so constituted cogent evidence against the survival hypothesis. Such a negative result would force us finally to realize that we have nothing but this life and that we cannot afford to fritter away our lives on insignificant things.

The positive or negative resolution of the question of whether a human mind survives death would surely affect psychology, which is the study of the mind and which is naturally interested in whether the mind can extend beyond the body and death, and would affect philosophy by stilling the mind-body issue that has plagued philosophers since Plato.

An attempt to push the case for survival off dead center with hard positive or negative data, and to resolve the question raised by the man of Uz, would be in keeping with the times and the interest now surging toward the subject. In order to make the attempt, however, serious investigators must be ready to pass through a twilight zone occupied by hopes, fears, superstitions and apathy. These confront investigators like the fiends and monsters who came at Bunyan's Christian when he entered the Valley of Humiliation. But if we have to use Myers' word, the "zeal" to prevent these forces from discouraging or deterring us from following a path of systematic and scientific investigation, new perspectives and a new model for it await us.

APPENDIX A
TABLES OF COMPARISON—
EXPLANATION OF CRITERIA

As stated earlier, two-by-two tables were constructed to compare the frequency of the special factors in each line of inquiry among good and poor communicators in the samples examined.

First Line of Inquiry: Personal Data

For the first line of inquiry, three tables of comparison were prepared. In the first, certain criteria were accepted as standards by which to judge factors relating to the six people in the special sample. $P = .1$ was the lowest possible value, and, if found, indicated that a factor was of the highest significance. Between $p = .1$ and $p = .15$, a result was considered "significant." A result of over $p = .15$ but less than $p = .2$ was "suggestive." Between $p = .2$ and $p = .25$ the result was considered "interesting." Larger values were considered of no interest.

In the second table, where six people comprising the general sample were studied, $p = .067$ was the smallest possible value. Between this level and $p = .12$ the result was "significant," above $p = .12$ but below $p = .17$, it was "suggestive," and over $p = .17$ but less than $p = .22$, it was "interesting."

In the third table, the smallest value that might have been produced in this investigation of the twelve people in the combined sample was $p = .00176$. Between this value and $p = .05$, the result was "significant." A result of over $p = .05$ but less than $p = .10$ was "suggestive" and between $p = .10$ and $p = .15$ it was "interesting."

Second Line of Inquiry:
Circumstances Relating to Death

Three two-by-two tables were prepared to show the frequency of these factors among the poor and good communicators. In the first table, the criteria of significance were the same as those set forth in connection with the first table in the first line of inquiry.

For the second table in the second line of inquiry, the p value standards are the same as those for the second table in the first line of inquiry.

The same criteria of significance used in the third table in the first line of inquiry were applied in the third table prepared for the second line.

Third Line of Inquiry: Postmortem Factors

A table was prepared to examine these factors. The smallest possible p value was $p = .00176$ so that the standards of significance stated above in connection with the third table in the first line of inquiry and the third table prepared for the second line of inquiry were repeated here.

APPENDIX B
CITATIONS FOR
MASS SURVEY CASES

The 100 cases examined were taken from the *Proceedings* of the Society for Psychical Research (abbreviated PS) and the *Proceedings* of the American Society for Psychical Research (abbreviated PAS). Following are 100 citations of the publications in which the cases examined will be found. Abbreviations are followed by year of publication, volume number and page numbers.

1. PS, 1890, 6, 478–481.
2. PS, 1890, 6, 455, 524, 540, 553.
3. PS, 1890, 6, 511, 554.
4. PS, 1890, 6, 503, 506, 515, 517.
5. PS, 1890, 6, 578.
6. PS, 1892, 8, 16, 45, 92–95.
7. PS, 1892, 8, 19, 106.
8. PS, 1892, 8, 111–114.
9. PS, 1895, 11, 82–86, 110.
10. PS, 1895, 11, 96–99, 110.
11. PS, 1895, 11, 103–104.
12. PS, 1898, 13, 286–287, 295.
13. PS, 1898, 13, 335–336, 417, 471–473.
14. PS, 1898, 13, 336–337, 480–482.
15. PS, 1898, 13, 337–339, 413, 439.
16. PS, 1898, 13, 475–478.
17. PS, 1898, 13, 342.
18. PS, 1898, 13, 343ff.
19. PS, 1898, 13, 447–449.
20. PS, 1898, 13, 502–510.
21. PS, 1898, 13, 527.
22. PS, 1898, 13, 351–352, 540–541, 550, 559–560.

23. PS, 1898, 13, 353–357.
24. PS, 1898, 13, 378–379, 517–519.
25. PS, 1901, 14, 12–22.
26. PS, 1901, 14, 31–33.
27. PS, 1901, 14, 31–33.
28. PS, 1901, 14, 9–10, 34–35.
29. PS, 1901, 16, 20–86, 307ff.
30. PS, 1901, 16, 27, 90ff., 316, 459.
31. PS, 1901, 16, 95ff., 427, 442.
32. PS, 1901, 16, 100–104, 309.
33. PS, 1901, 16, 105ff., 451.
34. PS, 1901, 16, 93ff., 445.
35. PS, 1902, 17, 79–81, 84, 89, 108–111.
36. PS, 1895, 11, 72–73.
37. PS, 1902, 17, 180–183.
38. PS, 1902, 17, 225, 228, 229, 232.
39. PS, 1906, 20, 2, 222–224, 234, 238, 239, 260.
40. PS, 1908, 21, 303ff.; PS, 1908, 22, 31ff.; PS, 23, 1909, 2ff.
41. PS, 1908, 21, 316ff., esp. 326–327.
42. PS, 1909, 23, 162ff.
43. PS, 1909, 23, 191ff.
44. PS, 1909, 23, 255ff.
45. PS, 1909, 23, 265ff.
46. PS, 1910, 24, 351ff.
47. PS, 1914, 27, 221ff.; PS, 1917, 29, 197ff.; PS, 1921, 31, 227.
48. PS, 1917, 29, 125.
49. PS, 1917, 29, 125.
50. PS, 1917, 29, 126ff.
51. PS, 1917, 29, 197ff.
52. PS, 1919, 30, 339ff.; PS, 1921, 31, 248–252.
53. PS, 1919, 30, 521ff.
54. PS, 1919, 30, 546.
55. PS, 1921, 31, 253–260.
56. PS, 1921, 32, 28–43.
57. PS, 1921, 32, 28–43.
58. PS, 1921, 32, 28–43.
59. PS, 1921, 32, 68–69.
60. PS, 1921, 32, 74.
61. PS, 1921, 32, 75.
62. PS, 1921, 32, 76.
63. PS, 1921, 32, 77.
64. PS, 1921, 32, 77–78, 130–132.
65. PS, 1921, 32, 78–79.

66. PS, 1921, 32, 82.
67. PS, 1921, 32, 85–86.
68. PS, 1921, 32, 86–87, 107.
69. PS, 1921, 32, 91–92.
70. PS, 1921, 32, 92.
71. PS, 1921, 32, 93–95.
72. PS, 1921, 32, 107–108.
73. PS, 1921, 32, 26.
74. PS, 1921, 32, 114–116.
75. PS, 1925, 35, 485–523.
76. PS, 1928, 36, 57–58.
77. PS, 1928, 36, 286–291.
78. PS, 1928, 36, 299–310.
79. PS, 1928, 36, 310–314.
80. PS, 1928, 36, 322–325.
81. PS, 1928, 36, 327–332.
82. PS, 1928, 38, 50ff.
83. PS, 1928, 38, 10–16.
84. PS, 1929, 39, 1–46.
85. PS, 1933, 41, 140, 180–185.
86. PS, 1933, 41, 163.
87. PS, 1933, 41, 148–149, 165.
88. PS, 1933, 41, 146–148.
89. PS, 1935, 43, 439–519.
90. PS, 1939, 45, 257–287.
91. PS, 1960, 52, 79–267.
92. PS, 1960, 52, 79–267.
93. PS, 1971, 55, 295–301.
94. PS, 1971, 55, 301–302.
95. PS, 1971, 55, 302–306.
96. PS, 1971, 55, 306–315.
97. PS, 1971, 55, 322–326.
98. PAS, 1907, 1, 548–552, 706–710.
99. PAS, 1907, 1, 552–554, 653–656.
100. PAS, 1907, 1, 558–562, 681–688.

APPENDIX C

Case No. 1. *John Jacob Astor IV*

James H. Hyslop, "A Further Record of Mediumistic Experiments," *Proceedings of the American Society for Psychical Research*, 1925, **19**, 1–451.

Case No. 2. *Samuel Langhorne Clemens (Mark Twain)*

James H. Hyslop, "The Return of Mark Twain," *Journal of the American Society for Psychical Research*, 1917, **11**, 361, 365.

James H. Hyslop, "Cross Reference Experiments for Mark Twain," *Proceedings of the American Society for Psychical Research*, 1920, **14**, 1–225.

Case No. 3. *Hannah Wild*

William James, "A Record of Observations of Certain Phenomena of Trance," *Proceedings of the Society for Psychical Research*, 1890, **6**, 651–659, p. 657.

Richard Hodgson, "A Record of Observations of Certain Phenomena of Trance," *Proceedings of the Society for Psychical Research*, 1892, **8**, 1–167.

Case No. 4. *Carroll D. Wright*

James H. Hyslop, "A Record of Experiments," *Proceedings of the American Society for Psychical Research*, 1912 (a), **6**, 17–976.

James H. Hyslop, "Summary of Experiments Since the Death of William James, Part II. Carroll D. Wright," *Journal of the American Society for Psychical Research*, 1912 (b), **6**, 345–384.

James H. Hyslop, *Contact with the Other World*, New York: Century, 1919.

Case No. 5. Isaac Kauffman Funk

James H. Hyslop, "Book Review," *Journal of the American Society for Psychical Research*, 1915, **9**, 536.

James H. Hyslop, *Contact with the Other World*, op. cit.

James H. Hyslop, "Cross Reference Experiments for Mark Twain," op. cit.

Walter F. Prince, "Chips from the Workshop," *Journal of the American Society for Psychical Research*, 1925, **29**, 95–98.

Case No. 6. Emma Fischer

Walter F. Prince, "The Doris Case of Multiple Personality," *Proceedings of the American Society for Psychical Research*, 1915, **9**, 1–700.

Walter F. Prince, "The Doris Case of Multiple Personality," *Proceedings of the American Society for Psychical Research*, 1916, **10**, 701–1419.

James H. Hyslop, "Experiments with the Doris Case," *Journal of the American Society for Psychical Research*, 1917, **11**, 463.

James H. Hyslop, *Contact with the Other World*, op. cit. pp. 392–397.

Walter F. Prince, "Mother of Doris," *Proceedings of the American Society for Psychical Research*, 1923, **17**, 1–216.

Case No. 7.

No cases reported.

Case No. 8. Henry Sidgwick

J.G. Piddington, "On the Types of Phenomena Displayed in Mrs. Thompson's Trance," *Proceedings of the Society for Psychical Research*, 1904, **18**, 104–307.

Mrs. A.W. Verrall, "On a Series of Automatic Writings," *Proceedings of the Society for Psychical Research*, 1906, **20**, 1–432.

Alice Johnson, "On the Automatic Writing of Mrs. Holland," *Proceedings of the Society for Psychical Research*, 1908, **21**, 166–391.

Case No. 9. F.W.H. Myers

J.G. Piddington, "On the Types of Phenomena Displayed in Mrs. Thompson's Trance," op. cit.

Mrs. A.W. Verrall, "On a Series of Automatic Writings," op. cit.

Alice Johnson, "On the Automatic Writings of Mrs. Holland," op. cit.

J.G. Piddington, "Three Incidents from the Sittings," *Proceedings of the Society for Psychical Research*, 1910, **24**, 86–169.

Oliver Lodge, "Evidence of Classical Scholarship and of Cross-Correspondence in Some New Automatic Writings," *Proceedings of the Society for Psychical Research*, 1911, **25**, 113–175.

W.H. Salter, "F.W.H. Myers's Posthumous Message," *Proceedings of the Society for Psychical Research*, 1958, **52**, 1–32.

Case No. 10. Edmund Gurney

William James, "A Record of Observations of Certain Phenomena of Trance," op. cit.

Mrs. A.W. Verrall, "On a Series of Automatic Writings," op. cit.

Alice Johnson, "On the Automatic Writings of Mrs. Holland," op. cit.

Oliver Lodge, "Report on Some Trance Communications Received Chiefly Through Mrs. Piper," *Proceedings of the Society for Psychical Research*, 1909, **23**, 127–285.

Case No. 11. Frank Podmore

James H. Hyslop, "A Record of Experiments," op. cit.

James H. Hyslop, "Some Larger Problems of Psychical Research," *Journal of the American Society for Psychical Research*, 1914, **8**, 505–525.

G.W. Lambert, "Our Pioneers, IV. Frank Podmore," *Journal of the Society for Psychical Research*, 1959, **40**, 1–4.

Case No. 12. William James

James H. Hyslop, "A Record of Experiments," op. cit.

James H. Hyslop, "A Case of Musical Control," *Proceedings of the American Society for Psychical Research*, 1913, **7**, 429–569.

John E. Coover, "Investigations with a 'Trumpet' Medium," *Proceedings of the American Society for Psychical Research*, 1914, **8**, 201–252.

James H. Hyslop, "Some Uncertain Phenomena," *Journal of the American Society for Psychical Research*, 1915, **9**, 512–523.

CHAPTER NOTES

1. THE MAN OF UZ

1. Arthur S. Berger, "Concepts of Survival: Towards Clarification, Evaluation and Choice." In *The Synergy of Religion and Psychical Research: Past, Present and Future, 1983.* Proceedings of the Academy of Religion and Psychical Research, 1984, 45–56.

2. L.E. Rhine, *Hidden Channels of the Mind*, New York: William Sloane Assoc., 1961, 260.

3. Frederic W.H. Myers, *Human Personality and Its Survival of Bodily Death*, London: Longmans, Green, 1903, 2 vols.

4. Corliss Lamont, *The Illusion of Immortality*, New York: Philosophical Library, 1959, 24.

5. Miguel de Unamuno, *Tragic Sense of Life*, New York: Dover Publications, 1954.

2. HUMAN MORTALITY

1. Miguel de Unamuno, *Tragic Sense of Life*, op. cit., 1.

2. Henry Sidgwick, "Address by the President at the First General Meeting," *Proceedings of the Society for Psychical Research*, 1882, 1, 7–12, p. 8.

3. "The Objects of the Society," *Proceedings of the Society for Psychical Research*, 1882, 1, 3.

4. Renée Haynes, *The Society for Psychical Research 1882–1982: A History*, London: MacDonald, 1982, 170.

5. Frederic W.H. Myers, "Edmund Gurney's Work: Experimental Psychology," *Proceedings of the Society for Psychical Research*, 1885, 5, 359–373.

6. Eleanor Sidgwick (Mrs. H), "On the Development of Different Types of Evidence for Survival in the Work of the Society," *Proceedings of the Society for Psychical Research*, 1917, 29, 245–259, p. 246.

7. Henry Sidgwick, "Opening Address at the Twenty-Eighth General Meeting," *Proceedings of the Society for Psychical Research*, 1888, 5, 271–278, pp. 272–273.

8. Henry Sidgwick, "Address at the General Meeting of January 25th, 1889," *Proceedings of the Society for Psychical Research*, 1889, 5, 399–402, p. 401.

9. "Formation of the Society," *Proceedings of the American Society for Psychical Research*, 1885, 1, 3–4.

3. THE CONTINUING SCANDAL

1. "First Report of the Committee on Mesmerism," *Proceedings of the Society for Psychical Research*, 1882, 1, 217–229.

2. "Report of the Committee on Thought-Transference," *Proceedings of the Society for Psychical Research*, 1885, 1, 6–49.

3. "First Report of the Committee on Haunted Houses," *Proceedings of the Society for Psychical Research*, 1882, 1, 99–115.

4. Edmund Gurney and F.W.H. Myers, "A Theory of Apparitions," *Proceedings of the Society for Psychical Research*, 1884, 2, 109–136, 157–186.

5. "Report of the Committee on Mediumistic Phenomena," *Proceedings of the American Society for Psychical Research*, 1889, 1, 320–322.

6. Richard Hodgson, "A Record of Observations of Certain Phenomena of Trance," *Proceedings of the Society for Psychical Research*, 1892, 8, 1–167; "A Further Record of Observations of Certain Phenomena of Trance," *Proceedings of the Society for Psychical Research*, 1898, 13, 284–582.

7. William James, "Report on Mrs. Piper's Hodgson-Control," *Proceedings of the Society for Psychical Research*, 1909, 23, 470–589.

8. James H. Hyslop, "Preliminary Report on the Trance Phenomena of Mrs. Smead," *Proceedings of the American Society for Psychical Research*, 1907, 1, 525–722; "A Record and Discussion of Mediumistic Experiments," *Proceedings of the American Society for Psychical Research*, 1910, 4, 1–785; "A Record of Experiments," *Proceedings of the American Society for Psychical Research*, 1912, 6, 17–976.

9. William F. Barrett, *On the Threshold of the Unseen*, New York: E.P. Dutton, 1918.

10. James H. Hyslop, *Contact with the Other World*, New York: Century, 1919.

11. Oliver Lodge, *The Survival of Man*, New York: George H. Doran, 1909.

12. F.W.H. Myers, *Human Personality*, op. cit.

13. William James, "Review of Human Personality," *Proceedings of the Society for Psychical Research*, 1903, 18, 22–33, p. 30.

14. Oliver Lodge, *Survival of Man*, op. cit., 17.

15. J.G. Pratt, *On the Evaluation of Verbal Material in Parapsychology* (Parapsychological Monographs, No. 10), New York: Parapsychology Foundation 1969.

16. Karlis Osis, "Linkage Experiments with Mediums," *Journal of the American Society for Psychical Research*, 1966, 60, 91–124.

17. Alan Gauld, "A Series of Drop-In Communicators," *Proceedings of the Society for Psychical Research*, 1971, 55, 273–379.

18. Ian Stevenson, *Twenty Cases Suggestive of Reincarnation*, 2d rev. ed., Charlottesville: University Press of Virginia, 1974; *Cases of the Reincarnation Type: Vol. I, Ten Cases in India*, Charlottesville: University Press of Virginia, 1975; *Vol. II, Ten Cases in Sri Lanka*, 1977; *Vol. III, Twelve Cases in Lebanon and Turkey*, 1980; *Vol. IV, Twelve Cases in Thailand and Burma*, 1983.

19. For death-bed visions, see Karlis Osis and Erlendur Haraldsson, *At the Hour of Death*, New York: Avon Books, 1977. Interest in near-death experiences was triggered by Raymond A. Moody, Jr.'s *Life after Life*, Atlanta, Ga.: Mockingbird Books, 1975. There have been many subsequent studies, including Kenneth Ring's *Life at Death: A Scientific Investigation of the Near-Death Experience*, New York: Coward, McCann & Geoghegan, 1980.

20. Karlis Osis and Donna McCormick, "Kinetic Effects at the Ostensible Location of an Out-of-Body Projection During Perceptual Testing," *Journal of the American Society for Psychical Research*, 1980, 74, 319–329; C.E. Green, "Ecsomatic Experiences and Related Phenomena," *Journal of the Society for Psychical Research*, 1967, 44, 111–130.

21. Konstantin Raudive, *Breakthrough*, New York: Taplinger, 1971.

22. W.H. Salter, *Zoar; or the Evidence of Psychical Research Concerning Survival*,

London: Sidgwick & Johnson, 1961; Alan Gauld, *Mediumship and Survival: A Century of Investigations*, London: Heinemann, 1982. Also see Gauld's "Discarnate Survival," in Benjamin B. Wolman et al. (eds.), *Handbook of Parapsychology*, New York: Van Nostrand Reinhold, 1977.

23. Gardner Murphy, "An Outline of Survival Evidence," *Journal of the American Society for Psychical Research*, 1945, **39**, 2–34; "Difficulties Confronting the Survival Hypothesis," *Journal of the American Society for Psychical Research*, 1945, **39**, 67–94; "Field Theory and Survival," *Journal of the American Society for Psychical Research*, 1945, **39**, 181–209.

24. C.J. Ducasse, *A Critical Examination of the Belief in a Life After Death*, Springfield, Ill.: Charles C. Thomas, 1961.

25. Charles Richet, "The Difficulty of Survival from the Scientific Point of View," *Proceedings of the Society for Psychical Research*, 1924, **34**, 107–113, pp. 108, 113.

26. E.R. Dodds, "Why I Do Not Believe in Survival," *Proceedings of the Society for Psychical Research*, 1934, **42**, 147–172, p. 170.

27. J.B. Rhine, "The Question of Spirit Survival," *Journal of the American Society for Psychical Research*, 1949, **43**, p. 44.

28. Ian Stevenson, "Comments on 'The Psychology of Life After Death'," *American Psychologist*, November 1981, 1459–1461.

29. Oliver Lodge, *Survival of Man*, op. cit., pp. 337, 341.

30. Curt J. Ducasse, *Paranormal Phenomena, Science and Life After Death* (Parapsychological Monographs, No. 8), New York: Parapsychology Foundation 1969, p. 63.

31. Ian Stevenson, "Research into the Evidence of Man's Survival After Death," *Journal of Nervous and Mental Disease*, 1977, **165**, 3, 152–183, pp. 167–168.

32. Gardner Murphy, papers cited in 23 supra.

33. Gardner Murphy, *Challenge of Psychical Research*, New York: Harper and Row, 1970.

34. Ibid., p. 273.

35. Alan Gauld, "Discarnate Survival," op. cit., p. 577.

36. H.H. Price, "Mediumship and Human Survival," *Journal of Parapsychology*, 1960, **34**, 199–219, p. 216.

4. NEW PERSPECTIVES

1. Byron, "Don Juan," Canto X.

2. George W. Meek, *After We Die, What Then?* Franklin, N.C.: Metascience, 1980, and Ian Currie, *You Cannot Die*, New York: Methuen, 1978 are two examples. A more sophisticated effort to treat the evidence seriously was made recently by two parapsychologists: Elizabeth E. McAdams and Raymond Bayless, *The Case for Life After Death: Parapsychologists Look at the Evidence*, Chicago: Nelson Hall, 1981. But even this book does not give the clear case against life after death and suffers, as was noted by one critical reviewer of the book, from "its authors' reluctance to consider alternative explanations" (Roger I. Anderson, "The Case for Life After Death," *Journal of Religion and Psychical Research*, 1982, **5**, 260–263, p. 261).

3. Corliss Lamont, *Illusion of Immortality*, op. cit.

4. Gardner Murphy, *Challenge of Psychical Research*, op. cit., p. 273.

5. Alice Johnson, "On the Automatic Writing of Mrs. Holland," *Proceedings of the Society for Psychical Research*, 1908, **21**, 166–391, p. 193.

6. Arthur S. Berger, "Death Comes Alive," *Journal of Religion and Psychical Research*, 1982, **5**, 139–147.

7. J.B. Rhine, "The Question of Spirit Survival," op. cit., p. 44.

8. George Zorab, "The Forlorn Quest," in William G. Roll, et al. (eds.), *Research in Parapsychology 1982*, Metuchen, N.J.: Scarecrow Press, 1983, 125–128, p. 128.

9. R.A. McConnell, "A Parapsychological Dialogue," *Journal of the American Society for Psychical Research*, 1977, **71**, 429–435, p. 431.

10. Blaise Pascal, "Pensees," in Saxe Cummins and Robert N. Linscott, *Man and Spirit: The Speculative Philosophers*, New York: Random House, 1947, p. 215.

5. THE NEGLECTED ANGLE

1. K. Ramakrishna Rao, *Experimental Parapsychology*, Springfield, Ill.: Charles C. Thomas, 1966, p. 25.

2. Ibid.

3. E.P. Gibson, "An Examination of Motivation as Found in Selected Cases from Phantasms of the Living," *Journal of the American Society for Psychical Research*, 1944, **38**, 83–105. He studied those who seemed to communicate as apparitions, but his study was restricted to an examination of motivations.

4. Ian Stevenson, "Some Psychological Principles Relevant to Research in Survival," *Journal of the American Society for Psychical Research*, 1965, **59**, 318–337. He studied mediumistic communicators but was concerned only with their motives and the difficulties they might encounter in remembering in their after-death state.

5. J.G. Pratt, "Prologue to a Debate: Some Assumptions Relevant to Research in Parapsychology," *Journal of the American Society for Psychical Research*, 1978, **72**, 127–139, p. 127.

6. C.W.K. Mundle, "Strange Facts in Search of a Theory," *Proceedings of the Society for Psychical Research*, 1973, **56**, 1–20.

7. Naomi A. Hintze and J. Gaither Pratt, *The Psychic Realm: What Can You Believe?* New York: Random House, 1975, p. 236.

8. Robert Crookall, *Intimations of Immortality*, London: James Clarke, 1965, p. 70.

6. THE DEMOCRACY OF THE DEAD

1. William G. Roll, "Poltergeists," in Wolman et al. (eds.), *Handbook of Parapsychology*, op. cit., 381–413.

2. Ian Stevenson, *Cases of the Reincarnation Type: Vol. 1, Ten Cases in India*, op. cit., p. 1.

3. Richard Hodgson, "A Further Record of Observations of Certain Phenomena of Trance," op. cit., p. 362.

7. SAINTS AND SCOUNDRELS

1. Bertrand Russell, *Authority and the Individual*, Boston: Beacon Press, 1949.

2. Arthur Koestler, *Roots of Coincidence*, London: Hutchinson, 1972.

3. Renée Haynes, *Society for Psychical Research*, op. cit., p. 64.

4. Ibid., pp. 6–7.

8. THE MAKING OF A COMMUNICATOR

1. V. Cowles, *The Astors*, New York: Alfred A. Knopf, 1979.
2. p. 7, col. 1.
3. *New York Times*, May 3, 1912, 2:6.
4. *New York Times*, May 1, 1912, 4:1.
5. H.N. Smith, *Mark Twain: The Development of a Writer*, New York: Atheneum, 1974.
6. Raymond Bayless, "Parapsychological Portraits: Mark Twain, A Pioneer in Telepathy," *Journal of the American Society for Psychical Research*, 1960, **54**, 81–86.
7. J. Kaplan, *Mr. Clemens and Mark Twain*, New York: Simon and Schuster, 1966.
8. L. Unger (Ed.), *American Writers IV*, New York: Scribner's, 1974.
9. A.B. Paine, "Mark Twain: A Biographical Summary," in *The Family Mark Twain*, Vol. 1, New York: Harper and Row, 1972 (orig. pub. 1893–1894).
10. James H. Hyslop, *Contact*, op. cit., p. 285.
11. Leslie A. Shepard (Ed.), *Encyclopedia of Occultism and Parapsychology*, Detroit: Gale Research, 1978, 2 vols., p. 364, vol. 1.
12. James H. Hyslop, "Book Review," *Journal of the American Society for Psychical Research*, 1915, **9**, 536.
13. James H. Hyslop, *Contact*, op. cit., p. 284.
14. Walter F. Prince, "The Doris Case of Multiple Personality," *Proceedings of the American Society for Psychical Research*, 1916, **10**, 701–1419, pp. 1292–1293.
15. Walter F. Prince, "Mother of Doris," *Proceedings of the Society for Psychical Research*, 1923, **17**, 1–216, p. 28.
16. Eleanor Sidgwick (Mrs. H), "Presidential Address," *Proceedings of the Society for Psychical Research*, 1908, **22**, 1–18, p. 18.
17. Eleanor Sidgwick (Mrs. H), "The Society for Psychical Research: A Short Account of Its History and Work on the Occasion of the Society's Jubilee, 1932," *Proceedings of the Society for Psychical Research*, 1932, **41**, p. 26
18. Alice Johnson, "Mrs. Henry Sidgwick's Work in Psychical Research," *Proceedings of the Society for Psychical Research*, 1936, **44**, 53–93.
19. G.R. Strutt, letter to the author, August 2, 1982.
20. F.W.H. Myers, *Human Personality*, op. cit.
21. Edmund Gurney, F.W.H. Myers and Frank Podmore, *Phantasms of the Living*, London: Kegan Paul, Trench and Trubner, 1918 (orig. pub. 1886).
22. Oliver Lodge, "In Memory of F.W.H. Myers," *Proceedings of the Society for Psychical Research*, 1902, **17**, 1–10, p. 5.
23. F.W.H. Myers, "The Work of Edmund Gurney in Experimental Psychology," *Proceedings of the Society for Psychical Research*, 1888, **5**, 359–373, p. 360.
24. Trevor H. Hall, *The Strange Case of Edmund Gurney*, London: Gerald Duckworth, 1964.
25. F.W.H. Myers, "Presidential Address," *Proceedings of the Society for Psychical Research*, 1900, **15**, 110–127.
26. See P. Grosskurth, *John Addington Symonds, A Biography*, London: n.p., 1964.
27. Trevor H. Hall, *Strange Case of Edmund Gurney*, op. cit.; M. Asquith, *The Autobiography of Margaret Asquith*, London: n.p., 1920.
28. Trevor H. Hall, *Strange Case of Edmund Gurney*, op. cit., p. 19.
29. Renee Haynes, *Society for Psychical Research*, op. cit., p. 40.
30. E.J. Dingwall, "Introduction," in Frank Podmore, *Mediums of the 19th Century*, New Hyde Park, N.Y.: University Books, 1963, 2 vols.

31. Alan Gauld, *The Founders of Psychical Research*, New York: Schocken Books, 1968, p. 316.

32. E. Rhys, *Everyman Remembers*, New York: n.p., 1931.

33. See, e.g., Alan Gauld, *Founders of Psychical Research*, op. cit.

34. E.J. Dingwall, "Introduction," op. cit.

35. L.R.N. Ashley, "Introduction," in Edmund Gurney et al. *Phantasms of the Living*.

36. William James, "Report on Mrs. Piper's Hodgson-Control," op. cit., p. 121.

37. The information from which I constructed the biographies described in this chapter came not only from some of the references cited above but also from the following sources of information: **Case No. 1** John Jacob Astor IV. *Who Was Who in America*, Vol. 1, 1887–1942, Chicago: Marquis-Who's Who of 1968, p. 34. **Case No. 2** Samuel Langhorne Clemens. D.B. Kesterson, *Critics on Mark Twain: Readings in Literary Criticism*, Coral Gables, Fla.: University of Miami, 1973. W.R. McNaughton, *Mark Twain's Last Years as a Writer*, Columbia: University of Missouri Press, 1972. *The Family Mark Twain*, op. cit. **Case No. 3** Hannah Wild. Letters to the author from Forestdale Cemetery, Holyoke, Mass., Oct. 26, 1982; Holyoke Public Library, Aug. 6 and Sep. 7, 1982; City Hall, Holyoke, Mass. (death certificate); and an obituary from an unnamed newspaper. Her death certificate merely says that her place of birth was England so I could specify in her biography no exact birth place in England. I indicated the year of her birth as 1835 because she was 51 when she died in 1886. **Case No. 4** Carroll D. Wright. *Standard Dictionary of Facts*, Buffalo: Frontier Press, 1922. Letter to the author from Clark University, November 22, 1982. *Carroll D. Wright*, booklet published by Clark University, Worcester, n.d. Obituary from unnamed newspaper from Worcester or Boston. **Case No. 5** Isaac Kauffman Funk. *Dictionary of American Biography*, Vol. IV, New York: Scribner's, 1931, 1932. *New York Times*, April 5, 9, 17, 1912. Letters to the author from: Wittenberg University, Nov. 9 and Dec. 10, 1982; the Greenwood Cemetery, Nov. 29, 1982, and Jan. 27, 1983; Funk and Wagnalls, Nov. 16, 1982. **Case No. 6** Emma Fischer. W.F. Prince, "The Mother of Doris," op. cit. **Case No. 7** Eleanor Sidgwick. Alice Johnson, "Mrs. Sidgwick's Work in Psychical Research," op. cit. E. Sidgwick, *Mrs. Henry Sidgwick: A Memoir*, London: Sidgwick and Jackson, 1938. Letters to the author from: Hon. G.R. Strutt, May 9, June 29, Aug. 2, 1982; the Society for Psychical Research, March 23, 1982. *Woking News and Mail*, Feb. 14, 1936. **Case No. 8** Henry Sidgwick. E.M. Sidgwick and A. Sidgwick, *Henry Sidgwick: A Memoir*, New York: Macmillan, 1906. C.D. Broad, "Henry Sidgwick and Psychical Research," *Proceedings of the Society for Psychical Research*, 1938, **45**, 131–161. Lord Rayleigh, "Some Recollections of Henry Sidgwick," *Proceedings of the Society for Psychical Research*, 1983, **45**, 162–173. **Case No. 9** Frederic W.H. Myers. *London Quarterly Review*, 1912. Oliver Lodge, "In Memory of F.W.H. Myers," op. cit. *Light*, Vol. FFF, Jan. 26, 1901. Letters to the author from: Allerdale District Council Cemetery Division, November 26, 1982. **Case No. 10** Edmund Gurney. Brighton Gazette and Sussex Telegraph, June 28, 1888. S.J. Kunwitz (Ed.), *British Authors of the Nineteenth Century*. New York: H.W. Wilson, 1936. Personal interviews Brighton Council Cemetery Authority and Attree and Kent, Ltd. **Case No. 11** Frank Podmore. S.J. Kunwitz and H. Haycroft (Eds.), *Twentieth Century Authors*, New York: H.H. Wilson, n.d. *Berrows Worcester Journal*, Aug. 27, 1910. *Malvern Gazette*, Aug. 19, 1910. *Light*, XXX, Jan. to Dec., 1910. Personal interviews Malvern Hills District Council. **Case No. 12** William James. G.M. Murphy and R.O. Ballou, *William James on Psychical Research*, London: Chatto and Windus, 1961. W.A. Gay, *William James*, New York: Viking, 1967.

9. COMPARISONS AND FINDINGS

1. Gardner Murphy, *Challenge of Psychical Research*, op. cit., pp. 272–273.
2. Robert Crookall, *Intimations of Immortality*, op. cit., pp. 72–73.
3. G.N.M. Tyrrell, *Science and Psychical Phenomena & Apparitions*, New Hyde Park, N.Y.: University Books, 1961, p. 139.

10. A THUMBNAIL SKETCH

1. H. Babington Smith, "On a Series of Experiments at Pesaro," *Proceedings of the Society for Psychical Research*, 1889, **5**, 549–565.
2. Ian Stevenson, "The 'Perfect' Reincarnation Case," in William G. Roll, Robert L. Morris and Joanna D. Morris (eds.), *Research in Parapsychology 1972*, Metuchen, N.J.: Scarecrow Press, 1973, 185–187.
3. G.N.M. Tyrrell, *Science and Psychical Phenomena & Apparitions*, op. cit., pp. 77–82.
4. Raymond A. Moody, Jr., *Life After Life*, New York: Bantam Books, 1975.

11. A STORY OF SURVIVAL

1. Alice Johnson, "On the Automatic Writing of Mrs. Holland," op. cit., p. 375.
2. Oliver Lodge, "Evidence of Classical Scholarship and of Cross-Correspondence in Some New Automatic Writing," *Proceedings of the Society for Psychical Research*, 1911, **25**, 113–303, p. 123.
3. J.G. Piddington, "A Series of Concordant Automatisms," *Proceedings of the Society for Psychical Research*, 1908, **22**, 19–416, p. 31.
4. J.G. Piddington, "Three Incidents from the Sittings: Lethe; Sibyl; The Horace Ode Question," *Proceedings of the Society for Psychical Research*, 1910, **24**, 86–169, p. 87.
5. Oliver Lodge, "Evidence of Classical Scholarship," op. cit., p. 174.
6. Alice Johnson, "On the Automatic Writing of Mrs. Holland," op. cit., p. 375.
7. Oliver Lodge, "Evidence of Classical Scholarship," op. cit., p. 174.

12. LOOKING TO THE FUTURE

1. Arthur S. Berger, "Better Than a Gold Watch: The Work of the Survival Research Foundation," *Theta*, 1982, **10**, 82–84; "Project: Unrecorded Information," *Christian Parapsychologist*, 1982, **4**, 159–161; "Project: Unrecorded Information: Toward a New Category of Survival Evidence," *Journal of Parapsychology*, 1983, **47**, 61 (abstract); "The Development and Replication of Tests for Survival," *Parapsychological Journal of South Africa*, 1984, **5**, 24–35.
2. Alice Johnson, "On the Automatic Writing of Mrs. Holland," op. cit., p. 208.
3. "Case of the Will of James L. Chaffin," *Proceedings of the Society for Psychical Research*, 1928, **36**, 517–524.
4. F.W.H. Myers, *Human Personality*, op. cit., vol. II, pp. 43ff.
5. Ibid., pp. 183–184.
6. "Opening of an Envelope Containing a Posthumous Note Left by Mr. Myers," *Journal of the Society for Psychical Research*, 1905, **12**, 11–13, p. 13.

7. W.H. Salter, "F.W.H. Myers's Posthumous Message," *Proceedings of the Society for Psychical Research*, 1958, **52**, 1–32.

8. Konstantin Raudive, *Breakthrough*, op. cit.

9. D. Scott Rogo and Raymond Bayless, *Phone Calls from the Dead*, Englewood Cliffs, N.J.: Prentice-Hall, 1979.

10. F.W.H. Myers, *Human Personality*, op. cit., Vol. II, p. 499.

11. Ibid., p. 182.

13. THE RISING WAVE

1. *Washington Post*, Oct. 28, 1985, p. B1.

2. *Congressional Record*, Oct. 31, 1985, *Proceedings and Debates of the 99th Congress*, 1st Session, Vol. 131, No. 148.

3. F.W.H. Myers, *Human Personality*, op. cit., Vol. II, p. 80.

4. Arthur S. Berger, "Death Comes Alive," op. cit., p. 142.

BIBLIOGRAPHY

Ashely, L.R.N. "Introduction." In E. Gurney et al., *Phantasms of the Living* (q.v.).
Barrett, W.F. *On the Threshold of the Unseen*. New York: E.P. Dutton Co., 1918.
Bayless, R. "Parapsychological Portraits: Mark Twain, A Pioneer in Telepathy." *Journal of the American Society for Psychical Research*, 1960, **54**, 81–86.
Berger, A.S. "The Development and Replication of Tests for Survival." *Parapsychological Journal of South Africa*, 1984, **5**, 24–35.
_____. "Project: Unrecorded Information: Toward a New Category of Survival Evidence." *Journal of Parapsychology*, 1983, **47**, 61 (abstract).
_____. "Concepts of Survival: Towards Clarification, Evaluation and Choice." *The Synergy of Religion and Psychical Research: Past, Present and Future*, 1983. Proceedings of the Academy of Religion and Psychical Research, 1984, 45–56.
_____. "Death Comes Alive." *Journal of Religion and Psychical Research*, 1982, **5**, 139–147.
_____. "Project: Unrecorded Information." *Christian Parapsychologist*, 1982, **4**, 159–161.
_____. "Better Than a Gold Watch: The Work of the Survival Research Foundation." *Theta*, 1982, **10**, 82–84.
Cowles, V. *The Astors*. New York: Alfred A. Knopf, 1979.
Crookall, R. *Intimations of Immortality*. London: James Clarke, 1965.
Currie, I. *You Cannot Die*. New York and Toronto: Methuen Publications, 1978.
Dingwall, E.I. "Introduction." In Frank Podmore, *Mediums of the 19th Century*. New Hyde Park, N.Y.: University Books, 1963, 2 vols.
Dodds, E.R. "Why I Do Not Believe in Survival." *Proceedings of the Society for Psychical Research*, 1934, **42**, 147–172.
Ducasse, C.J. *Paranormal Phenomena, Science and Life After Death* (Parapsychological Monographs, No. 8). New York: Parapsychology Foundation, 1969.
_____. *A Critical Examination of the Belief in a Life After Death*. Springfield, Ill.: Charles C. Thomas, 1961.
Gauld, A. "Discarnate Survival." In Benjamin B. Wolman et al. (eds.), *Handbook of Parapsychology*, 577–630. New York: Van Nostrand Reinhold, 1977.
_____. "A Series of Drop-In Communicators." *Proceedings of the Society for Psychical Research*, 1971, **55**, 273–339.
_____. *The Founders of Psychical Research*. New York: Schocken Books, 1968.
Gibson, E.P. "An Examination of Motivation as Found in Selected Cases from Phantasms of the Living." *Journal of the American Society for Psychical Research*, 1944, **38**, 83–105.
Green, C.E. "Ecsomatic Experiences and Related Phenomena." *Journal of the Society for Psychical Research*, 1967, **44**, 111–130.

Gurney, E., and Myers, F.W.H. "A Theory of Apparitions." *Proceedings of the Society for Psychical Research*, 1884, **2**, 109–136.

————, ————, and Podmore, F. *Phantasms of the Living*. London: Kegan Paul, Trench and Trubner, 1918; Scholars' Facsimiles and Reports, 1970 (orig. pub. 1886).

Hall, T. *The Strange Case of Edmund Gurney*. London: Gerald Duckworth, 1964.

Haynes, R. *The Society for Psychical Research, 1882–1982: A History*. London: Mac-Donald, 1982.

Hodgson, R. "A Record of Observations of Certain Phenomena of Trance." *Proceedings of the Society for Psychical Research*, 1892, **8**, 1–167.

————. "A Further Record of Observations of Certain Phenomena of Trance." *Proceedings of the Society for Psychical Research*, 1898, **13**, 284–582.

Hyslop, J.H. *Contact with the Other World*. New York: Century, 1919.

————. "Book Review." *Journal of the American Society for Psychical Research*, 1915, **9**, 536.

————. "Preliminary Report on the Trance Phenomena of Mrs. Smead." *Proceedings of the American Society for Psychical Research*, 1912, **6**, 17–976.

James, W. "Review of Human Personality." *Proceedings of the Society for Psychical Research*, 1903, **18**, 22–23.

————. "Report on Mrs. Piper's Hodgson-Control." *Proceedings of the American Society for Psychical Research*, 1909, **3**, 470–589.

Johnson, A. "Mrs. Henry Sidgwick's Work in Psychical Research." *Proceedings of the Society for Psychical Research*, 1936, **44**, 53–93.

————. "On the Automatic Writing of Mrs. Holland." *Proceedings of the Society for Psychical Research*, 1908, **21**, 166–391.

Kaplan, J. *Mr. Clemens and Mark Twain*. New York: Simon and Schuster, 1966.

Koestler, A. *Roots of Coincidence*. London: Hutchinson, 1972.

Lamont, C. *The Illusion of Immortality*. New York: Philosophical Library, 1959.

Lodge, Oliver. "Evidence of Classical Scholarship and of Cross-Correspondence in Some New Automatic Writing." *Proceedings of the Society for Psychical Research*, 1911, **25**, 113–303.

————. *The Survival of Man*. New York: George H. Doran, 1909.

————. "In Memory of F.W.H. Myers." *Proceedings of the Society for Psychical Research*, 1902, **17**, 1–10.

McAdams, E.E., and Bayless, R. *The Case for Life After Death: Parapsychologists Look at the Evidence*. Chicago: Nelson Hall, 1981.

McConnell, R.A. "A Parapsychological Dialogue." *Journal of the American Society for Psychical Research*, 1977, **71**, 429–435.

Meek, G. *After We Die, What Then?* Franklin, N.C.: Metascience, 1980.

Moody, R.A., Jr. *Life After Life*. Atlanta: Mockingbird, 1975.

Mundle, C.W.K. "Strange Facts in Search of a Theory." *Proceedings of the Society for Psychical Research*, 1973, **56**, 1–20.

Murphy, G. *The Challenge of Psychical Research*. New York: Harper and Row, 1970.

————. "Field Theory and Survival." *Journal of the American Society for Psychical Research*, 1945, **39**, 181–209.

————. "Difficulties Confronting the Survival Hypothesis." *Journal of the American Society for Psychical Research*, 1945, **39**, 67–94.

————. "An Outline of Survival Evidence." *Journal of the American Society for Psychical Research*, 1945, **39**, 2–34.

Myers, F.W.H. *Human Personality and Its Survival of Bodily Death*. 2 vols. London: Longmans, Green, 1903.

_____. *"Presidential Address." Proceedings of the Society for Psychical Research,*
1900, **15**, 110–127.

_____. "Edmund Gurney's Work in Experimental Psychology." *Proceedings of the*
Society for Psychical Research, 1888, **5**, 359–373.

Osis, K. "Linkage Experiments with Mediums." *Journal of the American Society for*
Psychical Research, 1966, **60**, 91–124.

_____. "Deathbed Observations by Physicians and Nurses." *Parapsychological*
Monographs No. 3. New York: Parapsychology Foundation, 1961.

_____, and Haraldsson, E. *At the Hour of Death.* New York: Avon Books, 1977.

_____, and McCormick, D. "Kinetic Effects at the Ostensible Location of an Out-
of-Body Projection During Perceptual Testing." *Journal of the American Society for*
Psychical Research, 1980, **74**, 319–329.

Paine, A.B. "Mark Twain: A Biographical Summary." In *The Family Mark Twain,* Vol.
1. New York: Harper and Row, 1972 (orig. pub. 1894).

Piddington, J.G. "Three Incidents from the Sittings: Lethe; Sibyl; The Horace Ode
Question." *Proceedings of the Society for Psychical Research,* 1910, **24**, 86–169.

_____. "On a Series of Concordant Automatisms." *Proceedings of the Society for*
Psychical Research, 1908, **22**, 19–416.

Pratt, J.G. "Prologue to a Debate: Some Assumptions Relevant to Research in Parapsychology." *Journal of the American Society for Psychical Research,* 1978, **72**,
127–139.

_____. "On the Evaluation of Verbal Material in Parapsychology." *Parap-*
sychological Monographs No. 10. New York: Parapsychology Foundation, 1969.

_____, and Hintze, N.A. *The Psychic Realm: What Can You Believe?* New York:
Random House, 1975.

Price, H.H. "Mediumship and Human Survival." *The Journal of Parapsychology,*
1960, **34**, 199–219.

Prince, W.F. "Mother of Doris." *Proceedings of the American Society for Psychical*
Research, 1923, **17**, 1–216.

_____. "The Doris Case of Multiple Personality." *Proceedings of the American*
Society for Psychical Resaerch, 1916, **10**, 701–1419.

Rao, K.R. *Experimental Parapsychology.* Springfield, Ill.: Charles C. Thomas, 1966.

Raudive, K. *Breakthrough.* New York: Taplinger, 1971.

Rhine, J.B. "The Question of Spirit Survival." *Journal of the American Society for*
Psychical Research, 1949, **43**, 43–61.

Rhine, L.E. *Hidden Channels of the Mind.* New York: William Sloane Assoc., 1961.

Richet, C. "The Difficulty of Survival from the Scientific Point of View." *Proceedings*
of the Society for Psychical Research, 1924, **34**, 107–113.

Rogo, D.S., and Bayless, R. *Phone Calls from the Dead.* Englewood Cliffs, N.J.:
Prentice-Hall, 1979.

Roll, W.G. "Poltergeists." In Benjamin B. Wolman et al. (eds.), *Handbook of Para-*
psychology, 382–413. New York: Van Nostrand Reinhold, 1977.

Russell, B. *Authority and the Individual.* Boston: Beacon Press, 1949.

Salter, W.H. "F.W.H. Myers's Posthumous Message." *Proceedings of the Society for*
Psychical Research, 1958, **52**, 1–32.

Shepard, L.A. *Encyclopedia of Occultism and Parapsychology.* Detroit: Gale Research,
1978, 2 vols.

Sidgwick, E. (Mrs. H). "The Society for Psychical Research: A Short Account of Its
History and Work on the Occasion of the Society's Jubilee, 1932." *Proceedings of*
the Society for Psychical Research, 1932, **41**, 1–26.

_____. "On the Development of Different Types of Evidence for Survival in the

Work of the Society." *Proceedings of the Society for Psychical Research*, 1917, **29**, 245–259.

————. "Presidential Address." *Proceedings of the Society for Psychical Research*, 1908, **22**, 1–18.

Sidgwick, H. "Address of the President at the First General Meeting." *Proceedings of the Society for Psychical Research*, 1882, **1**, 7–12.

————. "Address at the General Meeting of January 25, 1889." *Proceedings of the Society for Psychical Research*, 1889, **5**, 399–402.

————. "Opening Address at the Twenty-Eighth General Meeting." *Proceedings of the Society for Psychical Research*, 1888, **5**, 271–278.

Smith, H.B. "On a Series of Experiments at Pesaro." *Proceedings of the Society for Psychical Research*, 1889, **5**, 549–656.

Smith, H.N. *Mark Twain: The Development of a Writer*. New York: Atheneum, 1974.

Stevenson, I. "Comments on 'The Psychology of Life After Death'." *American Psychologist*, November 1981, 1459–1461.

————. "Research into the Evidence of Man's Survival After Death." *Journal of Nervous and Mental Disease*, 1977, **165**, 3, 152–183.

————. *Cases of the Reincarnation Type: Vol. I, Ten Cases in India*; Charlottesville: University Press of Virginia, 1975; *Cases of the Reincarnation Type: Vol. II, Ten Cases in Sri Lanka*, 1977; *Vol. III, Twelve cases in Lebanon and Turkey*, 1980; *Vol. IV, Twelve cases in Thailand and Burma*, 1983.

————. *Twenty Cases Suggestive of Reincarnation*, 2d rev. ed. Charlottesville: University Press of Virginia, 1974.

————. "The 'Perfect' Reincarnation Case." In W.G. Roll, R.L. Morris and J.D. Morris (Eds.), *Research in Parapsychology 1972*, 185–187. Metuchen, N.J.: Scarecrow Press, 1973.

————. "Some Psychological Principles Relevant to Research in Survival." *Journal of the American Society for Psychical Research*, 1965, **59**, 318–337.

Tyrrell, G.N.M. *Science and Psychical Phenomena & Apparitions*. New Hyde Park, N.Y.: University Books, 1961.

Unamuno, M. de. *Tragic Sense of Life*. New York: Dover Press, 1954.

Unger, L. (Ed.). *American Writers IV*. New York: Scribner's, 1974.

Zorab, G. "The Forlorn Quest." In W.G. Roll, J. Beloff and R.A. White (Eds.), *Research in Parapsychology 1982*, 125–128, Metuchen, N.J.: Scarecrow Press, 1983.

INDEX

199